THE SCIENCE AND FICTION OF AUTISM

THE SCIENCE AND FICTION
OF AUTISM

LAURA SCHREIBMAN

Harvard University Press

Cambridge, Massachusetts

London, England

2005

Library of Congress Cataloging-in-Publication Data

Schreibman, Laura Ellen.
The science and fiction of autism / Laura Schreibman.
p. cm.
Includes bibliographical references and index.
ISBN 0-674-01931-8 (alk. paper)
1. Autism.   2. Autism—Etiology.   I. Title.

RC553.A88S374 2005
616.85′882—dc22   2005046369

Acknowledgments

Many people have contributed to this book. I would like to thank particularly Dr. George Mandler, friend and colleague, who was so generous with excellent advice during the initial stages of this project. I also wish to thank Drs. Aubyn Stahmer, Brooke Ingersoll, Marjorie Charlop-Christy, and Karen Pierce for their helpful comments on earlier drafts of the manuscript. My husband, Dennis LaDucer, also provided editorial advice and unwavering support.

A special thank-you is owed my editor, Elizabeth Knoll, for her good judgment, knowledgeable editorial acumen, encouragement, and infinite patience.

I am greatly indebted to the National Institute of Mental Health, which has generously funded my research for almost thirty years. In particular, U.S.P.H.S. Research Grant #MH39434 has supported some of the research described in this book.

Most important are my thanks to the many children with autism and their families who have let me into their lives over the years. They have taught me a great deal about the experience of autism and have contributed to my continuing enthusiasm for the field. They have made autism much more for me than a label or a set of symptoms. They set me on the course of a very rewarding career, and for that I will be forever grateful.

Contents

Invisibility

We had gone back East
to visit my Aunt Brenda and Uncle Peter
I had been casually told that my cousin had something
    called autism.
Everyone was being so optimistic about it,
so I didn't think much of it.
I didn't think it was really a problem at all. Just something
    like a beauty mark
or a pimple on your face.

We drove from the airport to their house and we walked in
    the door.
I skipped over to Reed and bent down to kiss him.

But he didn't even bother to look at me.

Well, he did look at me,
but it was as if he were looking right through me,
        as if I were invisible.

I felt so sad
and frightened by this that I started to cry.

I tried again later that day.
I knelt down on the floor and brightly called out, "Reed!"
He turned and ran towards me.

My heart started to beat faster and faster, full of hope—
but he only ducked beneath my outstretched arm and ran
    right past me to his toy drum.
Bop-ta bop. Bop-ta bop.

Now I was starting to get angry.
Why did everyone tell me that autism wasn't that big
   of a deal?
It was a big deal.
It was like he was locked up in his own little world.
I wanted to hug the problem right out of his little body.

Later that day I was watching TV with my uncle and aunt,
   and I
suddenly felt someone hold my hand.
I looked down—and it was Reed!
He was gazing at something across the room, but
   at the same time
he was absent-mindedly holding onto my hand.
I grasped his hand
and looked at the side of his fragile, lonely face.
He wasn't looking at me at all,
but rather had simply reached out to hold onto something,
      anything.
He could have reached out and grabbed a stupid chair.
Even though it seemed like he couldn't love me,
I did—I loved *him*.
In this hard world, loving someone, even though they might
not love you the same way in return, can be enough.

And it was.

Julia Rose Ayeroff (age 12)

Introduction

Peter is a beautiful 5-year-old boy with blond hair, blue eyes, and freckles. He looks like many other very cute kids. He is well coordinated, active, and agile. However, while Peter looks perfectly normal, it soon becomes apparent as you watch him that Peter does not *behave* like a typical child. He does not interact with the other children in his class, and in fact he avoids contact with them. He is not attached to his parents or anyone else, preferring to be alone. Rather than playing appropriately with toys, he mouths them or flaps them in front of his eyes. He does not communicate but instead parrots TV commercial jingles or bits of conversation he hears from others. He throws frequent and intense tantrums, often lasting over an hour and precipitated by nothing more severe than the discovery of a drawer left open, the disruption of a precise line of toy cars he has arranged by color, or the removal of one of the McDonald's mustard packets that he insists on carrying with him at all times. Sometimes during these tantrums Peter bangs his head against the floor or wall or bites his hand. He has calluses on his hands from repeated biting. When not otherwise engaged, he will jump repeatedly while flapping his arms and whistling. The teachers in his school try a variety of techniques in an effort to help him. Understandably, his parents are immensely frustrated. They cannot reach their son emotionally despite endless attempts. Their lives are complicated further by the fact that they avoid taking him places because of his disruptive, bizarre, and embarrassing behavior. Their son has autism.

A child like Peter differs significantly from typical children, and does so in very challenging ways. It is also apparent that a child like Peter affects not only his parents but the extended family, scientists, the educational system, and indeed the entire community.

Autistic disorder, or autism, is a severe form of psychopathology evident before the age of 3 years. It is a disorder characterized by a unique constellation of severe and pervasive behavioral deficits and excesses, which have challenged and fascinated professionals and lay personnel for over fifty years. Because of the interesting and unusual characteristics of the disorder and the all-encompassing nature of its effects, autism has received a tremendous amount of attention from psychologists, psychiatrists, pediatricians, neurologists, speech and language specialists, educators, parents, and others whose responsibility it is to understand and help these children and adults. Attention has also come from the lay public, for whom autism seems to hold a special fascination, judging by the many depictions of the disorder in movies, television, and print media. Considering its relative infrequency, autism has attracted far more than its share of attention.

Autism is unique not only in its constellation of symptoms but in the extent to which it has generated controversy and strong competing factions among those professionally concerned with its understanding and treatment. From the very beginning, when Leo Kanner first described autism in 1943, controversies have raged about its specific behavioral features and etiology. Many aspects of the disorder remain highly controversial to this day, and new issues arise regularly. There is almost nothing concerning autism about which everyone agrees, except for the fact that it is a seriously debilitating disorder that affects almost all aspects of behavior.

What accounts for these controversies? Controversies are most likely to arise when things are poorly understood, and this is certainly the case with autism. Although we are much further along in our understanding of the disorder than we were even a few years ago, there is still a great deal we do not know. This poses a tremendous challenge to all those interested in, or responsible for, the care of these affected individuals.

Controversies are not necessarily problematic, however; indeed, they often can be the engine that keeps discovery moving forward. Disagreements often help us better understand a problem and also illuminate issues in related areas. Since autism has social, cognitive, linguistic, and developmental aspects (among others), any insight into the nature of autism will illuminate these areas. More specifically, asking questions about autism will require an examination or reexamination of basic principles in these areas. And new insights about autism will undoubtedly benefit our understanding of other disorders as well. Perhaps it is because of these contributions that autism remains at the forefront of research and clinical interest in the fields of developmental psychopathology and developmental psychology.

My intent in this book is to provide a comprehensive and informative account of autism in a manner that differs from standard treatments. Rather than presenting a general discussion of symptoms, etiology, treatment, and so on, I will look at the disorder in a manner organized around the controversies that have surrounded it. Thus while all the main aspects of autism are thoroughly covered, they are addressed within the contextual framework of the highly controversial, and at times contentious, nature of the field.

In structuring the book in this way, I had to determine what made an issue controversial and decide on specific criteria for inclusion. Some of the controversies were easy to identify; others were less obvious. Some controversies were embedded in other controversies. I came up with four criteria for the issues covered in this book: to be included, a particular issue had to (1) have a significant impact on the lives of individuals with autism and/or their families, (2) reflect at least two conflicting positions claiming some degree of ownership of the "truth," (3) point to theoretical and/or methodological issues important to the fields of autism and normal development, and (4) lead to important advances in research and treatment. I found no shortage of qualified candidates for inclusion.

One of the main goals of this book is to evaluate controversial issues and see if the application of scientific evaluation can lead to resolution, and thus it is necessary to describe how the various arguments are evaluated from a critical perspective. This requires applying an objective, scientific burden of proof as opposed to reliance on testimonials, anecdotes, single case histories, and subjective forms of substantiation. It also requires evaluating the quality of the science applied to bolster a position, for it is the case that *bad* science can lead to as much mischief as *no* science. We will see that some of the major controversies in the field have indeed been resolved, but they have historical importance in demonstrating the potentially serious negative consequences of failing to require objective substantiation. Some controversies are still actively in debate, and I will apply critical standards of proof to the opposing sides to see if resolution is possible at this point.

I begin with a discussion of how we use critical evaluation to differentiate between fact and fiction, which sets the stage for how we will look at the issues and controversies to be discussed throughout this book. Next I provide a description of autism, followed by issues of diagnosis and assessment. Some controversy will be evident even here, since there have been disagreements involving the specific behaviors required for the diagnosis of autism and the way it can be differentiated from other disorders that share common features. I then move on to other areas of controversy, beginning with one of the most difficult, the etiology of autism. This is followed by a discussion of the hypothesized "core" deficits that may underlie autism. The next general area covered, treatment issues, is a particularly fertile ground for debate; new controversies seem to emerge even as old ones are resolved.

I take evaluative stands on many of the existing controversies and do so on the basis of current science. Some of the debates in the field have been resolved; others have not. I hope the discussion in this book will help the reader evaluate the existing controversies as well as new ones that may arise. I have no doubt that some will disagree, perhaps vehemently, with some of the stands I take, but that is in the nature of this field. As I've noted, disagreements can be productive in moving a field forward.

I'll begin by mentioning one controversy that affects the terminology used in this book and that has led to a great deal of disagreement in the field: how individuals who are affected by autism should be labeled. Should we refer to "autistic children" or "children with autism"? The term "autistic children" was commonly used until several years ago, when some advocates expressed the view that this was not politically correct and insisted that the term "children with autism" was more appropriate. This terminology reflected the "person first" idea—that the primary characteristic of the young person was that he or she was a child and that autism was something the child had. To use "autistic" first suggested to these advocates that autism was the most important feature of the individual, and they believed that this was not the case. However, not everyone agrees with this position. Bernard Rimland, for example, the father of an autistic son and founder of the Autism Society of America, prefers the term "autistic child." His feeling is that autism is who his son is, not just a characteristic. I can see merits to both arguments, and thus I use both terms interchangeably throughout this book.

CHAPTER 1

Critical Evaluation of Issues in Autism

We believe that the field of autism will advance like other scientific fields that accept the standards of scientific research and the results of studies, wherever they may lead.

   —Donald J. Cohen and Fred R. Volkmar, *Handbook of Autism and Pervasive Developmental Disorders* (1997)

The mission of the National Institute of Mental Health (NIMH) is to diminish the burden of mental illness through research. This public health mandate demands that we harness powerful scientific tools to achieve better understanding, treatment and, eventually, prevention of mental illness.

   —NIMH Mission Statement, 2001

Nevertheless, mainstream medicine, by which I mean such groups as the American Academy of Pediatrics, the American Medical Association, the National Institute of Mental Health, the American Psychiatric Association, and similar organizations, have harmed rather than helped autistic children and their families from Day One.

   —Bernard Rimland, keynote address at the Autism Society of America, 2001

The field of autism is littered with the debris of dead ends, crushed hopes, ineffective treatments, and false starts. This has been frustrating and discouraging for everyone, including parents and professionals. Why has this situation developed? The field is susceptible to all sorts of false beliefs, snake-oil treatments, and potential "cures" because we are dealing with a devastating disorder for which we have relatively few answers to date. Ignorance provides a vacuum that sucks in all kinds of ideas—some right, some irrelevant, some dead wrong, and some even harmful.

The best hope for finding the correct and helpful answers, and our best defense against wrong answers, is to evaluate critically the information that is presented to us. A voluminous stream of information about autism comes at us daily from magazine and newspaper articles, television, movies, and, to an increasing extent, the Internet. The best way to evaluate this information objectively is to employ the principles of science: careful observation, systematic testing, and the cautious interpretation of information. It is extremely important to remember that the answers we *do* have regarding autism and its effective treatment are those that have been derived from sound, systematic, and well-conducted research.

One need not be a scientist in order to know how to evaluate information critically; one just needs to be appropriately critical. While few of us are trained researchers, all of us are capable of evaluating information analytically, especially once we know what to look for. When presented with claims, we need to ask solid, basic questions that will allow us to draw conclusions regarding the accuracy of those claims. Critical thinking empowers us to cut through all of the hype, dramatic claims, and wishful thinking. Sometimes the truth hurts (for example, finding out that a proposed cure is indeed bogus), but it certainly does no good to pursue dead ends. The pursuit of these fruitless avenues serves only to waste time, money, and emotional energy on theories that do not add up or cures that do not work.

Let's look at some of the consequences of *not* thinking critically. The field of autism is rife with examples of the negative consequences of uncritical acceptance of ideas. Probably the best-known unsound idea proposed in the field of autism was the early acceptance of the psychogenic hypothesis of etiology (discussed in Chapter 4). It was asserted that autism was the result of parental psychopathology, usually the "refrigerator mother" who failed to provide the emotional warmth required for the healthy development of her child. As we will see, this erroneous conception had three seriously negative effects. First, parents were essentially blamed for causing the disorder in their children. Second, on the basis of this erroneous conception, early treatments were focused in the wrong direction. Third, adhering to the psychogenic hypothesis served to delay for many years both the search for the biological basis of the disorder and the development of effective treatments. We wasted a lot of time, energy, and money looking in the wrong direction.

Or consider a much-hyped treatment. Facilitated Communication (FC) was touted as a "miracle" on national television.[1] The adherents of this form of treatment (to be discussed in detail in Chapter 8) claimed that many individuals with autism and/or mental retardation had communication abilities far beyond what we might expect given their poor performance on intellectual assessments. When another person "facilitated," or physically assisted, the individual to respond via a keyboard or communication board, unexpected levels of communication ability were apparent. Thus severely disabled children who could not speak or otherwise communicate were able, through FC, to tell their parents they loved them, write poetry, comment on current events, and in one case even declare a political affiliation ("I am a Democrat!"). This highly optimistic approach was heavily promoted and garnered quite a bit of high-profile publicity. One can certainly see why parents were eager to embrace a treatment that allowed them to communicate with their children at a level they could never achieve before.

When FC was subjected to objective, controlled experimentation, however, it was determined that it was, as in the title of a *60 Minutes* exposé, "less than a miracle."[2] FC was shown to be a situation where it was the "facilitator" (the individual providing the physical assistance) who in most cases was doing the communicating. In fact, the treatment proved to be bogus, and what had looked like a miracle led only to another major disappointment for parents and clinicians, whose hopes had been raised only to be ultimately dashed. As if this were not bad enough, some families were devastated by false claims of sexual abuse that had been "reported" via FC. This again illustrates that lack of critical evaluation can lead not just to negative situations but to tragic ones.

In fact, the main proponent of FC, Douglas Biklen, waving probably the largest red flag in the history of autism treatment claims, declared that any scientific study of FC would be impossible. Biklen said that subjecting the procedure to empirical testing violated the process and would render it ineffective; therefore it could not be tested.[3] It is important to be very wary of any treatment that "cannot be tested," since without testing, we cannot verify effectiveness.

Limitations of Testimonials and Anecdotal Reports

In the field of autism it is not uncommon to hear about effective, even amazing, treatments from reports by parents or professionals. These anecdotal reports, or testimonials, are typically single case histories presented in magazine articles or books. To choose just one example, a story appeared in a 1999 issue of *Ladies' Home Journal* magazine describing the experience of a family with an 8-year-old boy who had been diagnosed at age 2 with Pervasive Developmental Disorder (PDD, one of the autism spectrum disorders). The description of the boy's behavior does suggest an autistic spectrum disorder in that he was socially avoidant, did not make eye contact, disliked being held, fixated on objects, and hated unfamiliar things. He would use words once, only to never use them again.

He had severe tantrums as well as sleep difficulties. By the time he was 6 he had acquired some aggressive and destructive behaviors such as biting, kicking, and stuffing up the toilet. Understandably, his parents, who had three other children, were devastated and overwhelmed. Then the mother heard about a television report of a child who had shown dramatic progress after receiving treatments with a hormone called secretin. She arranged to have secretin given to her son and reported a dramatic improvement in the child's behavior. He began speaking spontaneously, was more socially engaged with the family and others, was calmer, and showed a variety of other positive changes. Needless to say, the family was thrilled, and they attributed their son's improvement to the secretin.

While stories such as these may be heartwarming, encouraging, and motivating, there are several potential issues that must be considered critically. Although it is possible that secretin had something to do with this youngster's behavioral improvement, we cannot definitely draw this conclusion. First, there is a real danger in generalizing from one person's experience. Just because one child may have showed improvement after receiving treatment X (for example, secretin), this does not mean that another child—or any other child—will benefit. Of course, this is particularly true of autism since the well-known heterogeneity of this population usually results in heterogeneity of treatment outcome.

Second, it is important to remember that it is typically the positive experiences and outcomes that are reported. People who experience failures are not those likely to write magazine articles or chat with Katie Couric on the *Today Show*. Yet failures may be just as frequent or perhaps more frequent than the successes. Thus there is a reporting bias in that a particular type of experience is more likely to come to our attention. I know of no magazine articles in which parents report the failure of secretin to lead to behavioral improvement of their child (even though we know that many children have not responded to secretin). Failures are certainly not as interesting or dramatic as successes.

Third, single-case or anecdotal reports are difficult or impossible to verify. If we hear a report of a child with autism showing major clinical improvement or perhaps being "cured" after the adoption of a specific treatment regimen, several questions must be asked. What objective, independent information do we have to suggest that the child improved? Often the outcomes consist of subjective reports of improvements with no independent verification. For example, while we know that parental reports and description can be very useful, the parents in the case described above already knew about the secretin treatments and had certain hopeful expectations about the effects, and thus their impressions may have been colored by these expectations. Independent observations or assessments conducted by individuals unaware of the secretin treatments would serve to validate the parents' impressions. Was the child truly autistic? In our example, the child did have a diagnosis of PDD and therefore, assuming an appropriate professional provided it, we may be fairly confident in this case. In addition, the description of the child's behavior is consistent with such a diagnosis. However, anecdotal reports often fail to provide enough verification of initial diagnosis or behavioral profile. Was the child also receiving other treatments at the same time (such as a special education program, one-on-one training, or medication)? If so, could improvement be attributed to these other treatments? In our example, it is apparent that the child was receiving a variety of interventions, and without a controlled study to determine the impact of each, it is impossible to isolate a specific intervention as necessarily leading to behavioral improvement. If there was substantial improvement in the child's condition, was this due to the intended treatment or to some incidental, unspecified aspect of the treatment? Could maturation have led to some of the reported changes? These are only some of the important questions we must ask.

We all wish so much for positive outcomes that we may be tempted to believe these reports. It is also important to realize that anecdotal reports that turn out to be false are most likely not intended by the reporting parent or professional to be misleading. Most often these outcomes are reported with the greatest optimism and best intentions. The mother who shares the story of her son and secretin certainly does this to provide hope to other parents in the same difficult situation. However, best intentions are not sufficient for us to invest our efforts and resources. We must require a much higher standard of proof.

Correlational Research

A definite step up from anecdotal reports and testimonials is a form of science called correlational research, where we measure one behavior or event and look for concurrent variation in another event—a correlation. We do not manipulate anything; we just measure two (or more) things of interest and see if they move together in a systematic way. For example, mothers of juvenile delinquents have been generally reported to be depressed and more rejecting of their youngsters. Thus high levels of delinquency are associated with increased levels of rejection, while low levels of delinquency are associated with less rejection. In another more recent example, it was reported that statistically Academy-Award-winning actors live three to five years longer than actors who have not won an Oscar. In fact, statistics show that actors who have won multiple Oscars live longer than single Oscar winners. This is another positive correlation: the more Oscars, the longer the life expectancy.

Although correlational research is better than anecdotal reporting, it, too, has its limitations. A clear example of these limitations can again be found in the early days of autism research, when the psychogenic hypothesis was influential. A look at this situation reveals two of the main potential problems with correlations.

As we will see in Chapter 4, the psychogenic hypothesis was based on the observation that parents of children with autism tended to lack warmth and affection when interacting with their child. That is, unaffectionate parents were correlated with the presence of autism. It was concluded that the parents of these children were cold, unemotional, overly rational people who failed to provide the nurturing environment so essential for normal child development. This unwelcoming and even threatening environment led the child to "withdraw" into autism. Because of this observation, and the acceptance of psychodynamic thought, the idea that parental behavior *caused* child behavior seemed quite natural. However, one could argue that this is a case where the opposite is true: is it not possible that the parents' behavior was influenced by their child's autism? How warm and affectionate would you expect parents to be after learning from repeated experience that their loving overtures toward their child would at best be ignored and at worst actively rebuffed? Thus one of the possible limitations of correlations (in this case unaffectionate parents and autism were correlated) is *direction of causality:* we may not know in which direction the causal relationship occurs.

Of course, this assumes that there *is* a causal relationship. A second potential limitation of such a correlation is that one may assume a causal relationship between two events when no relationship exists. To continue with the example of the psychogenic hypothesis of autism etiology, another reported correlation was between the presence of autism and certain demographic features of the families. Leo Kanner noted that many of the parents of the first group of autistic children he observed were of high socioeconomic status, had advanced educational degrees, and were very logical in their thinking (for example, many were scientists). This was interpreted at the time as support for the psychogenic hypothesis in that the parents were seen as being overly logical, rational, and achieving, to the detriment of their emotional warmth toward the child. But other factors may be responsible for this correlation. What type of parent is most likely to bring his child to the most famous child psychiatrist of the day at Johns Hopkins University? One could well argue that it would be the parent who is well educated and has the financial means to seek out the best expert at an internationally renowned university. Thus the observed correlation between the presence of autism and family demographic characteristics was likely caused by other, unrelated variables.

To return to the examples cited earlier, the correlation between maternal rejection and juvenile delinquency is another situation where direction of causality may be an issue (might not a parent become rejecting because of her child's delinquent behavior?). Moreover, it might be the case that another variable, poverty, leads both to an increase in delinquent behavior and to maternal rejection and depression. And while we can be fairly certain that long life does not cause an individual to win an Academy Award, it is likely that such actors live in safe, even privileged, environments and can afford the very best life-style and health care.

Thus correlational research is not ideal for our purposes, but it does have some usefulness. Looking at correlations often gives us ideas of possible causal relationships that we can investigate further using other methodologies. Another example from autism research will serve as an illustration. I was once trying to determine what environmental factors led to an autistic child's delayed echolalia (repetition of what is said by other people). Jerry would repeat TV game show lines such as "You've just won $10,000!" or "Let's make it a true daily double, Alex!" Since the echolalia was delayed, he would say these things at what appeared to be random times during the day. Because the speech was stigmatizing and served to further isolate Jerry from his peers, we wanted to eliminate it. To give us an idea of where to begin our study, we observed Jerry for an extended period of time and noted what was occurring when he echoed his game show lines. We found that when he was aroused (either very happy, anxious, or upset) he would say the lines. This correlation (high arousal associated with high rate of "game show" talk) suggested the possibility of a relationship between the two.

This led us to consider emotional arousal as the stimulus for his delayed echo. We conducted a more controlled study and determined that we were correct.

Controlled Studies

In a controlled study, rather than accepting anecdotal reports or testimonials, or looking for correlations, the researchers design an experiment in which they perform some experimental manipulation under controlled circumstances and then look for some change in measured behavior. In the case of Jerry, since we guessed that a condition of emotional arousal cued his echolalia, we systematically manipulated his arousal to see if the echolalia occurred. To do this, we set up several conditions where Jerry was exposed to situations that elicited high arousal (in this case, positive arousal) alternated with situations that did not. Thus in the positive conditions he was allowed to play with his very favorite set of crayons, use his mother's mixing bowls to stir food, and watch his favorite Disney videos. We also intermixed conditions that were relatively neutral for Jerry in that he was not particularly excited. These included playing with a set of blocks, working on school-related tasks, and watching nonfavorite videos. We exposed Jerry to these various conditions in random order and measured how much delayed echoing he engaged in during each exposure. We found that during the high-arousal (happy) conditions, he echoed much more often than he did in the neutral conditions. This allowed us to conclude that arousal was a condition that tended to evoke game-show talk.

This experiment was superior to the correlational observation because it satisfied three main criteria that are required in order to determine if researchers have proven a relationship. These criteria are ones that all of us should consider before accepting the findings of an experiment as we consider its validity. The three criteria, as applied to the experiment described above, are the following:

(1) We have *demonstrated the direction of causality:* we know that the introduction of high arousal was followed by the increase in echolalia rather than vice versa (that is, the echolalia did not evoke playing with crayons). Also, we know that echolalia did not cause Jerry's positive high arousal because we introduced the arousal first and then watched for the appearance of the echolalia.

(2) We *replicated the demonstration* of the causal relationship. We accomplished this by having several instances where we presented high-arousal situations and showed that an increase in delayed echolalia followed each time, whereas an increase did not occur during the instances where we presented the neutral situations. Therefore we can be confident that our observed relationship was not a fluke, or a one-time or chance occurrence. Replication is very important and indeed has been called the essence of believability. Replication is not just important in any one experiment but is also important to demonstrate across other experiments. This is why we often wait until different researchers in different laboratories demonstrate that their experiments show the same results; such a demonstration allows us to be confident in our findings. If it becomes apparent that a particular finding only occurs in one laboratory or with one researcher, despite the efforts of other laboratories or researchers to replicate the result, we have reason to be very cautious about accepting the findings as fact.

(3) We *controlled for potential confounding variables,* which are other variables that may affect our findings but are really not responsible for the observed relationship (for example, the variables of educational level and socioeconomic status of the parents in Kanner's original report, described earlier). In the experiment with Jerry, we controlled for potentially confounding variables such as actively playing with toys. Thus we had two active toy play conditions (crayons versus blocks) assigned to the two different arousal conditions. If active toy play was indeed the variable responsible for echolalia, the speech would have occurred during both conditions:

the crayons and the blocks. In fact, it was only the highly arousing toy play condition, crayons, that was associated with the increase in echolalia. The experiment similarly controlled for the potentially confounding variables of engaging in a work task (mixing food versus doing school tasks) and watching videos (favorite versus non-favorite videos). Thus we sought to systematically control for all variables except the one we were interested in, positive arousal.

This example illustrates that one can set up "tests" for suspected relationships. These tests all include one common element: the existence of *control*. By control we simply mean that we have demonstrated that we understand the relationship because we can control it (in our example with Jerry, we can "cause" echolalia by instituting positive arousal). Control means knowledge and understanding, and this is our goal. There is also something about control that gives one a sense of power, in that if we can control something we are not surprised, confused, or fooled by it. In the field of autism research (or any other field for that matter), we definitely do not want to be surprised, confused, or fooled. We want understanding.

The Role of the Professional versus the Parent

Everyone dealing with the population affected by autism seeks understanding. Everyone wants to find the answers, and everyone wants to improve the lives of these children and their families. The professionals in the field of autism seek answers not only to satisfy intellectual curiosity but also to discover information that will eventually lead to the prevention, treatment, and cure of the disorder. Parents and other family members may not share the motive of satisfying intellectual curiosity, but they certainly seek answers leading to effective treatment and a cure. The general public wants all of the above.

There are many professionals working in the field of autism, including psychologists, psychiatrists, pediatricians, neurologists, geneticists, speech and language specialists, special education teachers, and a host of others. Many of these individuals are scientists who use controlled methodology to answer some of the most vexing questions in the field. As a rule scientists are respected in our society, and their work, while perhaps of some debate within their own fields, is likely to be accepted and given credibility by the community at large. However, such widespread acceptance is relatively unusual in the study of autism. Findings in autism research are not only debated within the scientific community but may lead to heated fights among various constituents within the nonscientific autism community. (Indeed, some years ago one of my colleagues attended a meeting of parents of children with autism and was astounded when two parents, both over 50 years old, argued to the point of actual blows over some purported "cure" for autism.) In addition to claims about the effectiveness of various treatments, other recent contentious topics include whether federal research dollars should go to behavioral treatment research or to research on etiology, whether parents should refuse to have the measles-mumps-rubella (MMR) vaccine administered to their children, and whether intensive treatment should be provided in the classroom versus the home. These are just a few examples of ongoing debates.

Thus it seems that professionals are frustrated, parents are frustrated, and these populations are frustrated with each other. It is not a very happy situation. The existence of this frustration and skepticism may be attributed to several factors. First, despite years of research, particularly in the area of physiological substrates of autism, we have precious little in the way of answers regarding either etiology or cure. There is no doubt that the seemingly glacial pace of finding the answers, and the fact that so many of them continue to elude us, serves as fuel for the frustration. Science by its very nature is often a slow, methodical, and painstaking process, requiring many variations and replications of studies. The problem is compounded by the extremely complex nature of autism, which is not a single or homogenous disorder but rather a behaviorally defined syndrome which may consist of several different disorders with distinct etiologies, courses, and so on. Moreover, because autism affects almost every aspect of behavior, it is a monumental task to study and understand all of its aspects. It must be remembered, however, that although our findings may be slow in coming, this is infinitely better than the alternative: quick-fix answers derived from uncritical adoption of questionable "facts." We have learned some very painful lessons going down that road.

Second, it must be acknowledged that some of the findings to date are not good news. Finding evidence of genetic involvement and distinctive neurological abnormalities does not suggest that a "quick fix" to the problem will be forthcoming any time soon. Moreover, the fact that we seem to be finding an increase in the range, severity, and pervasiveness of deficits in the population afflicted with autism certainly is not encouraging.

Adding to the frustration and skepticism is the existence of confusing and opposing claims. For example, do megavitamins lead to improvement in the behavior of children with autism? Do wheat-free diets make a difference? Does the MMR vaccine cause autism? These are debates that will not be settled by those who shout the loudest or who bring the largest number of professionals to the table to make statements; they will be settled only by sound science. And the debates likely will not be solved quickly.

Unfortunately, a distinctly troubling trend has emerged, which is the atmosphere of distrust and suspicion that has arisen between some professionals in the autism field and some parents. There are some sources of great frustration to parents: the historical issue of professionals mistakenly "blaming" the parents for causing autism, the slow pace of research, the paucity of answers to questions of etiology, and the fact that existing treatments are not cures. In addition, parents may feel left out of the process when it comes to making decisions regarding their child's treatment. One parent reported that she felt as if she had no say as professionals dictated the course of her child's treatment; she said she felt "like a passenger on the train as we were being railroaded through the process." Sometimes the parents may feel that their children are guinea pigs being used by professionals who are interested not so much in helping the children as in obtaining lucrative research grants, advancing their careers, or lining their pockets. Parents may also feel the professionals are uncaring and insensitive. This, of course, is not the case.

On the other side, some scientists may see the parents as unsophisticated when it comes to understanding the scientific approach to autism and generally too demanding of immediate answers. They may be frustrated that parents want them to accept findings derived from "unscientific" sources such as anecdotal reports. I have attended many a professional meeting where parents have indeed expressed open hostility at the refusal of a scientist to embrace an unproven fact. The quote from Bernard Rimland at the beginning of this chapter perhaps best exemplifies this hostility. Scientists may see the parents as being too emotionally invested to be objective when it comes to their children. They may resist the efforts of parents to "drive the science," meaning they feel that parents should not be the people to dictate what the research questions ought to be and certainly not the people to determine ways to study the questions. In short, some scientists may see parents as having little to contribute to the study of autism. This, of course, is not the case.

Certainly the lack of trust and the negative attitudes that have just been described are not true of all parents and professionals. Yet there is no doubt that distrust and suspicion exist, and this atmosphere does nothing to help either side or to advance the cause. One need only visit autism-related Web sites to see evidence of this problem and the real anger that some people feel. One parent/researcher lamented in a Web site comment that this field is difficult enough without having an adversarial relationship between the two main constituencies involved: the scientific community and the consumers of the science. One can only imagine how much more fruitful it would be if the parents felt more trust of the scientific community and if the scientific community appreciated the sophistication of parents and were more likely to make use of the valuable input that parents can provide.

Perhaps a change will eventually occur in this adversarial relationship, as was the case in the relationship between the AIDS community and the medical community.[4] This was a situation that shared some of the features we see in the autism arena: there was a devastating disorder and a slow response from the scientific community. While the reasons for the slow response from the medical community differ in the two situations (with autism it was a focus on the wrong theoretical basis, whereas with AIDS it was more of a political issue), the fact remains that much frustration resulted. Gay activists were frustrated by the slow pace of research and were pushing for more active investigations into effective treatments and more drug trials. There was a good deal of hostility directed toward the federal government, drug companies, and scientists. This adversarial relationship, often quite intense, raged on until the various factions realized something very important: they needed one another. The fact was that true progress was going to require significant contributions from all parties involved. There was a growing realization that each of the parties had significant and unique perspectives and abilities that would be essential if answers were to be forthcoming.

In the case of AIDS, eventually the various parties found common ground and a common language. Gay activists and AIDS patients who had been so vehement in their criticisms determined they were not going to get the help they sought so desperately without the government and drug companies providing the funding and scientists doing the research. At the same time, the scientists realized how important the activists and patients were in assisting the research in terms of recruiting research subjects, enrollment of subjects in the studies, and promoting compliance with research protocols. All this led to more focused discussions between the groups and a better outcome for the research. Activists began holding their own conferences to bring in various disciplines important in the search for the treatment and cure of AIDS. The focus gradually shifted from one of an adversarial nature to one of a cooperative nature. This situation can now be studied from a historical perspective since the negativity once so rampant in the field has largely abated. This may be attributed not only to the increased cooperation and collaboration of the parties but also to the fact that more effective treatments have been developed. The availability of treatments has served to mitigate the pressing emergency in the sense that although a vaccine or cure has not been found, treatments that greatly increase life expectancy are now available.

The AIDS saga can be seen as a hopeful sign of what can be accomplished when scientists and consumers (whether they are AIDS patients, gay activists, parents of children with autism, or others) learn to value the contributions of all the parties concerned. The field of autism will likely go in this direction, and indeed there are signs that more cooperative efforts are emerging. For example, organizations such as the Autism Society of America (ASA) are composed jointly of parents and professionals. The ASA holds a national conference every year, with state and local chapters also holding conferences, and professionals from the scientific community are invited to these meetings. In addition, scientific conferences on autism are including more input from parents and teachers, who are invited to speak to the research community. In another example of joint efforts, the federal funding agencies such as the National Institute of Mental Health are including parents and other community members on review panels that evaluate the merits, feasibility, and potential contribution of research grants.

Autism activism shares another feature with activism in other disorders. In recent years, offshoot groups have formed to advance particular causes within the autism arena. For example, Cure Autism Now (CAN) and Defeat Autism Now! (DAN!) are organizations formed to focus activism and attention on identifying the biological bases of autism and biologically based treatments. CAN (founded in 1995) is an organization of parents, physicians, and researchers that promotes public awareness about autism as well as funding research that focuses on finding the biological cause of autism, its prevention, and the development of medical treatments. One of the best examples of parents joining hands with professionals is the establishment of the M.I.N.D. (Medical Investigation of Neurodevelopmental Disorders) Institute at the University of California, Davis campus. This institute was started and inspired by parents who wanted a set of comprehensive answers to the causes and treatment of autism and other neurodevelopmental disorders. The Institute brings together a diverse set of disciplines—genetics, neuroscience, behavioral and cognitive psychology—and a diverse set of groups including parents, educators, physicians, and scientists, all committed to collaborative work to find some of these answers. The M.I.N.D. Institute supports the work of resident scientists and clinicians as well as providing grants to others engaged in promising research. Here we can see a concerted parent-professional effort at increased understanding of autism and its treatment.

One can attribute the development of these organizations at least partially to dissatisfaction with the main ASA organization, which is often seen as too broad-based and bureaucratic to be relevant to more narrowly focused agendas. Largely because of its broad constituency (over 20,000 members including parents, teachers, scientists, and other interested persons) and its central role in the many areas of autism treatment and research over the years, the organization by necessity has played host to many points of view and strong opinions. Since it comes as no surprise that the many controversies associated with autism have in some way entered the discussions of the ASA, it is also not surprising that the organization historically has been associated with episodes of rather strident infighting between factions that promoted specific types of treatments or research. In many ways it is impressive that the ASA has been able to accomplish all that it has over its forty-year existence.

Another area where professionals (in this case, educators) and parents have had an adversarial relationship is the issue of school programs for autistic children. As I will discuss in Chapter 10, prior to the mid-1970s there were no special education programs for children with autism. Since these youngsters were not classified as mentally retarded or physically handicapped, they fell through the cracks in the educational system. The situation was essentially that the schools had no programs for them, the educational system was not legally required to provide an education, and the parents often found themselves unable to care for the children at home. Sadly, many were institutionalized before they reached adolescence.

Finally the families had had enough. They began using the legal system to further their cause. Class-action lawsuits were filed against school districts demanding appropriate educational opportunities for children with autism. Bumper stickers with the message "Educate Autistic Children!" adorned vehicles across the country. The strategy worked, and school districts began providing special classrooms to meet the needs of these children. Finally, in 1974 California governor Reagan signed into law legislation mandating classrooms for children with autism. In a tremendous victory by parents and advocates, these children were no longer excluded from the educational process. Although it must be acknowledged that many of these early classrooms were not as effective as one might hope (the teaching methodology was just beginning to be developed), it was certainly a very important start and provided the framework for the future.

Thus we can see that the educational community, the research community, and parent-professional organizations such as the ASA are all having an impact, and that they are doing so by means of the critical evaluation of information about autism. This is the avenue that has allowed for the progress to date, and that will lead to progress in the future. But it has been a stormy process. Autism is a lightning rod for the best and the worst because the emotional issues are profound, because the science is hard, and because so many mistakes have been made in the past.

CHAPTER 2

Characteristics of Autism

He seemed to regard people as unwelcome intruders to whom he paid as little attention as they would permit. When forced to respond, he did so briefly and returned to his absorption in things. When a hand was held out before him so that he could not possibly ignore it, he played with it briefly as if it were a detached object. He blew out a match with an expression of satisfaction with the achievement, but did not look up at the person who had lit the match.

—Leo Kanner, "Autistic Disturbances of Affective Contact" (1943)

The most impressive thing is his detachment and his inaccessibility. He walks as if he is in a shadow, lives in a world of his own where he cannot be reached.

—Kanner, "Autistic Disturbances of Affective Contact"

He almost never says a sentence without repeating it. Yesterday, when looking at a picture, he said many times, "Some cows standing in the water." We counted fifty repetitions, then he stopped after several more and then began over and over.

—Kanner, "Autistic Disturbances of Affective Contact"

In 1943 the child psychiatrist Leo Kanner of Johns Hopkins University provided the first detailed account of what he called "autistic disturbances of affective contact." He described a group of eleven children who seemed quite similar to each other but qualitatively different from children who were more adequately described by other clinical diagnoses.[1] In this initial report he provided a richly detailed description of each of the children and in so doing gave us the first fascinating glimpse of what we now call autistic disorder or autism.

The central characteristic of these children, as described by Kanner, was what he called "extreme autistic aloneness," demonstrated by an inability to develop normal social relationships or relationships with the environment. This feature led him to use the term "autism" because the word is related to "self" and had been used by Eugen Bleuler to describe the extreme withdrawal and lack of environmental involvement in people with schizophrenia.[2] Other main features of children with autism were (1) a delay or failure to acquire speech, (2) the noncommunicative nature of speech if it did develop, (3) stereotyped and repetitive play activities, (4) a compulsive demand for the maintenance of "sameness" in the environment, (5) good memory for rote material, and (6) lack of imagination. Kanner emphasized that behavioral abnormalities were apparent even in infancy but that despite these impairments the children had a normal physical appearance.

Given the fact that many years have passed and there has been some debate over the behavioral criteria for the diagnosis, it is a testament to Kanner's skill as a perceptive observer and recorder that the major symptoms required for a diagnosis of autism remain basically unchanged. Most of the debate has focused not so much on the nature of the main symptoms but rather on the relative importance of the symptoms for the diagnosis.

Let us first look closely at the main behavioral characteristics associated with autism. The severity of these symptoms varies widely among individuals. Not every affected child or adult exhibits all of these characteristics, and some of the characteristics are also noted in individuals who are not in fact autistic. It is the unique constellation of symptoms that characterizes the disorder.

Deficits in Social Behavior and Attachment

He seems to be self-satisfied. He has no apparent affection when petted. He does not observe the fact that anyone comes or goes, and never seems glad to see father or mother or any playmate. He seems almost to draw into his shell and live within himself. (Kanner, description of Donald, p. 2)[3]

The mother . . . recalled that while her younger child showed an active anticipatory reaction to being picked up, Richard had not shown any physiognomic or postural sign of preparedness and had failed to adjust his body to being held by her or the nurse. (Kanner, description of Richard, p. 12)

She has no relation to children, has never talked to them, [tried] to be friendly with them, or to play with them. She moves among them like a strange being, as one moves between the pieces of furniture of a room. (Kanner, description of Elaine, p. 32)

Perhaps the hallmark feature of autism, and one of the most dramatic, is the profound and pervasive deficit in social behavior and attachment. Children with autism often do not bond with their parents, do not play with other children, may ignore or avoid the social initiations of others, and prefer to be alone.

It is not uncommon to hear a mother report that as an infant her child did not hold up his arms in anticipation of being picked up, did not look at her when held, or was "stiff" or "rigid" to hold. The infant might be described by the parent as a "good baby" because he was nondemanding and quite content to be left alone in the crib.

The baby may have cried if wet or hungry, but not just to have the parents come for company and comfort. At the other extreme, the child might engage in constant, inconsolable crying.

The parent may describe the slightly older child as not wanting to be held, cuddled, or kissed, sometimes actively resisting or avoiding expressions of affection or other social overtures. Typically the child is not upset when the parent leaves or particularly happy when the parent returns after an absence; he seems, in fact, not to notice. Children with autism usually do not come to the parent for comfort if frightened or injured, nor are they likely to be consoled by the parent's efforts to comfort them. The parents are not used as a "secure base" when the children are in new or strange settings. Rather, the parents have to be very careful to keep the child close because if they become separated, the child most likely will not be distressed nor try to locate the parent.

Many parents come to feel that their child does not love them or need them as people, but simply relates to them as objects that provide what the child wants. Consider Donnie, a 3-year-old child who was with his mother in a room full of toys. When his mother called to him, trying to get him to come to her or look at her, he persisted in ignoring her while repetitively lining up a toy Ping-Pong net along the edge of a table. He never acknowledged her presence until she finally touched his arm to get his attention. At this time he very purposefully walked away from her and pressed his face against the opposite wall in an apparent effort to shut her out completely. His almost total detachment and avoidance were striking to witness but not unusual for a child with autism.

Children with autism may not engage in social eye contact. Sometimes they actively avoid such eye contact (termed "gaze aversion"), or they seem to look "through" another person. These children rarely engage in "peek-a-boo" games or other social teasing games. Significantly, they fail to develop, or are delayed in developing, "joint attention"—that is, using their eye gaze to direct the attention of others. Joint attention is an important prerequisite for the development of more complex forms of communication and social interaction, and its absence is a significant feature of autism.

As one might expect from someone who is not socially involved, individuals with autism typically fail to show empathy or to understand the feelings of others. An autistic child returning from school to find her mother in tears would be unlikely to try to comfort her but would more likely respond inappropriately (for example, laughing or touching the mother's tears with curiosity), or would fail to notice at all. Children with autism seldom share the enjoyment of others or seek to share their own enjoyment.

Autistic children are as unresponsive to their peers as to their parents. Other children are typically ignored or actively avoided. When asked how their child might be differentiated in a group of children, parents of a child with autism often say that she is the one off by herself, playing alone. If the autistic child expresses interest in peer play, it is usually only to watch the activity without social interaction or reciprocation. If the child does initiate play with a peer, it often consists of a socially inappropriate overture such as scattering toys or saying something odd or irrelevant (for example, interrupting peers' game of catch by throwing the ball away while yelling "I'll risk a thousand, Alex!").

Since toy play is learned from the social environment, it is not surprising that children with autism are deficient in play skills. These children might ignore toys altogether, use the toy in a manner other than that for which it was intended, or become engaged with only a part of the toy. For instance, when given a toy car the autistic child does not run it along the ground while making motor noises, but might ignore it, wave it in the air repetitively, or spin the wheels in front of his eyes.

Children with autism often fail to engage in imaginative, pretend, or sociodramatic play. Play that appears imaginative is often rigidly "scripted"; the child will repeat the same script over and over, with little or no variation. For example, a child who is given a toy car set complete with little people, a house, and other accessories might do the following: drive the car to the house, put two people in the car, drive to another house, and take the people out. This precise sequence of actions would be repeated in an identical manner again and again, with no changes or elaboration. Or perhaps the child likes to draw, but only draws the same picture every time.

Even high-functioning individuals with autism remain uninterested in establishing friendships, prefer being alone, fail to consider the interests of others, and may be unresponsive or totally oblivious to subtle social cues. For example, one 22-year-old autistic man who had just earned a master's degree in engineering would talk almost exclusively and at great length about bridges and elevators. The obvious boredom of his audience and repeated efforts to change the direction of the discussion went completely unheeded, and the pedantic monologue continued until he was pointedly asked to stop talking about bridges and elevators. At no time during this "conversation" did the young man ask anything about his conversational partner's interests or activities. Either he had no interest in, or appreciation of, the social needs of others, or if he indeed had the interest he lacked the skill to engage in appropriate social discourse.

Deficits in Communication

He always seemed to be parroting what he had heard said to him at one time or another. He used the personal pronouns for the persons he was quoting, even imitating the intonation. When he wanted his mother to pull his shoe off, he said: "Pull off your shoe." When he wanted a bath, he said: "Do you want a bath?" (Kanner, description of Donald, p. 4)

Words to him had a specifically literal, inflexible meaning. He seemed unable to generalize, to transfer an expression to another similar object or situation. If he did so occasionally, it was a substitution, which then "stood" definitely for the original meaning. Thus he christened each of his watercolor bottles by the name of one of the Dionne quintuplets— Annette for blue, Cécile for red, etc. Then, going through a series of color mixtures, he proceeded in this manner: "Annette and Cécile make purple." (Kanner, description of Donald, p. 4)

Some of those exclamations could be definitely traced to previous experiences. He was in the habit of saying almost every day, "Don't throw the dog off the balcony." His mother recalled that she had said those words to him about a toy dog while they were still in England. (Kanner, description of Paul, p. 15)

Kanner considered the delay or failure in the acquisition of language to be primary to the disorder, and this opinion is still held today. Approximately half of children with autism fail to develop functional speech. Those children who do acquire speech often develop noncommunicative speech patterns that are qualitatively different from those of ordinary children or those with other specific language disorders.[4] Although parents are also concerned about their child's social unresponsiveness, it is often the delay or failure to develop speech that really alarms parents and suggests to them that something may be very wrong with their child.

In addition to failing to develop speech, nonverbal communication such as communicative gestures may be absent. Autistic children often do not shake their head to indicate "no" or nod to indicate "yes." They seldom wave "bye-bye," blow a kiss, or use other conventional social gestures. A frequently noted early sign of potential trouble is that these children do not use pointing to direct the attention of others. They may take their mother's hand, lead her to what they want, and place her hand on the object rather than point to it (*protoimperative* pointing). Similarly, they typically do not point to things in their environment to share an experience (*protodeclarative* pointing) such as seeing a fire truck or airplane. As already noted, these children often fail to use their eye gaze to direct the attention of others, which can be seen as an early nonverbal way of saying "look at that" (joint attention). They are unlikely to be able to pantomime an action to communicate, such as pretending to pour a liquid to indicate that they would like juice.

Without intensive treatment, many children remain nonverbal, using neither receptive nor expressive language. Others develop early speech using a few words or perhaps simple phrases, only to lose this speech at around 18 to 30 months of age. Thus the children may use words or phrases like "mama," "cookie," "go car," or idiosyncratic phrases such as a word from an amusement ride but suddenly (usually in a matter of days or weeks) lose the acquired speech and fail to progress linguistically. Often parents report that their child said a word or phrase very clearly on one occasion, never to do so again.

Autistic children who do speak typically exhibit distinctively pathological speech patterns. Many display *echolalia,* the repetition of words or phases spoken by others.[5] One basic form of echolalia is *immediate* echolalia, where the child parrots immediately what has just been heard. For example, in response to the question "Where is your jacket, Susan?" the child responds "Where is your jacket, Susan?" In *delayed* echolalia, the individual repeats speech that has been uttered a few minutes, a few hours, a few days, or even years in the past. Because the speech is remote in time, it is most often contextually inappropriate and may sound quite bizarre. Sometimes the original speech stimulus is identifiable, as when the child repeats a phrase from a TV commercial, an instruction heard from her teacher at school, or a parental reprimand—for instance, Paul's "Don't throw the dog off the balcony." One can usually identify a verbal statement as an echo if it can be tied to something one knows the child has heard and/or if the statement is too advanced for the child's current level of linguistic development. Most often this speech is noncommunicative: the children do not comprehend what they are saying, nor do they use this speech functionally in their environment.

We do know some of the conditions under which these children are most likely to echo. One condition that often leads to immediate echolalia is the incomprehensibility of the stimulus.[6] The child is more likely to immediately echo a verbal stimulus if he cannot come up with a response. For example, a child asked to touch his head may do so. Yet if asked to "indicate your cranium" he would likely echo "indicate your cranium" since he does not understand the command.

The conditions leading to delayed echolalia are less well understood. However, anecdotal reports suggest that it is more likely to occur under conditions of high arousal. For example, I knew an autistic child, Bobby, who was very frightened of dogs. When confronted by a dog one day the terrified child blanched, backed away, and loudly declared: "It's not going to hurt you, Bobby." "Pet the nice doggy, Bobby." It is quite likely that these are reassuring phrases he had heard in similar circumstances when he had been frightened or aroused. There are other times, however, when the reasons for the specific delayed echolalic response are unclear. Thus on another occasion when Bobby was confronted by a dog he also exclaimed, "It's not a glass paperweight!" and "I said get to bed *right now!*" Obviously any connection between the immediate environmental stimulus and the original verbal stimulus was remote.

Probably related to echolalic speech is the often observed pattern of *pronominal reversal,* in which the individual refers to himself as "you" or by his name rather than "I" or "me." The quotes from Donald given above are examples of this speech anomaly. Undoubtedly Donald heard his parent say "Do you want a bath?" in situations where he was given a bath. Children who use their echolalia to communicate may produce statements such as "Do you want to go outside?" or "Do you want a cookie?" to indicate that these are their wishes. These are direct echoes of statements they have heard on occasions when they have been given what they wanted. It is interesting to note that early in the history of autism research, psychodynamic observers often saw great significance in the failure of these children to use the words "me" or "I" and suggested this was because the child was denying the existence of the "self." However, the more modern, and reasonable, perspective views this speech anomaly as a function of echolalic speech.

Idiosyncratic speech and *neologisms* are also frequently noted in these individuals. Idiosyncratic speech occurs when a person consistently uses an unusual word or phrase to express a label or concept. Donald's use of the Dionne quintuplet names rather than the accepted color names for paints is an example. Another child consistently referred to a particular mechanical toy as a "Cow says." When activated in a particular way, this toy produced a prerecorded voice that said, "The cow says moo." Another child referred to any reel-to-reel tape recorder as a "self-destruct in five seconds" (obviously related to the television program *Mission: Impossible*). Neologisms occur when an individual consistently uses a novel, made-up word or phrase to express a label or concept. One child used the neologism "pling" to refer to any pencil.

The speech of most speaking autistic individuals is characterized by *dysprosody,* meaning that the melodic features of the speech are irregular. Their speech may be monotonic (often described as similar to the speech of the deaf), poorly articulated, and unusual in rhythm, pace, or inflection. Thus the speech may be too rapid or too slow, may have incorrect emphasis on syllables within a word, or may otherwise be abnormal. Unfortunately, even those autistic individuals who have relatively good language skills may still sound abnormal because of the prosodic errors in their speech.

Communication may be deviant in other aspects as well. Often language comprehension is severely impaired, and speech may serve noncommunicative purposes such as self-stimulation, where it serves primarily to function as a means for receiving sensory feedback.[7] Thus autistic children may repeat specific sounds, words, or phrases over and over, not to communicate but rather for the stimulation that such repetition provides. Further, communicative language is often limited to the here-and-now, with distinct difficulty shown in communicating past, future, or hypothetical events.

The language of children with autism may be restricted to the very literal; analogies, metaphors, and humor are essentially incomprehensible. An autistic child told that it is "raining cats and dogs" may run outside to watch for the falling animals. Humor frequently falls flat, as the children just do not "get" the joke. Literalness can interfere with even the simplest of interactions. I remember one autistic child, Danny, who was receiving treatment in our program. An undergraduate student named Rick worked with Danny for several months. For some reason Danny kept referring to Rick as "Poster" despite numerous corrections from Rick. Finally one day Rick became frustrated and told the child very intently, "Danny, my name is NOT POSTER!" The result (as one might have guessed) was that Danny referred to him as "Not Poster" ever after.

The speech of even high-functioning and linguistically skilled individuals with autism is often devoid of emotion, abstraction, or imagination. Attempts to elicit statements of feelings are typically met with noncommittal answers, such as "It was good," "It was bad," and the perennial favorite, "I don't know." Sometimes even the most direct query will elicit a highly concrete and odd response. For example, one adult with autism was asked how he felt when his mother died. He responded, "She was 68." It is startling to hear conversation that is based almost completely on the concrete, lacking in color or emotion, yet such is the case with many of these individuals.

Restricted, Repetitive, and Stereotyped Patterns of Behavior

The major part of his "conversation" consisted of questions of an obsessive nature. He was inexhaustible in bringing up variations: "How many days in a week, years in a century, hours in a day, hours in half a day, weeks in a century, centuries in half a millennium," etc., etc.; "How many pints in a gallon, how many gallons to fill four gallons?" Sometimes he asked, "How many hours in a minute, how many days in an hour?" etc. (Kanner, description of Donald, p. 7)

Another of his recent hobbies is with old issues of *Time* magazine. He found a copy of the first issue of March 3, 1923, and has attempted to make a list of the dates of publication of each issue since that time. So far he has gotten to April, 1934. He has figured the number of issues in a volume and similar nonsense. (Kanner, description of Donald, p. 8)

He persistently refused to take fluid in any but an all-glass container. Once, while at a hospital, he went three days without fluid because it was offered in tin cups. . . . He became upset by any change of an accustomed pattern: If he notices change, he is very fussy and cries. (Kanner, description of Herbert, p. 20)

The behavior of many children with autism is compulsive, ritualistic, repetitious, obsessive, and stereotyped, which may involve gross- and fine-motor behaviors or highly sophisticated verbal rituals. These behaviors are usually idiosyncratic and rarely serve any function other than to provide the child with sensory feedback or to reduce the anxiety often displayed when the behaviors are blocked.[8]

At the gross-motor level, one often sees rhythmic body rocking, rocking from foot to foot, head bobbing or weaving, arm and/or hand flapping, jumping, spinning, pacing, or posturing. At a fine-motor level one might observe finger wiggling, gazing at or "regarding" the cupped hand at the side of the face, grimacing, finger posturing, eye crossing, saliva swishing, or hair twirling. Often objects are incorporated in these movements, as when the child repeatedly taps something, twirls saucepan lids or pieces of string, flips the pages of a book, waves objects in front of the face, or spins the wheels of a toy car. Repetitive vocalizations such as nonsense sound patterns, repetitive production of words or phrases, or snippets of songs are also common. These behaviors are typically referred to either as "self-stimulation," to connote that the function of the behavior is to provide sensory stimulation, or as "stereotypy," to reflect the repetitive and stereotyped nature of the activity.

Self-stimulation presents several problems. First, many of these children spend a great deal of their time in such self-stimulatory activity. While the amount of time may vary, some children spend most of their waking hours so engaged, often to the exclusion of almost everything else. Second, the behavior often appears bizarre and thus it stigmatizes the individual. Finally, there is substantial research that suggests self-stimulation interferes with responsiveness to the environment and with learning. Accordingly, a good deal of research has focused on the nature of self-stimulation and on how it may be eliminated. Unfortunately, it remains one of the most difficult and poorly understood behaviors that are observed in autistic individuals.

Other compulsive and ritualistic behaviors are seen as well. We observe children who compulsively line up objects, follow patterns in floor tiles or wallpaper, or build the identical block form repeatedly. Rather than playing with toy cars in the usual way, a child with autism may arrange them in perfect rows, categorized by color, and all facing the same direction. Any disruption of this arrangement by adding, subtracting, or rearranging the cars is met with distress (often a tantrum). The child will probably repeat the car arrangement over and over, with no variation.

Autistic children may insist on collecting and carrying particular objects (such as small rocks, sticks, a piece of cloth, or a particular toy) at all times, and strongly resist any attempt to remove them. Children I have known have insisted on carrying items such as fast-food condiment packets, Tinker Toy dowels (one in each hand at all times), leaves, pages from a phone book, and bottle caps. I remember one little boy who was not attached to a teddy bear or blanket but rather took a hand-held vacuum cleaner to bed with him every night, and a girl who insisted on carrying a stop sign with her everywhere she went.

Children with autism may strongly resist changes in the physical environment—what Kanner described as an "anxiously obsessive desire for the maintenance of sameness." Changes in furniture arrangements, for example, are often noted immediately, with the child attempting to return the furniture to its original position. If this is impossible, the child may be quite upset until the disruption is corrected. Sometimes even the most minute detail is detected, as when the child notices that a particular figurine has been moved a few inches on a table or a package of cookies has been placed in the wrong position on a pantry shelf. To illustrate, one little girl became extremely upset if any of the following occurred: the Cheerios box was left open, any drawer in the house was left open, her father's reclining chair was left in the reclining position, or the dining room drapes were left in the halfway open position. Needless to say, her tantrums had her parents and siblings racing around the house to fix the offending problems.

Changes in daily routine or familiar routes of travel also may be very upsetting. Alterations to expected schedules are not well tolerated, and maintaining routines becomes imperative for parents. If the child is used to riding in the car and taking a specific route to school or other familiar destination, changes in the route or travel pace may lead to a tantrum. One mother reported receiving several traffic citations for failing to stop at a stop sign in her neighborhood. The stop sign had only recently been placed at that location, but since her autistic son was used to maintaining speed there, any stop on her part was followed by a screaming tantrum.

Ritualistic preoccupations are also observed, when the children memorize information that may be trivial or of little functional value. They may rigidly pursue rote learning of train or bus schedules, TV schedule grids, maps, consecutive numbers in a telephone book, or dates. Donald's preoccupation with cataloging issues of *Time* magazine is a good example of this behavior. One may be amazed at the individual's ability to retain such information, and at its practical pointlessness. The individual may never take the trains or buses whose schedules are memorized, watch the television shows, or call the phone numbers. Rather, it is the act of memorizing and maintaining the information that seems to be of utmost importance.

Compulsions and rituals involve behaviors that must be performed in a particular manner. Such behaviors include, for example, insisting on watching a particular TV program every day at the same time, tapping a door jamb three times before crossing the threshold, only using certain eating utensils (like Herbert with his glass cups), wearing only red clothing, or folding the bedspread into an exact square. Many autistic children have compulsive food rituals: they will only eat one or two specific foods, or may only eat foods of a particular color, or only if the food is placed in a specific section of a plate. These behaviors can be extremely disruptive for the parents and family; for example, one child insisted on licking the license plate of every car he passed while walking in a parking lot. Needless to say, this family avoided parking lots whenever possible, and when forced to use one, they found a parking space as close as possible to their destination.

Linguistically advanced individuals with autism may exhibit compulsive behaviors when they engage in conversations. Repetitive questions are common, as is the insistence that the listener respond in a particular manner or provide a specific answer. The child may become very agitated until the listener does in fact respond in the expected fashion. When a person with autism engages in conversation involving a favored topic, it is extremely difficult to divert the direction of the conversation (as with the engineer who was preoccupied with elevators and bridges). I remember one autistic child who was completely obsessed with Volvo automobiles. He carried around a Volvo brochure describing the models, looked for Volvos on the street, and would work very hard for the reward of visiting a Volvo dealership and being allowed to walk down the aisles of cars. Another young man was obsessed with the television news anchorman Dan Rather and spoke of little else.

Abnormalities in Response to the Physical Environment

But usually, when spoken to, he went on with whatever he was doing as if nothing had been said. Yet one never had the feeling that he was willingly disobedient or contrary. He was obviously so remote that the remarks did not reach him. (Kanner, description of Paul, p. 14)

He displayed "an abstraction of mind which made him perfectly oblivious to everything about him." (Kanner, description of Donald, p. 3)

One puzzling and discouraging thing is the great difficulty one has in getting his attention. (Kanner, description of Richard, p. 12)

Children with autism are often described as showing deficient or unusual responsiveness to their sensory environment. Parents often suspect sensory impairment such as blindness or deafness because a child may be very unresponsive to loud noises, the calling of her name, or other auditory stimuli. The failure to develop language is another reason parents and others may suspect deafness. Similarly, the child may be unresponsive to visual stimuli; she may not respond to people entering a room, nor track the progress of people or things across her visual field. This is not true sensory impairment, however, as shown by the fact that the unresponsiveness may be highly variable. Thus the child who does not respond to the calling of her name or a loud noise may respond to the crinkle of a candy wrapper or may repeat commercial jingles. The child also may be hypersensitive to noises and cover her ears at the sound of a cat's meow. The child who appears to be blind may not respond to people coming and going in his environment, but will spot a small piece of candy several feet away or be transfixed by watching pieces of lint fall through a beam of light. Clearly the unusual responsiveness observed in these children is behavioral and not due to basic deficits at the receptor level.

Unusual sensory interests are also frequently observed. Autistic children may seek to run their hands across certain textures, mouth or lick objects, sniff people or objects, or put their ear against sound stimuli such as stereo speakers. One little girl I knew would go up to unfamiliar adult men, raise up their pants cuff, and feel their socks, much to the embarrassment of her parents. These children may gaze intently at spinning objects such as flushing toilets, tops, washing machines, and fans. Some stimuli are attractive and sought out; others are avoided at all cost.

Autistic children may also be over- or under-responsive to touch, pain, or temperature. An attenuated response to pain is often reported, as when the child falls and skins his knee or bumps his head and fails to cry (or, of course, to seek comfort from a parent). Often the child's response to such an injury is to get up and continue with what he was doing, to the amazement of those watching. In fact, many parents find this particular feature of the disorder very unsettling since they fear the child may suffer a serious injury of which the parent might be unaware. In contrast to this under-responsiveness, some children display a hypersensitivity to physical contact with other people and become quite agitated when touched ("tactile defensiveness").

The unusual responsiveness of these children to their sensory environment is interesting not only because of their sometimes unusual behaviors but also because this sensory deficit has significant implications for learning. Since learning from the environment requires attention to relevant stimuli, deficits in this area have a direct impact on learning. As we shall see later in the book, some interesting controversy exists around the issue of patterns of attention and cognitive development.

Abnormalities of Affect

He had many fears, almost always connected with mechanical noise (meat grinders, vacuum cleaners, streetcars, trains, etc.). (Kanner, description of Alfred, p. 24)

He was "tremendously frightened by running water, gas burners, and many other things." (Kanner, description of Herbert, p. 20)

He frets when the bread is put in the oven to be made into toast, and is afraid it will get burned or be hurt. He is upset when the sun sets. He is upset because the moon does not always appear in the sky at night. (Kanner, description of Alfred, p. 22)

The emotions expressed by individuals with autism are frequently odd. Their emotional responses may be excessive and exaggerated, or may be relatively stable and minimal ("flat"). Some autistic children are extremely labile, shifting rapidly between hysterical laughter and inconsolable sobbing with no apparent provocation. Parents often complain that their children "fly into" intense tantrums or laugh uncontrollably, and there is nothing the parent can do to predict or ameliorate the problem. The affect may be quite mismatched to the situation, as when the child laughs when someone else is hurt, or cries when given a birthday present. The children displaying flat affect may seem to be "cruising in neutral" despite the varying conditions in the environment. This flat affect is typically accompanied by little variation in facial expression.

The lack of connection between the affect and the environment is well described by Bernard Rimland.[9] He notes that while childhood schizophrenics may be described as "disoriented," in that their response to the environment is apparent but confused, children with autism can be described as "unoriented" in that they fail to respond directly to their environment.

Irrational fears are frequently noted, and often these are related to the children's demand for sameness. Their extreme responses to changes in environment, routes of travel, or routine often take the form of fear or anger. These children may be frightened by objects or events that to other people are completely innocuous, as can be seen with Alfred and Herbert in the quotes given above. I have known children who have been intensely frightened of balloons, felt, tortillas, ferns, yellow ducks, sesame seed hamburger buns (regular buns were fine), Bill Cosby, the Channel 7 *Eyewitness News*, and the theme song from the television show *Family Ties*.

Intellectual Functioning

He gave the impression of silent wisdom to me. (Kanner, description of Richard, p. 12)

Formal testing could not be carried out, but he certainly could not be regarded as feebleminded in the ordinary sense. After hearing his boarding mother say grace three times, he repeated it without a flaw and has retained it since then. He could count and name colors. He learned quickly to identify his favorite [V]ictrola records from a large stack and knew how to mount and play them. (Kanner, description of Paul, p. 15)

Even though most of these children were at one time or another looked upon as feebleminded, they are all unquestionably endowed with good cognitive potentialities. (Kanner, general discussion, p. 39)

Kanner felt that the excellent rote memories of the children he studied, together with their intelligent, serious facial appearance and their lack of physical abnormalities, suggested normal intellectual abilities. In his opinion, the appearance of mental retardation (that is, poor performance on standardized intellectual assessments and learning difficulties) was the result of the social and communicative impairments that characterized the children and of the difficulties encountered when administering standardized tests to them. However, despite Kanner's optimistic original assessment, we now know that normal cognitive ability is by far the exception in the case of autism. The majority of these children are in fact cognitively impaired to some extent, most to a serious degree. In fact, estimates from various studies agree that approximately 75 percent of autistic children are mentally retarded.[10]

One of the main distinctions between children with autism and children whose primary diagnosis is mental retardation is the fairly distinctive and variable profile exhibited by autistic children on subtests of intellectual ability. While children with mental retardation tend to score at a depressed level across all areas, the pattern of performance on different tests and/or subtests for children with autism typically shows a distinctive pattern. These children tend to score poorly on assessments of symbolic thought (such as language) and abstract reasoning, and to score higher on assessments of visual-spatial ability and rote memory.

There is another argument for the view that poor scores on standardized assessments reflect a genuine cognitive impairment in these children, which is that IQ in autistic children has the same properties as it does for other children. Thus the score tends to be relatively stable in childhood and adolescence and to be predictive of future educational accomplishments.

An additional reason why Kanner and others originally thought children with autism were not mentally retarded was the presence of "splinter" skills, or special abilities that stood in stark contrast to the severe deficits seen in other areas of functioning. Many of these children display isolated, and usually quite narrow, areas of exceptional skill. In a minority of cases these skills may be at the savant level,[11] but it is usually the case that the skill is at a normal or near-normal level for the child's age; it appears exceptional because of the child's low level of ability in other areas. These special abilities most commonly lie in the areas of rote memory, mathematical calculations, mechanical skills, or musical ability. Parents are often amazed when their young autistic child proves adept at operating the VCR, memorizes nursery rhymes, or remembers the exact location of an object in a store after not visiting the store for years.

Not surprisingly, the true savant skills seen in a small percentage of autistic individuals have attracted a great deal of attention. Consider the movie *Rain Man*, which depicts a young man with autism who is adept at performing complicated mathematical calculations in his head, card counting in Las Vegas, and other impressive counting feats. This depiction is not an exaggeration; indeed, the actor Dustin Hoffman based his characterization on a compilation of three known autistic savants. Other such individuals have shown their ability to rapidly complete complicated jigsaw puzzles (picture side down), memorize schedules from *TV Guide*, assemble complex mechanical apparatus, or reproduce musical pieces after only one hearing. Some savants can determine on which day of the week a particular date will fall (a skill called "calendar calculation").

These special skill areas tend to be narrow and isolated, and completely nonpredictive of the child's overall level of functioning. For example, one 7-year-old musical savant could hear a melody once and subsequently play the melody on any of six musical instruments. He could also instantly play complex harmonies to the melody. However, this same child was not toilet-trained, could not respond to a simple question like "What's your name?" and could not respond to an instruction such as "Close the door." He was very gifted in his musical ability, but one could not imagine how this skill would benefit him in life, especially in the absence of more adaptive skills. Despite his immense musical talent, he was functionally mentally retarded and required constant supervision.

Disruptive Behaviors

Although not diagnostic of autism, other behavioral features are important to describe since they can be important aspects of a child's functioning and may have a significant impact on the child, various treatment providers, and the family. These are the severely disruptive behaviors exhibited by many autistic children. These behaviors are also observed in other populations such as the mentally retarded.

Probably one of the most dramatic of these is self-injurious behavior (SIB), which occurs when the child purposely inflicts physical damage to his body. The most common forms of SIB are head banging and self-biting of the hands or wrists. Other common SIB behaviors include self-slapping of the face or sides, hair pulling, eye gouging, and self-scratching. The intensity of SIB varies widely across individuals. Some individuals who slap their faces, bite their wrists, bang their heads, or otherwise injure themselves leave bruises, redness, or calluses. Others, however, engage in SIB so intensely that they may suffer major injuries such as fractured skulls, detached retinas, broken noses, or the loss of large chunks of flesh. In fact, it is possible for an individual to die from injuries sustained from SIB, as when the child runs headfirst into a concrete wall or head-bangs to the point of severe brain damage. I remember one little boy who sought out metal bed frames on which to bang his head. Despite the best efforts of his caretakers and the presence of almost continuous physical restraints, he managed to continue this behavior until he suffered major brain damage and died from his injuries. It is important to remember that the child was not "suicidal" in the sense that he was seeking death; rather, the death was a tragic result of engaging in this behavior.

While not usually as dangerous to the individual, severe tantrum behavior can be a serious problem with many autistic children. These tantrums look pretty much like the standard, everyday tantrums of all children except for their intensity and, to some extent, their unpredictability. These children may throw violent, screaming tantrums that persist for many hours. On a trip her parents will certainly never forget, one 3½-year-old girl had a nonstop 13-hour tantrum while on a flight from California to Germany.

The tantrums may be set off by very idiosyncratic and seemingly benign events such as the misplacement of a piece of furniture, the alteration of a daily routine, or a particular scene in a video. As discussed earlier, some of these youngsters may be quite upset in response to violations of rituals or compulsions, and a major tantrum may result. In some cases the child may engage in aggression or property destruction (although children with autism are neither more aggressive nor more destructive than other populations with severe behavior problems).

As one can imagine, raising a child with autism is a daunting, frustrating, and often discouraging challenge. These children suffer from a severe life-span disability that affects just about every area of functioning. Given the enormity of the burden of raising such a child, it is not surprising that the parents of these children are often reported to suffer from high levels of depression and stress. As bad as this situation is, however, it used to be even worse. In the past the parents often had to face an additional burden—the accusation that they caused the disorder in their child.

CHAPTER 3

Diagnosis and Assessment

It might seem safe to infer . . . that there would be little controversy about the existence of infantile autism as a clinical entity, and little confusion as to its diagnosis. Nothing could be further from the truth.

> —Bernard Rimland, *Infantile Autism* (1964)

Today, among the complex psychiatric or developmental disorders, autism probably has the best empirical basis for its cross-national diagnostic criteria.

> —Fred R. Volkmar, Ami Klin, and Donald J. Cohen, in *Handbook of Autism and Pervasive Developmental Disorders* (1997)

These data suggest that improvements in detection and changes in diagnosis account for the observed increase in autism; whether there has also been a true increase in incidence is not known.

> —Lisa A. Croen, Judith K. Grether, Jenny Hoogstrate, and Steve Selvin, in *Journal of Autism and Developmental Disorders* (2002)

As with most areas in autism, diagnosis and classification of the syndrome have been complicated topics. The complications have arisen largely because of the heterogeneity in the expression of the disorder, earlier diagnostic schemes that intertwined theories of etiology with diagnosis, and the fact that autism shares features with many other forms of childhood disorders. All of these factors led to disagreements which in fact had the ultimately positive effect of promoting the development of objective and empirically based diagnostic classification.

Psychologists, psychiatrists, and researchers have persevered in their efforts to develop diagnostic criteria and a classification system for autism because such a system is critical for many reasons. First, for research in the field to advance in an effective and influential manner, it is essential that researchers ensure they are working with comparable populations. Both etiological and treatment research require that scientists be able to communicate clearly the nature of study populations. In the past, such comparisons were often meaningless because the heterogeneity of the population and the broad, rather poorly defined diagnostic categories meant that individuals in these studies could indeed be very different yet have the same diagnostic label of "autism." One scientist could be studying a group of children with no language while another scientist could be studying a group of children with language, yet all of the children might be labeled "autistic." These two groups were probably quite different. The more precise, comprehensive, and detailed a classification system is, the more valuable it is as a means of communication for researchers.

Second, diagnostic precision is important to clinicians for the development, implementation, and evaluation of treatment. Such a diagnostic system provides the clinician with a clear picture of what types of behaviors are likely to be present or absent, which behaviors may be most important for treatment focus in terms of prognostic importance, and what behavioral changes are important for the best outcome. In addition, diagnostic precision and clarity help communication between clinicians, thus allowing the treatment field to progress in a systematic manner (although, as we shall see later, this goal is far from completely achieved).

Third, educators and other community service providers depend upon diagnosis and classification systems for appropriate placements for children and adults with autism. Many classroom placements are made on the basis of diagnosis (although this is not necessarily the best course to pursue in every case). Again, a good diagnostic system will allow the service provider to anticipate the behavioral characteristics present in the individual, and it is hoped these very characteristics will lead to the design and development of a specific program (for example, an autism classroom) appropriate to the needs of each individual.

Fourth, diagnosis and classification are always important to other community entities such as governmental agencies, the legal system, and insurance companies. Individuals with various diagnostic labels typically have certain legal entitlements, access to specific government programs, and also perhaps insurance coverage. Of course, diagnosis can be a two-edged sword in that it can just as easily be used to deny as to qualify individuals for services.

Historical Debate

Today "autistic disorder" is recognized as a general label covering many constituent subdisorders, perhaps with distinct etiologies and/or courses as yet undetermined. However, this has not always been the case. The earliest diagnostic system involved Kanner's original description, which presented the syndrome as characterized by six main features: extreme "autistic aloneness," language abnormalities, obsessive desire for the maintenance of sameness, good cognitive potential, normal physical development, and highly intelligent, obsessive, and cold parents. Unfortunately, Kanner's relatively general description proved to be problematic because no clear and objective criteria were proposed for making the diagnosis.

In fact, it was left to subjective clinical judgment to determine when social withdrawal was severe enough to be pathological (or what Kanner called "autistic aloneness"). Similarly, the determination of parental obsessiveness or coldness was a subjective clinical judgment, since the parents were not given any standardized tests for these characteristics. This lack of diagnostic precision often led to some debate as to whether a particular child met enough of the individual criteria to qualify for the diagnosis.

One of the main reasons for this element of imprecision was of course the fact that autism was, and remains, a phenomenological diagnosis. That is, the diagnosis is made on the basis of the observed behavioral characteristics of the individual rather than the more definitive assessment of a biological marker. Given the well-known heterogeneity of expression of autism, one can easily see the potential for disagreement. To look at a different example, the diagnosis of Down syndrome can be very specific because a genetic analysis will show the trisomy of the 21st chromosome. Thus the diagnosis is definite, and the range of expression of Down syndrome is relatively narrow (although there is some variation). In contrast, we have as yet no biological marker for autism, and the expression of the disorder is very broad. It is likely that what we call "autistic disorder" is really a diagnostic category made up of several as-yet-undetermined subgroups. The subgroups may present with similar features, yet it may be the case that each subgroup is caused by different genetic interactions and each will be traced to a separate set of biological markers.

Another problem complicating the process was that early diagnostic schemes (most importantly, Kanner's) included erroneous assumptions that no doubt interfered with the development of accurate classification systems. One such assumption was the inclusion of parental characteristics such as socioeconomic level, education, emotional aloofness, compulsiveness, mechanical thinking, and the like. Since it was originally believed that autism was a result of parental pathology, the existence of parents exhibiting these characteristics was considered important in the diagnostic process. As we shall see, subsequent study did not support these assumptions. Empirical studies have demonstrated that when one controls for potential biasing factors in subject selection, autism is found in families from all social classes and educational levels. It is now known that autism is a neurologically based, as opposed to a psychogenically based, disorder.

A second early assumption was that children with autism had normal intelligence, or in Kanner's words "good cognitive potential." He based his opinion on the fact that the children in his initial cohort were very attractive, exhibiting none of the unusual physical characteristics typically seen in other populations such as children with Down syndrome or other forms of mental retardation. In addition, he was influenced by the fact that the performance of these children on intelligence tests was not uniformly poor. Unlike retarded children, who typically do poorly on all subtests of intelligence instruments, autistic children exhibit a variable profile; they may do relatively well on subtests assessing visual-spatial skills and rote memory despite their poor performance on tests of verbal skill and abstract reasoning. Kanner attributed the children's poor performance on these latter subtests to a basic social motivation problem. This optimistic view suggested that these children had the capacity for normal intellectual functioning but the nature of the tests was such that it was not being measured. However, we now know that this assumption is incorrect: the majority of autistic individuals have some degree of cognitive impairment.

A third assumption held by Kanner was that autism was not related to any specific medical condition. As the years passed it became apparent that autism was not wholly independent from other conditions, and indeed several medical conditions are often seen in conjunction with autism (although they are not necessarily a cause of autism). Some of these conditions include fragile X syndrome, rubella, and tuberous sclerosis.

Another problem was the early tendency to apply existing classification systems to these children. Kanner's rather unfortunate choice of the label "autism" created some confusion. When he used the term, he was emphasizing the extreme social withdrawal of these children. But Bleuler had earlier used "autism" to describe the idiosyncratic, self-centered withdrawal into an active fantasy life exhibited by schizophrenics.[1] Ironically, Kanner was expressing the opposite view—that it was the *absence* of any creative fantasy life that characterized the social isolation in autism. However, given the behavioral similarities between Kanner's cohort of children and individuals with schizophrenia, it is perhaps not surprising that the two were seen as related. Lauretta Bender and others thought that autistic children represented the earliest expression of adult schizophrenia,[2] and thus the diagnostic label "childhood schizophrenia" was used for many years. This view was not shared by Kanner, who steadfastly asserted that autism was distinct from childhood schizophrenia. Today the diagnosis of childhood-onset schizophrenia is not commonly confused with autism.

These early classifications were heavily based on psychodynamic influences that reflected the world of psychiatry at that time (primarily the 1940s and 1950s). This meant that very early childhood experiences, particularly attachment relationships with parents, were seen as directly leading to the development of psychological disorders. An influential child psychoanalyst, Berta Rank, talked about "atypical ego development"—the failure of early experiences and relationships to allow for the developmental progression to a normal, healthy self.[3] Margaret Mahler described autistic children as suffering from "symbiotic psychosis" and thus emphasized the hypothesized pathological mother-child relationship.[4]

These existing classification systems proved to be of relatively little value in the ultimate classification of the disorder. Erroneous assumptions regarding cognitive abilities and parental psychopathology, attempts to shoehorn these individuals into existing diagnostic classifications, and the heterogeneity in expression of the disorder all contributed to the delay in accurate and helpful diagnostic systems.

Current Diagnostic Issues

Although the years between Kanner's original report and the present have been characterized by numerous disagreements and debates regarding diagnostic criteria, it is now the case that a fairly good consensus exists. Over the past forty years the reliance on the clinical description and subjective diagnostic classifications has been reduced, and the process of diagnosis has been augmented or sometimes completely changed as a result of empirical research aimed at both refining important diagnostic features and developing objective assessments. The move from subjective impressions to empirically based diagnostic criteria reflects a general change in the field of psychopathology. The need for consensus and communication among researchers and clinicians called for a uniform classification system, and such a system had to be developed systematically.

First, decisions had to be made regarding which features were specific to autism and which features were often associated with the disorder but were not differentially diagnostic. For example, the severe and pervasive social deficits are differentially diagnostic in that such deficits seem to be largely unique to autism. In contrast, while self-stimulatory behavior is often observed in autistic children, it is also observed in children with mental retardation and those with sensory impairments, and thus this feature alone is not diagnostic of autism.

In addition, the whole diagnostic issue had to be put into a developmental perspective. This means that the process of diagnosis and the diagnostic requirements must consider the normative development of the individual. To what extent is a particular feature developmentally inappropriate, and to what extent is it inappropriate regardless of age? To give an example, echolalia is a speech anomaly associated with autism (although not in and of itself diagnostic). However, typical children of around 2 or 3 years of age also engage in verbal echoic behavior. The typical youngster who echoes is merely going through an early stage of the normal progression of language development, and the echoing disappears as more sophisticated speech is acquired. In children with autism, however, the echoing persists past the age where typical peers have moved on to more advanced speech. In contrast, some behaviors exhibited by autistic children, such as severe social isolation, are inappropriate at any age and normal children never exhibit them.

There is now agreement that autism is in fact a distinct disorder (or set of disorders, known as Autistic Spectrum Disorder) and that it is characterized by several specific behavioral features. This specificity of behavioral features is intended to reduce ambiguity as to the presence or absence of important diagnostic requirements. Evidence that consensus has been reached is the fact that the two most accepted diagnostic systems are now in almost complete agreement regarding the diagnostic features of autism. These two systems are the American Psychiatric Association's *Diagnostic and Statistical Manual of Mental Disorders, Fourth Edition* (DSM-IV; 1994)[5] and the 10th edition of the World Health Organization's *International Classification of Diseases* (ICD-10; 1993).[6] This consensus has been achieved over many years of field testing of diagnostic schemes and the continual refinement of specific behavioral criteria. Once the field let go of the schemes that relied upon erroneous assumptions of etiology and inaccurate characteristics and embraced empirical testing as a means of refinement, the establishment of diagnostic systems with validity and reliability became possible. In fact, we can now say that of all the major forms of psychiatric and developmental disorders, autism has probably the strongest empirical basis for its diagnostic criteria. A common "language" of diagnosis is finally available which can clarify communication among the rele-

Table 3.1 DSM-IV Diagnostic Criteria for Autistic Disorder

A. A total of six (or more) items from (1), (2), and (3), with at least two from (1), and one each from (2) and (3):
   (1) Qualitative impairment in social interaction, as manifested by at least two of the following:
   (a) marked impairment in the use of multiple nonverbal behaviors such as eye-to-eye gaze, facial expression, body postures, and gestures to regulate social interaction;
   (b) failure to develop peer relationships appropriate to developmental level;
   (c) a lack of spontaneous seeking to share enjoyment, interests, or achievements with other people (e.g., by a lack of showing, bringing, or pointing out objects of interest);
   (d) lack of social or emotional reciprocity.
   (2) Qualitative impairments in communication as manifested by at least one of the following:
   (a) delay in, or total lack of, the development of spoken language (not accompanied by an attempt to compensate through alternative modes of communication such as gesture or mime);
   (b) in individuals with adequate speech, marked impairment in the ability to initiate or sustain a conversation with others;
   (c) stereotyped and repetitive use of language or idiosyncratic language;
   (d) lack of varied, spontaneous make-believe play or social imitative play appropriate to developmental level.
   (3) Restricted repetitive and stereotyped patterns of behavior, interests, and activities, as manifested by at least one of the following:
   (a) encompassing preoccupation with one or more stereotyped and restricted patterns of interest that is abnormal either in intensity or focus;
   (b) apparently inflexible adherence to specific, nonfunctional routines or rituals;
   (c) stereotyped and repetitive motor mannerisms (e.g., hand or finger flapping or twisting, or complex whole-body movements);
   (d) persistent preoccupation with parts of objects.

B. Delays or abnormal functioning in at least one of the following areas, with onset prior to age 3 years: (1) social interaction, (2) language as used in social communication, or (3) symbolic or imaginative play.

C. The disturbance is not better accounted for by Rett's Disorder or Childhood Disintegrative Disorder.

Source: Reprinted with permission from the *Diagnostic and Statistical Manual of Mental Disorders,* Fourth Edition, Text Revision, copyright 2000, American Psychiatric Association.

vant parties and agencies concerned with research and practice with this population. Table 3.1 presents the precise diagnostic criteria for Autistic Disorder as listed in the DSM-IV (1994).

One important measure of the value of a diagnostic categorization system is the extent to which it not only identifies individuals who should be *included* within a diagnostic category but also determines which individuals should be *excluded* from the category. In other words, it is important that the diagnostic scheme be able to distinguish among disorders that indeed may be very similar in that they share common features. Thus differential diagnosis is extremely important, and over the years some debate has centered on these issues. Although we have firmly established that autistic disorder and childhood-onset schizophrenia are distinct, and we no longer speak of "atypical ego development" or "symbiotic psychosis," there are still some areas in which consensus has not been achieved.

Currently the DSM-IV makes distinctions between autistic disorder and other specific forms of pervasive developmental disorders with which it shares features. The three other forms of pervasive developmental disorder are Rett's Disorder, Childhood Disintegrative Disorder (formerly known as Heller's Disorder), and Asperger's Disorder.

Rett's Disorder

Rett's Disorder has to date been definitively diagnosed only in females (in contrast to autistic disorder, which is heavily weighted toward males). It is characterized by deceleration in head growth, progressive loss of purposeful hand skills, and poorly coordinated gait or trunk movements. In the early years, children subsequently diagnosed with Rett's Disorder may at first be diagnosed with autistic disorder because they exhibit social deficits and stereotypical hand movements ("hand wringing") as well as other difficulties similar to those found in autism. It may only be later in development when the physical symptoms of Rett's Disorder become apparent that the correct diagnosis is determined. (The recent discovery of a genetic marker for Rett's Disorder now allows for a test that will permit an earlier diagnosis.) The long-term prognosis of children with Rett's Disorder is poor, with most victims suffering severe deterioration in motor abilities, loss of ambulative ability, and subsequent reduced life span.

Child Disintegrative Disorder

Child Disintegrative Disorder (CDD) is extremely rare—only 100 cases have been reported since 1908 when it was first described. While it is characterized by some of the same features one sees in autistic disorder, CDD differs primarily in the fact that the distinctive regression in development occurs after approximately two years of normal development. In contrast, symptoms of autistic disorder are typically evident within the first year of life. The clinical outcome for children with CDD is reported to be quite variable. In approximately three-quarters of the cases, there is the characteristic marked deterioration with no further improvement. In some other cases the initial deterioration may be followed by some improvement, and in a very limited number of cases, the recovery may be significant.[7]

Asperger's Disorder

While the distinctions between autistic disorder and the two disorders just described are readily accepted, the same cannot be said of Asperger's Disorder. Asperger's Disorder was first described by the Austrian physician Hans Asperger in 1944,[8] around the same time when Kanner was writing to describe "infantile autism." Because World War II was going on, the two men were unaware of each other's reports. Despite being in the literature for as long as autism, Asperger's Disorder has attracted widespread attention only relatively recently and is now being diagnosed at the rate of about 1 in 250 children. (I will return to the subject of incidence later in this chapter.) There is still ongoing debate regarding the validity of a diagnostic distinction between Asperger's Disorder and "high-functioning" autism. Asperger's Disorder is characterized by many of the behavioral features of autistic disorder except two: children with Asperger's typically are not generally delayed in language development, nor are they cognitively impaired. Since some children with autistic disorder are likewise not cognitively impaired, and some develop sophisticated speech, there are professionals in the field who argue that there is no essential difference between the two. However, those who believe Asperger's Disorder is a distinct form of disorder argue that other differences between the two populations are significant.

First, children with Asperger's Disorder are likely to exhibit deviance as opposed to delay in language and communication. It has been noted that while they are not delayed in the acquisition of language *form* (semantics, syntax, phonology), other aspects of their communication are distinctly disordered. These other aspects relate to the *use* of language, generally referred to as pragmatics. Their use of language for social intercourse may be characterized by one-sided, pedantic, egocentric "conversation" in which they are quite verbose regarding a topic of their own (perhaps idiosyncratic) interest. Their conversation is typically devoid of real emotion and may be largely objective and practical. They may also engage in long, detailed monologues while exhibiting no appreciation of the listener's interests or needs. This characteristic has earned them the label "little professors." One young man I knew, at the slightest opportunity (or even without any obvious cuing context), would begin a long, detailed description of all 79 episodes of the television series *Star Trek*. This usually left the listener overwhelmed with details (and grateful the series' run was limited to 79 episodes). Any attempts to change the subject were futile. The following excerpt from the letter of a young man with Asperger's Disorder to his mother will illustrate the type of discourse noted in this population. Rather than the type of personal information a mother would probably expect to receive from her son, the mother is given an overly detailed, objective discussion of something about which she has little interest:

Dear Mom,

Have you heard about sunglasses that come in all styles? The solarshields are the big ones and come in all colors to suit the users' preference. All must claim to block 100% UV rays. Polycarbonate is plastic and not as good as Borosilicate glass at 1 cm. thick to block ultraviolet radiation. The tinted, hard, thick glass with gold particles (as in space suit blocks UV and X rays). New picture tubes are that way also to reduce X-rays.

The color filters of sunglasses are grey, clear, neutral, which reduces all colors, violet (reduces yellow), blue (reduces orange), green (reduces red, but still see traffic lights safely) yellow/amber (reduces violet) orange (reduces blue) red/pink (reduces green). All colors you see must combine to be white. The tint you see on white is the color of the sunglasses . . .[9]

Second, individuals with Asperger's Disorder exhibit fewer symptoms of social difficulties, and their social problems, while clinically significant, are not as severe as those seen in individuals with autistic disorder. Whereas children with autism may at best be passive or aloof in social situations, and at worst actively avoidant of social contact, children with Asperger's tend to be just socially clueless. As described earlier, some of the conversational behaviors of these children affect their social interactions, as when they launch into one-sided monologues that do not take into account the social needs of the listener. Whereas most people would change or adjust the topic of their conversation if they noted boredom, embarrassment, or other social cues from their listener, this is not the case with these children. When these children are quite young, their social relations with family members are not typically noted to be highly unusual (although in retrospect their social behavior may be identified as limited or odd); as children they may be more likely to be diagnosed with Attention Deficit Hyperactive Disorder (ADHD) or Obsessive Compulsive Disorder (OCD). As the child matures, it is clear that there is indeed a social interest on his part, but serious skill deficits usually make successful interaction unlikely. In contrast to an autistic child, who typically has no interest in relating to other children or adults, a child with Asperger's Disorder may exhibit a desire for interaction but his attempts are more likely to be odd and inappropriate. Thus the child may approach a child or adult and begin a "little professor" monologue.

A third distinction often mentioned is that children with Asperger's Disorder may exhibit clinical depression when older. They know they are "different" and are concerned about this. They may even be able to articulate their concern, as when they make statements like "I do not know how to act" in various situations or "I cannot read what other people are thinking or feeling." They know they have to be taught how to socialize in ways that come so naturally and effortlessly for other people. In fact, two-thirds of adolescents with Asperger's have a secondary mood disorder. In contrast, it is more likely that a child with high-functioning autism will see his accomplishments as successes and be happy about them.

Finally, while children with autistic disorder typically display a pattern of cognitive functioning in which performance skills are superior to verbal skills, children with Asperger's may exhibit the opposite. In addition, while autistic children are often reported to be physically coordinated and agile, Asperger's children tend to be more clumsy.

Nevertheless, there are some social features that children with Asperger's share with high-functioning autistic children. Both are inept when responding to the social and emotional expression of others. They cannot read others' emotions, and their responses are either severely limited (that is, they may not notice) or inappropriate. Tony Attwood describes one young man with Asperger's who when confronted with the furrowed brow of his angry mother said "Look, it's an eleven!"[10] Moreover, both types of children have great difficulty in describing characteristics of people. When asked what their mother is like, they may respond with statements such as "She likes ranch dressing."

Although the debate regarding the distinction between these two forms of developmental disorder continues, its importance depends on the function of the distinction. On one hand, if a researcher is conducting a study and thus must be extremely careful about the diagnosis of participants, then the distinction may be critical. On the other hand, the distinction may not be useful in terms of the delivery of clinical services. It is likely that the needs of "Asperger's" and "high-functioning autism" cases would be quite similar and would necessitate the same sorts of interventions.

Pervasive Developmental Disorder, Not Otherwise Specified (PDD-NOS)

Since the diagnostic categories discussed above are phenomenologically determined at this point, as opposed to being biologically determined, there is also a category for those children who do not fit neatly in any of the previously described categories. PDD-NOS is a diagnostic category used for those children who do not meet the criteria for a specific pervasive developmental disorder, nor the criteria for other disorders such as schizophrenia, schizotypal personality disorder, or avoidant personality disorder. Thus the children in this category may exhibit severe impairment in the development of social relating as well as impairment in the development of verbal and nonverbal communication, and may exhibit stereotyped and re-

stricted behaviors. As indicated in the DSM-IV, this category includes "atypical autism," which does not meet the criteria for autistic disorder because the symptoms may not be as severe or may be a
bit different than in autistic disorder, and/or the age of onset is later
than three years.

Comorbidity

Another set of debates focuses on issues of comorbidity (that is,
multiple conditions occurring at the same time) in autism. As we
have seen, autism is a life-span disorder and one with multiple features. It should not be surprising that as the child matures into adolescence and adulthood, these features may change. While retaining
the autism diagnosis, it is not unusual for these individuals to receive other diagnostic labels as they develop. Anxiety disorders, obsessive-compulsive disorder, attention deficit hyperactivity disorder,
specific speech and language disorders, social difficulties, and cognitive impairments are common comorbid diagnoses given to this
population, and some may not be applied until later in life (the exception being mental retardation, which is common in autistic disorder and identifiable early on).

The decision of whether or not to apply another diagnostic label
is motivated by a number of possible factors. The relatively recent
successes in pharmacological treatment of obsessive-compulsive
disorder and various anxiety disorders have served to increase the
profile of these clinical features in autism. This raises the issue of
whether obsessive-compulsive disorder in the nonautistic population is indeed the same as the obsessive-compulsive nature of the
perseverative and ritualistic behaviors seen in autism. On a theoretical level, this question can be (and is) debated. On a clinical level,
it is relatively unimportant as long as the same treatment regimen
is effective. Indeed, there is evidence that many individuals with
autism do respond to the pharmacological agents used with nonautistic patients, and do so without any autism-specific side effects.

Another factor is the relative salience of a behavioral feature and the need to make it a focus of intervention. A young child with autism is likely to exhibit perseverative and ritualistic behaviors but also to be essentially nonverbal. At this stage of development, the focus on language intervention takes precedence since language is the basis for the development of so many other aspects of behavior. Without language, a child is at a severe disadvantage for acquiring complex cognitive and social skills. While perseverative and ritualistic behaviors may be disruptive and stigmatizing, their presence or absence will have a less dramatic impact on future development. Later in life, however, the treatment emphasis will likely shift as the relative salience of behavioral features changes. As the child matures into adulthood and language skills have likely stabilized (at some level), it may be important to focus more intensely on socially stigmatizing behaviors such as perseverative, ritualistic interests. The absence of these behaviors may be very important in the successful placement of the individual into a community setting. Thus a young adult with autism who is experiencing difficulties in this area may receive a diagnosis of anxiety disorder, and this may become a main focus of intervention (behavioral and/or pharmacological).

Attempts to Identify Subgroups

The issue of comorbidity is often tied to the efforts to define subgroups of autism.[11] Since autism is such a heterogeneous disorder, any progress toward allowing for more discrete and specific distinctions within the population would be very welcome. The recognition that autism may indeed not be a single disorder but rather a cluster of disorders, perhaps with different etiologies and courses, has spurred efforts to identify subtypes. An identification of such subtypes would of course have tremendous theoretical and practical implications. Not surprisingly, the efforts to identify subgroups in this population have so far been controversial and have met with limited success.

A common methodology for determining subgroups of a population involves the use of statistical approaches such as cluster analyses, factor analyses, and multivariate analyses. While this is normally a robust way to address the issue of subgroups, the efforts to do so in the area of autism have yielded little to date. A major problem with most of these statistical methods is that in order for them to be effective, one needs to deal with populations whose important characteristics are known and measured. It is the measures of these characteristics that are entered into the analyses. In the area of autism, the problem of wide heterogeneity in expression of symptoms, the fact that symptoms vary with age and cognitive level, and the availability of only relatively small sample sizes have hampered work in this area. In order to identify valid subgroups, one must utilize fairly sizable, truly representative samples. Moreover, these statistical methodologies assume that the behaviors measured and included in the analyses are the behaviors relevant to various subgroups. Since we do not yet know the important behavioral variables (for example, neurological features) to look for, we do not know if we are measuring them. Although various researchers have nonetheless used statistical procedures to identify potential subtypes, there has as yet been no formal replication or consensus.

Another approach to identifying subtypes is to apply clinical observation and judgment. Perhaps the best-known such attempt was that of Wing and Gould, who proposed three subtypes of autism based upon social interaction patterns.[12] The *aloof* subgroup is composed of the most severely socially detached; these individuals are likely to avoid social interaction and reject physical or social contact. As small children they do not come to their parents for comfort when hurt or upset, do not seek affection from their parents, and do not actively greet the parents after an absence. The understanding and use of verbal and nonverbal communication are severely impaired (or absent) in this group, as is toy play. The *passive* subgroup includes individuals who are less severely impaired. Although they do not seek out social contact or affection, they will not actively reject the social initiatives of others. Their communication skills are better than those seen in the aloof group, but their speech often reflects the typical "autistic" abnormalities (such as echolalia, pronoun reversal, dysprosody) and is not usually used for pure social communication. Play is limited and may consist of imitation of the play of others, repetitive behavior, and unimaginative action. The *active-but-odd* subgroup contains individuals who may actively seek social contact but do so in an odd, often inappropriate, manner. They may approach another child and say something inappropriate or disrupt the other child's play, all in an attempt to socially engage the child. (I remember one child who would approach a peer, do something disruptive such as knock a toy train off its tracks, and then yell "Call 911!"). The language of these individuals is typically delayed and characterized by the usual autistic characteristics. Some develop rather sophisticated speech and extensive vocabularies, yet their speech is literal, repetitive, and typically devoid of colloquialisms, metaphors, and the like. Their play is characterized as stereotyped, repetitive, and "pseudo-imaginative" in that they may adopt the role of another or engage in symbolic play but will not vary from the rigid play pattern.

These subgroupings based on observed behaviors may have the benefit of helping to guide treatment interventions, since the specific needs of the groups may differ. However, it has been found that these subtypes seem to be highly correlated with level of cognitive impairment. Thus children in the *aloof* group tend to be the most cognitively impaired, while children in the *active-but-odd* category tend to be the least cognitively impaired. When level of cognitive impairment is controlled, the group differences tend to disappear.

The Issue of Assessment

There is no doubt that we have made substantial progress in the differential diagnosis of autistic disorder and its various relatives. This progress has been possible because diagnostic assessment has moved from the subjective to the objective. Rather than relying solely on the clinical impressions of professionals whose conclusions may potentially be affected by training biases or theoretical leanings, we now have at our disposal a number of empirically derived, objectively based assessment instruments. Even here, however, we have debates regarding which assessments are the most useful and which are best at distinguishing children with autism from children with other developmental disorders.

Early assessments consisted primarily of checklists that asked the respondent (usually a parent, teacher, or clinician) to rate the child on the occurrence of specific, objective behaviors known to be indicative of autism. The most popular of these were Rimland's E-2 Checklist,[13] the Autism Behavior Checklist (ABC), and the Childhood Autism Rating Scale (CARS).[14] Many of these are still in use today, with the CARS rating being the most frequently used. A newer assessment, the Checklist for Autism in Toddlers (CHAT),[15] has shown sensitivity to detecting autism in children at 18 months of age.

These checklists have the advantage of ease of administration—minimal or no training is required of the respondent or examiner—and they are useful for preliminary screening of autistic children. However, none of these instruments is comprehensive enough to be used alone, though unfortunately they often have been. This may be one reason for the lack of consistency in diagnosis and in research findings: different diagnosticians and researchers may be using different diagnostic assessments, and these different assessments may not correlate well.

It is easy to see that given the complexity of autism, only a very comprehensive instrument would be appropriate. Such an instrument would need to be a broad-based assessment in terms of gathering information from the parents (and perhaps other caregivers such as teachers) as well as obtaining observational information directly from the child in a variety of situations.

More recently a set of comprehensive diagnostic assessments, backed by extensive empirical foundation, has become available. These assessments are the Autism Diagnostic Interview–Revised (ADI-R)[16] and the Autism Diagnostic Observation Scale–Generic (ADOS-G).[17] The ADI-R is a detailed interview conducted by a trained examiner with the child's primary caregiver, usually the mother or father. Detailed information is obtained regarding the child's development in relation to the main behavioral areas significant for autism (such as social attachment and behavior, communication, stereotyped behavior). This is a lengthy interview, usually requiring over 2 hours. This parent-report measure is usually (and ideally) complemented by the ADOS-G, which involves a trained examiner working with the child in a prescribed set of interactions designed to elicit behaviors known to be important to an autism diagnosis. For example, the examiner will try to get the child to engage in imitation, joint attention, pretend play, and various language behaviors. The assessment is scored for these elicited behaviors as well as other behaviors such as affect, eye contact, and inappropriate behaviors such as self-stimulation.

The ADI-R and the ADOS-G have the advantage of gathering information from multiple sources (caregiver report and direct observation) and doing so in a highly systematic and objective manner. The empirical validation of these instruments is good, and they are specifically geared toward assessing areas required for both the DSM-IV and the ICD-10 diagnostic schemes. The disadvantage of these instruments is that extensive training is required to conduct and score them, which makes them unavailable to a wide array of potential users.

It should be obvious that the issue of assessment is a complicated one. Which assessment(s) the clinician or researcher chooses to use will depend upon the purpose of the assessment. Will it be used for screening purposes to determine eligibility for services? Is it for research purposes, where diagnostic precision is essential? Will it be used in determining detailed behavioral description for developing specific treatment interventions? Most centers that focus on autism conduct a battery of assessments including not only the diagnostic measures described above but also standardized cognitive, language, and motor assessments as well. All this is necessary to gain a comprehensive understanding of a difficult and complex disorder.

Increased Incidence of Autism

One of the hottest current issues in the field of autism is the reported tremendous increase in the incidence and prevalence of the disorder. Over the past several years, a truly dramatic increase in the number of children diagnosed with autism has been reported worldwide. Clinicians, the educational community, speech and language specialists, and developmental-disabilities service agencies as well as epidemiological studies have reported this increase.[18] One can easily see the substantial increase in the reported incidence of autism by looking at a chronological comparison of epidemiological studies. In the 1960s and 1970s, studies reported an incidence of autism of 4 to 5 cases per 10,000 births. This increased in the 1980s to 2.5 to 16 cases per 10,000, and in the 1990s to 5 to 31 cases per 10,000. In 2004 one routinely reads incidence reports claiming that 1 in every 150–200 children is autistic. The California State Department of Developmental Services (one of the few state agencies to report such extensive data) reported that between 1988 and 1998 there was a 610 percent increase in autism cases. In April 2002, a congressional hearing declared autism a national health emergency. It is estimated that today autism affects as many as 1,500,000 individuals in the United States and is rising at an annual rate of 10 to 17 percent. These statistics are indeed staggering.

The impact of the autism "epidemic," as it has been called, is substantial not only in terms of the emotional burden but in terms of cold, hard economics. The increased load on the community to support educational and clinical services is straining even the most affluent of areas. Given the cost estimate of $5 million per individual across his or her lifetime, it is apparent that in ten years we are looking at an estimated annual cost associated with autism of between $200 and $400 billion.[19]

The fact that the number of children being diagnosed with autism is on the rise is undisputed. However, is there indeed such a large increase in the incidence of autism, or is the reported increase a result of other factors such as public and medical awareness, diagnostic changes over the years, improvements in detection, diagnostic requirements for access to services, and the like? While we know that there have been significant changes in all of these areas, as well as others, we cannot yet determine whether such factors completely account for the huge increase in the incidence of autism.

It is certainly true that compared to forty, thirty, or even five years ago, there is a tremendous increase in awareness of autism. When I first entered the field as an undergraduate student in the 1960s, it seemed that very few people outside of the professional communities had ever heard of autism. In fact, I can remember early in my professional career giving presentations to pediatricians and finding that not only had they never seen a child with autism, but they had rarely even heard of the disorder. Of course, now the situation is very different. Pediatricians typically have an idea of what autism is and are aware of the early signs. Moreover, given the increased incidence, many pediatricians can report at least one autistic child in their caseload. This increased awareness is not limited to the medical and professional community. Autism is a frequent topic in the popular media, appearing in books, magazines, newspapers, movies, and television. Today almost everyone has at least heard of autism, even if their knowledge is limited (or, perhaps, incorrect). Given this increased professional and general awareness, is it possible that more cases are being detected and coming to the attention of the service agencies that report the number of cases? If so, this could cause an increase in reported cases even if no real increase in the incidence of autism exists.

The existence of broader diagnostic criteria and the availability of diagnostic instruments (such as those described earlier) might also have an impact on the number of identified cases of autism. It is possible that the greater clarity and precision of diagnostic evaluation and assessment may contribute to this increase. Some have speculated that recently diagnosed children may represent a broader behavioral expression than those diagnosed years ago.

Another potentially contributing factor is that children are being diagnosed at a younger age now, and this may help to account for the increased number of cases reported by service agencies. This early-diagnosis trend is likely due to the emphasis on early treatment intervention and the impact of the Individuals with Disabilities Education Act (IDEA), first implemented in 1975, which mandates that the states must provide intervention services to children aged 0–3 years who either have, or are at risk for, developmental delay or disability. To give an example, a study of autism cases reported in California found that the mean age of entry into the service delivery system decreased from 6.9 years among children born in 1987 to 3.3 years among those born in 1994.[20]

Another potential contributor to the increased prevalence of autism is the role of diagnosis in accessing services. It has always been the case that educational and medical services have been unequally distributed to populations with differing diagnoses. When I first entered this field, the educational system (in California) provided special classrooms for children with mental retardation and for children with various physical disabilities, but not for children with autism. (In fact, this situation contributed greatly to the fact that many autistic children were institutionalized by the time they were adolescents because there was little available for them in public education, and the parents simply could not handle the children when they got older.) Understandably, this led parents to actively "shop" for specific diagnoses that would enable their children to receive the best services. At that time parents wanted to avoid an autism diagnosis and "preferred" a diagnosis of mental retardation so that their child would be eligible for special education services unavailable to children with autism. It is also likely that professionals were more lenient about using the "mental retardation" diagnosis, knowing that this diagnosis would increase the likelihood the child would receive special services.

The situation changed greatly when special education programs were mandated for children with autism. Now it was the autistic child who had the advantage for special education services—programs that were specifically geared to the needs of these children. Largely as a result of parent advocacy and lobbying at various government agencies as well as lawsuits filed by parents, more and more money was earmarked for autism services. In response, the field changed; now it was an autism diagnosis that was preferred because it was less stigmatizing and yielded more intensive and appropriate services than did a diagnosis of mental retardation. In fact, the California study cited earlier found that the increase in incidence reported for children with autism was accompanied by a concomitant *decrease* in reported cases of children with mental retardation. Specifically, the prevalence of autism increased by 9.1 per 10,000 whereas the prevalence of mental retardation of unknown cause declined by 9.3 per 10,000. One cannot avoid the fact that there is money and there are services associated with an autism diagnosis, and this may play some part in the increase in diagnosed cases.

Yet another possibility relates the increase in incidence to increased environmental toxins. It may be the case that while the organic factors responsible for autism have remained consistent over the years, changes in the environment may now lead to autism expression in individuals who are organically predisposed. That is, it is possible that more recent environmental pollutants serve to inter-act with genetic or other organic propensities, with the result that more individuals develop autism.

Any or all of these potential factors may, or may not, be related to the undeniable large increase in the number of reported cases of autism. Could these factors completely account for the increase? We do not yet know. A recent review of many of the epidemiological studies that have been conducted, in several countries, concludes that the increase in estimates of the prevalence of autistic spectrum disorders likely represents changes in the concepts, definitions, and awareness of both the lay and professional public. Nevertheless, the author of this review points to the need for additional studies to test the idea that autism is on the rise.[21]

In fact, many new studies are currently underway as part of the attempt to isolate important factors in the increased incidence of autism. Several studies are now being conducted by the Centers for Disease Control and Prevention in Atlanta in order to develop and enhance programs to monitor the prevalence of autism spectrum disorders. The goal of these studies is to provide comparable, population-based estimates of the prevalence rates of autism and related disorders in different sites over time. We hope that such studies will shed light on the unresolved questions in autism research.

Whatever these new studies may find, one thing is clear: the number of autism cases is definitely on the rise, and the impact of this phenomenon on our service delivery systems is enormous. The pressures on our ability to detect, diagnose, evaluate, and of course treat an increasing number of individuals will require intensive research efforts and the collaborative efforts of the diverse constituencies involved in autism. Given the fact that the field of autism has not always been characterized by consensus and collaboration, the challenge will be substantial.

CHAPTER 4

What Causes Autism?

It's a dull month that goes by without a new cause for autism.

—Michael Rutter, Address to the Second Annual International
Meeting for Autism Research, 2002

Throughout this book I state my belief that the precipitating factor in infantile autism is the parent's wish that his child should not exist.

—Bruno Bettelheim, *The Empty Fortress* (1967)

It may be concluded that, in the great majority of cases of autism, genetic influences predominate in the etiology of autism.

—Michael Rutter, Anthony Bailey, Emily Simonoff, and Andrew
Pickles, in *Handbook of Autism and Pervasive Developmental
Disorders* (1997)

When a definitive etiology for a disorder is unknown, theories of etiology proliferate. Nowhere is this more apparent than in the field of autism. As suggested by the quotations given above, there have been some major theoretical differences regarding the etiology of autism. In many ways, the different views have reflected the evolu-

tion of psychology as a whole, involving the prevailing conceptual-
izations of the times in which they appeared. Thus theories of etiology have ranged from the original conceptualization implicating
the parents as the cause of the disorder to the view that the disorder
is an entirely organically based syndrome independent of parental
influence.

Autism as a Result of Faulty Social Environment

Psychogenic Theory

> We did not fit the classic mold for autism, which is white, upper middle
> class, and very, very bright. According to my doctors, my son could not
> be autistic. I was not white and it was assumed that I was not educated.
> Therefore he was labeled emotionally disturbed. Here your child has a
> disability that you recognize and they said "No, you can't be that." You
> can't even be a "refrigerator mother." The irony of it all. (African-Ameri-
> can mother of an autistic son, from the film *Refrigerator Mothers*)[1]

With the advantage of hindsight, we can see that the psychogenic
theory that implicated the parents in the etiology of autism was certainly one of the saddest chapters in the history of autism. As one
can imagine, the issue of parental causation has been at the center
of highly charged debate in the field. Bitterness, anger, despair, and
guilt on the part of the parents were a direct result of a theory
strongly promoted by professionals who failed to subject that theory to critical investigation and validation. Eventually, however,
empirical study failed to support this theory, and although it was
popular from the early 1940s into the 1960s, it has relatively few
proponents today.

How did things get off to such an unfortunate start? There were
two basic elements that converged to provide the atmosphere in
which the psychogenic theory of autism could flourish. First, in
1943 when autism was first described, psychoanalytic theory was

very influential in the understanding of mental disorders. Essentially, this theory held that overt symptoms of both mild and severe mental disorders were manifestations of internal underlying conflicts based in very early childhood experiences, primarily relationships with parents. Thus if a child exhibited behavior disorders for which no physical basis could be found, professionals typically looked to the child's very early social experiences for an explanation. Since the main controllers of a child's early social experiences are the parents, particularly the mother, it followed that the parents must be responsible for the disorder.

Second, in his early assessments of the parents of autistic children, Leo Kanner described these parents as aloof, cold, obsessive, intellectual, disdainful of frivolity, humorless, socially insulated, and emotionally detached.[2] They were also described as compulsive to the point of being mechanistic in their child rearing and as failing to demonstrate warmth and affection in their interactions with their children. Such a social environment could hardly be conducive to the development of a normal parent-child attachment. Since very early attachment is considered to be extremely important for subsequent growth and functioning in a wide range of areas, it is no wonder that this apparent lack of attachment might have been thought to lead to the pervasive and severe symptoms characteristic of autism.

It is only fair to point out, however, that Kanner himself did not feel that parents were the sole cause of the disorder. Rather, he saw the etiology as probably resulting from the interaction of a biologically based (genetic) predisposition for autism coupled with the existence of unfavorable social conditions provided by the parents. He also suggested that the disorder might be an exaggerated version of a familial tendency toward social isolation.

Regrettably, many psychoanalysts and psychiatrists were not so willing to let the parents off the hook. These professionals took Kanner's description of parental personality and related it directly to the development of autism. A number of theories emerged which all related autism to family environment. For instance, some of the factors proposed as influential in the development of the disorder included parental rejection, insufficient stimulation, faulty communication patterns, family stress, and the child's response to deviant parental personality characteristics. This last proposed factor represents the most influential of these theories. Specifically, many psychoanalysts saw autism, characterized by the absence of normal relations with the social and physical environment and preoccupation with inner stimuli, as akin to the first stage of normal development. The shift from what is described as "primary narcissism" to object relations is thought to be accomplished through nurturing maternal acts. Thus it followed that a failure to progress through this stage of development could be attributed to inadequate or deviant mothering.

The most influential proponent of this theory was the well-known Viennese psychoanalyst Bruno Bettelheim, who brought the existing parent-causation position to its unfortunate full fruition by focusing wholly on the parents as the cause of the disorder.[3] Bettelheim used Kanner's term "refrigerator mothers" to describe the cold and emotionally insulated personalities of the mothers of children with autism. He proposed that, in contrast to the parents of nonautistic children, parents of autistic children had a psychological pathology that led them to react abnormally to their infant's normal behaviors. In the course of normal development an infant is actively exploring her environment and reaching out to people and objects. During this process the child passes through several critical developmental stages (which include nursing, recognition of parents, toilet training, and so on). Along the way, the child inevitably encounters a number of real or imagined threats and frustrations from the new environment she is exploring, and her response at these times may be to withdraw or to become less responsive. Under these circumstances a mother with no psychopathology is likely to react to her child with increased "mothering acts" such as cuddling, stroking, rocking, and feeding. The child interprets these acts as reassurance, and this increased mothering is seen as essential in the continuation of the emotional bonding between mother and child.

In contrast, Bettelheim suggested, mothers of autistic children respond to their infant's unresponsiveness pathologically. Specifically, these parents respond with extreme negative feelings, rejection, and even counterwithdrawal. The child interprets this behavior as hostility and responds in turn with despair and inner rage, and ultimately feels powerless in a hostile and threatening environment. This results in an intensification of the withdrawal. The cycle continues until the child retreats into what Bettelheim referred to as "chronic autistic disease." Thus, in this view, while the child's initial withdrawal is part of the normal developmental process, it is the mother's extreme negative response to this withdrawal and her unconscious rejection of the child that compound the situation and lead to the child's downward spiral into autistic withdrawal. (Not surprisingly, controversies existed even within the basic psychodynamic theory, with other theorists expressing modified versions of the theory where it is not maternal psychopathology but rather the child's misinterpretation of the mother's behavior that causes the withdrawal.)[4]

The basic assumption of Bettelheim's theory, therefore, is that the child's withdrawal, or retreat, into autism occurs in response to what is perceived as a threatening and hostile reality represented by the mother. Indeed, some of the symptoms of autism are seen in this view as specific responses to this hostile reality. As the child's withdrawal intensifies, all libidinal energy is channeled into defenses. Since experiencing certain environmental events would be too painful, the child keeps these events out of awareness by avoiding interaction with the environment. This avoidance is manifest in characteristic autistic symptoms such as self-stimulation, echolalia, and insistence on sameness, all of which can all be viewed as ways of maintaining a homeostatic psychic environment.

One can see why this theory was widely held at one time. It followed the prevailing conceptualization of the day, psychodynamic theory, and it neatly incorporated the personality characteristics described by Kanner with the known symptoms of autism. However, as with most theories that are not grounded in empirical validation, this theory cannot be sustained when subjected to critical review. Let's consider how this theory has failed the test of scientific scrutiny.

First, the theory rests heavily upon the assumption that the parents of children with autism exhibit specific abnormal personality characteristics. However, reports of these abnormal parental characteristics have typically been anecdotal in nature, rather than determined in scientifically controlled studies. Controlled investigations of parental personality and interactions have generally reported no difference between parents of children with autism and parents of typical children or parents of children with other disabilities. For example, one study compared the parents of normal-IQ autistic children with parents of normal-IQ receptive aphasic children and found no differences between the parent groups on measures including psychiatric illness, obsessional behavior, emotional warmth toward their children, and empathy.[5] While these investigators did find some degree of neurotic or depressive disorder in about half of the mothers in both groups, these were seen as reflecting the stress of raising a handicapped child rather than as a causative factor in the child's disorder. Another study compared the personality profiles of parents of autistic children on an empirically derived and well-established instrument (the Minnesota Multiphasic Personality Inventory; MMPI) and found that the parents' profiles did not differ significantly from the normal profile on this instrument. Nor was there any difference in family interaction style.[6]

A second problem with the psychogenic theory is that any differences seen in the personality characteristics of the parents may indeed be a *result*, rather than a *cause*, of the disorder. Autism is a profoundly debilitating disorder, and the challenges that it presents to parents cannot be overestimated. It is reasonable to think that some of the parental characteristics noted by Kanner might be a response to the child's behaviors. How warm, cuddly, and affectionate might any mother be if she knew her child would actively resist such overtures by screaming, biting, or pulling away? After a while the parent may understandably reduce her attempts to show affection. Further, if a child was very demanding of order in the environment and engaged in ritualistic behavior, it is not surprising that a parent might adopt an orderly environment so as to reduce the chances of an outburst by the child. Is it not also understandable that the parents might be "disdainful of frivolity" or "humorless" in the face of raising such a child? In short, a correlational relationship between autism and parental behavior does not allow us to draw conclusions regarding direction of causality, if any causality in fact exists.

A third problem with this theory is that the deviant interactions hypothesized to be the basis for the autistic "withdrawal" have never been systematically observed. One would assume that parental behavior that is so abnormal as to cause a disorder of the magnitude of autism would be very apparent to an observer. Yet such observations have not been reported. This means that any relation between parental interaction style and subsequent disorder in the child is a *post hoc* theory lacking in empirical support. Some professionals have inferred parental deviance or rejection on the basis of the parents' responses on self-report or projective assessments (such as the Rorschach inkblot test), but the reliability and validity of these methods have been called into serious question.

Fourth, Kanner's description of the parents of autistic children as intellectual, highly rational, objective, and disdainful of frivolity was apparently supported by his observation that most of the parents of his original sample of children tended to be of higher intelligence, socioeconomic status (SES), and professional achievement than would be expected of the general population. Although a great deal of research has addressed this issue, the fact remains that there is little solid substantiation of the view that the parents of children with autism differ systematically from parents of nonautistic children on the basis of IQ, SES, race, ethnicity, or occupational level. Further, as some have pointed out, there may have been a sampling error in Kanner's first group of parents. It is certainly more likely that an intelligent, well-educated parent would have been aware of Leo Kanner, the leading child psychiatrist of his day, and that a parent who could afford to take his child to Johns Hopkins University to be seen by Dr. Kanner must have had above-average financial resources.

Finally, if mechanical, overly structured interaction styles were sufficient to cause autism, then one would expect a very high rate of autism to occur in institutional environments such as orphanages and foster care settings. In such environments child-rearing practices are typically highly routinized and structured, and there is little opportunity for the children to develop close and stable relationships with caregivers. Yet children in such environments very infrequently develop the symptoms of autism.[7]

Thus it is now well accepted that the parents are not the cause of autism. However, this change of opinion was a long time in coming, and the tremendous guilt and pain inflicted on these parents for many years was perhaps one of the cruelest aspects associated with the diagnosis of autism. It was not bad enough that these parents had to deal with the burden of raising a child with such a challenging disability; they also had to deal with the guilt associated with "causing" the disorder.

If there is anything positive that arose from the "parent-causation" theory, it is that it provided the impetus for the parents to organize and become a strong force in refuting the theory. The National Society for Autistic Children (now called the Autism Society of America) was founded by Dr. Bernard Rimland (himself the father of a boy with autism) in 1965. The organization is composed of parents and professionals dedicated to disseminating information to families, supporting research into the etiology and effective treatment of the disorder, and advocating for educational and research funding. The members of this organization have been, and continue to be, extremely active and influential, and the organization is a very powerful force.

The parents of autistic children have not only initiated comprehensive efforts to change professional views but have also engaged in small, but very symbolic, acts of defiance. I remember one mother with whom I worked twenty years ago who responded to an autism diagnosis for her child by attempting to read everything on autism she could get her hands on. She visited the local public library and was horrified to find that the only books on the subject in the library's collection were *The Empty Fortress* and *Love is Not Enough*—both books by Bruno Bettelheim that laid out in great detail the parent-causation hypothesis. This mother did not want any other parent to be exposed to this material, and she asked the library to take the two books off the shelves. When the library refused, she simply checked out the books and subsequently threw them away. Some time later she returned to the library only to find that they had restocked the Bettelheim books. Again she checked them out and threw them away. When the library refused to lend her any more books, she sent another parent who also threw away the Bettelheim books. Additional parents were recruited as needed. To this day, I would be surprised if that library has any of Bettelheim's books. Another example of the parents' defiance of Bettelheim and his cohorts was demonstrated at their very first national meeting in 1968. There were numerous speeches criticizing Bettelheim and the pain he had caused. However, a sense of humor also permeated the meeting. Anti-Bettelheim jokes abounded, and it is widely rumored that these first parent attendees wore name tags in the shape of little refrigerators.

Learning Theory

In many respects psychodynamic theory and learning theory could not be more different. Psychodynamic theory focuses on the relationship between inferred, unobservable intrapsychic conflicts and disturbed behavior, whereas learning theory focuses on the relationship between observable, objective events and behavior. Nonetheless, learning theory also had an unpleasant chapter to contribute to the early search for an etiology of autism. Here again the parents were implicated as directly contributing to the disorder in their child. Mercifully, however, since learning theory was not nearly as influential as psychoanalytic theory in the 1940s through the early 1960s, the impact of the learning-theory approach to autism etiology was quite limited. Yet it merits some discussion not only because it represents another point of view that implicated the parents in the cause of autism but also because, unlike psychodynamic theory, it ultimately made important positive contributions to the development of effective treatment.

Charles Ferster was an eminent learning theorist who conducted significant work in the area of animal operant learning, primarily in the 1950s and 1960s. Like most advocates of a theory, he would often attempt to demonstrate that the theory had widespread implications. He sought to show how the basic principles of learning that had been convincingly demonstrated with animal subjects in the laboratory could be extended to help understand human behavior. Probably because autism represented such an extreme form of human behavior, it was an attractive area for researchers who wanted to speculate on how a certain type of learning environment might lead to autistic behaviors in children.

Ferster described how the infant's early social environment could in fact build the behavioral repertoire characteristic of autism.[8] He attempted to account for the specific behavioral deficits and excesses of autism in terms of the learning environment during the first years of life. Ferster pointed out that it was not necessarily the existence of specific *behaviors* that characterized autism, but rather the *relative frequency* of these behaviors within the child's repertoire. For example, all children engage in tantrums, and all spend some time staring into space, standing still, trying to manipulate adults, and the like. However, when compared with typical children, autistic children spend comparably more time in relatively nonfunctional behaviors (such as self-stimulation) and relatively less time in appropriate communication. This disordered pattern of frequency, Ferster argued, is the result of a specific learning environment characterized by reinforcement (strengthening effect) for some behaviors and a paucity of reinforcement (weakening effect) for other behaviors.

As an example, we can look at two forms of verbal behavior, mands and tacts. *Mands* are behaviors that benefit the speaker. "I want cookie," "Candy!" and "Go bye-bye" are all examples of mands because the consequence of the behavior (mediated by the listener) directly benefits the child. In contrast, *tacts* are responses that primarily benefit the listener and generally involve descriptions of the environment. Examples of tacts include "There's an airplane" or "That car is red." Children with autism do not use tacts frequently; if they use any speech, it more often takes the form of a mand. Ferster believed that this was the case because mands required a response from the audience (the parent, who often reinforces the mand by fulfilling the request), whereas tacts did not require any response from the audience. Further, he pointed out that mands could escalate in form until they became aversive if the parent did not respond to the milder form of the mand. Asking for a cookie might not be enough to get the cookie; but screaming, kicking, and head-banging might be so aversive to the parent that a cookie is delivered in order to halt the behavior. In contrast, tacts may not lead to any direct benefit for the child and do not require a response from the listener; thus they are weakened as responses in the child's repertoire.

In essence, Ferster was saying that the relative frequencies of specific behaviors in children with autism are determined by the amount and frequency of reinforcement associated with each. Behaviors that are reinforced by attention, access to desired objects/ activities, or avoidance of aversive situations are strengthened. Behaviors that do not lead to reinforcement (that is, behaviors that are ignored or punished) are weakened. Therefore, to understand the pattern of behaviors in these children, it is necessary to look at the learning environment within which the child's repertoire is shaped. Since the parents are the main mediators of the child's early environment, Ferster believed it was reasonable to consider how their responses to the child's emerging behaviors might strengthen or weaken these behaviors.

Ferster looked at factors in the parents' behavioral repertoire that might affect the frequency and pattern of their reinforcement of the child's behavior. He speculated that the parents of autistic children are predisposed to depression, are preoccupied with other life events, or otherwise are led to give a rather low priority to reinforcing their child's behavior. The parents are thus less likely to positively reinforce the appropriate aspects of their child's emerging social and communicative behavior. In contrast, the parents are more likely to attend to the child's atavistic behaviors, such as tantrums, because such behaviors are so unpleasant they cannot be ignored. As the parents adapt to disruptive behaviors, attention is delivered only when the child escalates these behaviors. This leads to a systematic shaping and differential reinforcement of more severely disruptive behaviors. Behaviors such as self-stimulation have essentially no impact upon the parents and are thus ignored and uninterrupted.

According to Ferster, the ultimate effect of these unfortunate reinforcement contingencies is the gradual establishment of a behavioral repertoire that we label autistic. Appropriate behaviors such as language and social interaction are not consistently reinforced, so their emergence is not strengthened. Inappropriate behaviors such as tantrums are reinforced, which leads to their establishment and strengthening. Behaviors such as self-stimulation lead to immediate reinforcement (sensory consequences for the child) and thus are strengthened particularly in the absence of interventions to reduce them.

Ferster also attempted to use learning theory to account for the development of other behaviors characteristic of the disorder. A hallmark feature of autistic individuals is the failure of other people to become important to them. The children are typically described as nonsocial, unaffectionate "loners" who are not emotionally bonded with parents or other significant people in their environment. In learning theory terms, we would say that these individuals had not acquired conditioned reinforcer properties. This means that affection, praise, and other forms of social consequences are not potent in terms of strengthening behavior. Whereas hearing remarks like "good job!" "good girl," or "I love you" would likely be powerful reinforcers for typical children and thus likely to strengthen behaviors they follow, these consequences remain essentially meaningless and nonfunctional for children with autism. Ferster explained that people become conditioned reinforcers by virtue of their association with a variety of reinforcers in many different situations. Since the parents of autistic children do not provide frequent or consistent reinforcement, according to Ferster, they fail to become generalized conditioned reinforcers.

In Ferster's view, then, the severe behavioral deficits and excesses exhibited in autism are due to faulty conditioning history, and since the parents are the early providers of reinforcers, one can view this theory as implicating the parents in the etiology of the disorder. However, as in the case of the psychogenic theory, the learning-theory model of etiology also comes up short when subjected to critical scrutiny.

The main problem with the theory is the same as with the psychogenic theory—namely, that the hypothesized parent-child interactions considered important in the development of the disorder have not been directly observed. While Ferster provided an intriguing view of how parental behavior *might* shape specific behaviors that one sees in autism, no one has reported observations showing that the parents do indeed act in this manner. A second problem is that while Ferster assumed the parents were "depressed" or preoccupied, it has never been shown that these parents are more depressed or preoccupied than are parents of nonautistic children or parents of children with other forms of disability. And if they are depressed, it could certainly be the result, rather than the cause, of having an autistic child. A third issue is that Ferster's theory does not explain other severe problems in autism, such as the particular and widespread cognitive deficits seen in autistic individuals.

In the early 1960s when Ferster presented his ideas, learning theory was not the predominant conceptual approach in vogue. In fact, it was mainly other researchers, not clinicians or parents, who read these early works in learning theory. This limited the impact of Ferster's arguments, and thus his ideas did not have the widespread negative effect on parents as the psychogenic theory did. Nevertheless, Ferster's focus on learning theory did pave the way for the later design and implementation of very effective treatments. In fact, he and his colleague, Marian DeMyer, provided the first studies demonstrating that autistic children could learn new behaviors when the training was conducted in a basic operant paradigm.[9] As we will see later in the book, these studies provided the earliest foundation for what is now the most popular form of treatment for children with autism. It is important to keep in mind, however, that the effectiveness of treatments based on a learning-theory model does not mean that the early learning environment *caused* the disorder. A potent illustration of this is Down syndrome. Although educational and behavioral interventions help individuals with Down syndrome, there is no doubt as to its genetic etiology.

Arguments against the Social Environment as Causal in Autism

In addition to failing to meet scientific scrutiny, these early etiological theories also faced strong opposition from parents and professionals, who saw compelling evidence both to refute the idea that parental environment was responsible for autism and to support a biological foundation for the disorder. These arguments included the following: (1) There have never been controlled observations of a specific behavioral pattern or personality of parents of children with autism. (2) Parents who supposedly fit the "refrigerator" parent description usually have normal, nonautistic children. (3) Most parents of even classically autistic children do not fit the pathological personality pattern. (4) Most of the siblings of autistic children are normal. (5) Children with autism are often noted to be different from birth, likely too early for parental pathology to have an effect. (6) Autism shares some symptomatology with specific types of known brain damage. (7) The consistently reported ratio of 3:1, 4:1, or even 5:1 males to females reported in the autism literature is consistent with that of other organic disorders and reflects the increased vulnerability of males to organic conditions. (8) Concordance for autism among monozygotic (MZ) twins is much greater than that for dizygotic (DZ) twins.

Because of these arguments, and also as a result of an increased ability to systematically identify and study genetic, neurological, and other biological aspects of behavior, the search for the etiology of autism has shifted from the parents' behavior to organic causes of the disorder.

Autism as a Biologically Based Disorder

Today some experts believe that "autism" is in fact most likely composed of subgroups of disorders, with each subgroup potentially having a distinct etiology (or etiologies), different courses, and different prognoses. Since the disorder is a behaviorally defined syndrome, it is likely that these different subgroups present with similar symptomatology, and this has led to the use of the same diagnostic label for all of them. (Not incidentally, this may also explain the heterogeneity associated with the diagnostic category.) However, other experts feel that autism, PDD, and Asperger's Disorder exist on a continuum and are not necessarily characterized by distinct etiologies. Whichever of these two views one holds, there is agreement on one thing: all of these disorders (or subgroups) are organically based, and the parents are in no way responsible for the development of autism in their children.

Genetic Involvement in the Etiology of Autism

The idea that biological factors might be responsible for autism was first noted by Kanner in his original description of the disorder. Even though he clearly implicated the parents as playing a significant role, he suggested that autism might ultimately be the result of "inborn" physiological defects. Nevertheless, it took many years before genetic involvement in autism was seriously considered. This delay was undoubtedly due both to the prevailing psychodynamic ideas that focused on the parents as etiological agents and to the lack of an understanding or technology to fully investigate the role of genetics. Moreover, early geneticists discounted the idea of genetic transmission of autism because autistic individuals rarely had autistic parents (no vertical transmission). This is not surprising, of course, since few autistic people have love relationships, marry, or have offspring. However, more recent theoretical and technical advances have provided clear and compelling evidence for genetic involvement in the etiology of many cases of autism. In fact, Sir Michael Rutter emphatically states that autism is probably "the most strongly genetic of all non-Mendelian psychiatric disorders."[10]

The genetic argument is supported by several findings. First, the fact that siblings of children with autism have a 2 to 7 percent probability of also being autistic represents a 50- to 100-fold increase in risk over that expected in the general population. Second, the concordance rate for identical (or monozygotic; MZ) twins has been variously reported to be between approximately 60 and 90 percent, while the concordance rate for fraternal (or dyzogotic; DZ) twins has been reported at between 5 and 10 percent. (The variability in reported concordance rates is undoubtedly the result of different studies using different inclusion rules for "autism"—some studies are more conservative, including only children who exhibit "classic" autism, while other studies include children with PDD and Asperger's Disorder.) Since MZ twins share the same genes whereas DZ twins do not, this difference in concordance rate strongly suggests a genetic loading for autism. Still, it is important to note that since even MZ twin concordance rates are not 100 percent, the role of various environmental determinants cannot be dismissed.

Third, a closer look at the twin data suggests that what is inherited may be a "broader phenotype" (expression) of the disorder. That is, while the concordance rate for MZ twins is lower than 100 percent, it is indeed the case that many of the nonautistic children in these twin sets exhibit other forms of disorder. The most frequent problems involve social relations, communication, cognitive difficulties, and anxiety disorders. Many researchers believe that a broader form of the disorder is inherited, of which classic autism is the most severe expression. What remains unclear, however, is what determines the expression of the disorder. Some have speculated that a more general liability for autism is inherited and that other factors, either organic or environmental (such as environmental toxins), act to influence the ultimate form of difficulties.

Finally, support for the inheritability of a general phenotype is provided by the fact that many first-degree relatives (parents, children, siblings) of autistic individuals are at higher risk for some of the difficulties mentioned above (that is, manifestations of the broader phenotype).

The existence of a "broader phenotype" or "lesser variant" of autism is interesting from a variety of standpoints. The major contribution of this finding is it allows a fuller understanding of the complexity and heterogeneity of the disorder. The research on this broader phenotype suggests that individuals with this type of disorder have social and communicative difficulties and also may have circumscribed and restricted interest patterns. In this respect they share features with individuals who have "pure" autism. Yet they differ in that these features may be significantly milder and are not accompanied by mental retardation. One wonders if this is what Leo Kanner was seeing back in the 1940s when he was describing personality characteristics of the parents of his sample of autistic children. If so, one might argue that these personality characteristics (such as aloofness, compulsiveness, being emotionally withdrawn), rather than "causing" autism, may instead have been manifestations of the broader genetic phenotype.

Another important contribution of this finding is that it reinforces the idea that classic autism results from the contributions of both a genetic liability *and* the effects of other risk factors that have yet to be determined. Of course, much work remains to be done: it is necessary to untangle the genetics of autism as well as identify these risk factors and how they work to amplify or "turn on" the genetic loading. This is a huge task, and one that is not likely to be completed very soon. We are undoubtedly looking at many years of focused and intensive research.

Clearly the existence of a genetic involvement in autism is now indisputable. We still have much to learn, however, about the specifics of where the causative genes are located and how the genetic effect takes place. Although it is possible that there is a single gene transmission for some cases of autism, that idea is losing favor. It is now widely believed that the vast majority of cases involve the complex interaction of a number of different genes. Still to be determined is precisely how the genetic endowment is translated into autistic symptomatology—that is, how the genes control the expression of the disorder.

The results of continued genetic research will undoubtedly be significant for several reasons. Rutter has pointed out several important implications of this research for clinical and preventive purposes,[11] including the following: (1) genetic research has already affected prevailing concepts of the nature of autism; (2) genetic findings raise the need for genetic counseling for families; (3) there is the potential for molecular genetics to provide a better identification of the broader phenotype; (4) genetic findings may provide leads regarding the causal neurological processes underlying the development of autism; (5) genetic findings may provide leads on possible protective factors, including an understanding of mechanisms that involve the transition from the broader phenotype to autism proper; (6) genetic findings may provide leads on effective drug treatments, and (7) genetic findings may aid in the identification of environmental risks.

It is important to keep in mind, however, that while genetic research has great potential in a number of areas, genetics will not have a major impact on the treatment of individuals already afflicted with autism. The treatment implications of genetic research are many years in the future. Although some geneticists, whom Rutter calls "genetic evangelists," seem to imply that clinical and preventive measures will quickly and automatically follow genetic findings, this is not the case.

Neurobiological Clues to the Etiology of Autism

Another fruitful area of research supporting the organic basis of autism is neurobiological studies. These studies have provided suggestive evidence for distinct neuroanatomical and neurochemical anomalies associated with autism, and in some instances we are beginning to see biobehavioral ties between specific identified neurological features and specific behaviors characteristic of the syndrome. As in the field of genetic influences in autism, the neurobiological area is one of rapid and exciting advances as well as occasional disputes.

Early studies of neurobiological anomalies in autism were frustratingly inconsistent. Although initial findings raised hopes that *the* distinctive feature of autism might have been isolated at last, subsequent studies by different researchers typically failed to replicate the original findings. Unfortunately, the desire of parents and professionals to find such a feature, and the popular appeal such a finding would have, could all too easily lead to an optimism that ultimately would prove to be unfounded. A case in point is the research conducted in 1961 by Schain and Freedman, who were the first to report elevated levels of the neurotransmitter serotonin in urine and whole blood samples of autistic children (a condition known as hyperserotonemia).[12] This finding was subsequently replicated in other investigations. In 1982 researchers at UCLA also reported hyperserotonemia in their sample of children. These investigators administered a serotonin-inhibiting drug called fenfluramine to three of these youngsters and reported that after receiving the drug, the children exhibited improvement in cognitive ability and language and a reduction in autistic symptoms such as social withdrawal.[13] Despite the researchers' appropriate cautions that the findings were preliminary and awaited replication, the popular media picked up the story and reported it widely as a promising treatment. As one can imagine, this very hopeful story led to many autistic children receiving treatment with fenfluramine. However, despite some initially promising results in several studies, it became apparent as more research accumulated and more children received the drug that fenfluramine typically did not lead to improvements in autism, and in fact it had some rather serious side effects in some cases. As is typical with autism, there was considerable variability across autistic individuals in their response to fenfluramine. Given the lack of strong evidence that significant improvement may be expected, and the potential for serious side effects, fenfluramine is rarely considered a viable treatment option today. Obviously this proved to be quite a disappointment to all those who had high hopes for the drug.

In the early days of the neurobiological study of autism, research methodology and technology were rather crude and did not always lead to careful and accurate studies. For example, early neuroanatomical studies depended on postmortem examination of the brains of autistic individuals. Problems arose because of the limited number of brains available for research, limited information regarding the behavioral characteristics of the deceased individual (for example, was this a case of classic autism? was the individual cognitively impaired?), the condition of the brains, how the brain tissue was preserved, and so on. Such information is essential when considering whether a specific brain should be included in a study.

Advances in our ability to study the structure of living brains via magnetic resonance imagery (MRI), to examine on-line brain activity via functional magnetic resonance imagery (fMRI), and our increasingly precise analyses of biochemical processes have allowed the field to progress. Indeed, developments in this field occur so rapidly that new findings seem to be reported almost daily. It is significant that geneticists, neurobiologists, and neuropsychologists are working together in appreciation of the interrelated aspects of autistic functioning.

What has our improved technological capability allowed us to discover about the neuroanatomy of autism? Certainly not as much as we would like, but a number of promising, and in most cases replicated, findings have recently come to light. While further substantiation and clarification will be needed in the future, several findings have received a good deal of empirical support.

To date, the cerebellum is the most consistently documented location of neuroanatomical abnormality in autism.[14] Specifically, both autopsy and MRI findings support Purkinje cell loss and/or cellular pathology in the neocerebellar vermis and the cerebellar cortex. Other replicated studies have reported abnormalities in the cerebral cortex, limbic structures (such as the amygdala), and additional sites.

Some very intriguing converging evidence is suggesting an unusual pattern of brain growth in autism. A particularly interesting study found that in a comparison of head circumference at birth, approximately 75 percent of children with autism showed a smaller head size than that of other infants.[15] Moreover, this was followed by a tremendous increase in head circumference following birth, so that by the age of 6 to 14 months the children with autism had a larger head circumference than typically developing children and children with PDD-NOS. Specifically, it appears that when brain volume is measured in very young (2- to 3-year-old) autistic children, many show a developmental macroencephaly, meaning that their brain volume is larger than that of typically developing youngsters of the same age. By the time the children are older, however, this difference disappears.[16] This finding has led some to speculate that abnormal regulation of brain growth in autism leads to overgrowth of neural matter that does not become appropriately differentiated into functional areas, which would explain many of the cognitive and behavioral anomalies associated with the disorder. In fact, there are two recent findings that may relate to the observed increase in brain volume and head circumference in autistic individuals. One finding is that there appears to be substantial overgrowth of white matter primarily in the frontal lobes of the cerebrum in young children with autism. This initial overgrowth is subsequently followed by a period of abnormally slow growth of white matter, suggesting a paring away of ineffective connections. Another finding is the presence of inflammation in the areas associated with overgrowth of white matter. Researchers in this area are intrigued by what these findings suggest regarding connectivity of different parts of the brain and how this relates to autistic functioning.[17] It is thought that genetic factors are likely responsible for this abnormal pattern of brain development. Whatever the basic cause of these abnormalities may be, results like this are exciting not only for their contribution in understanding the etiology of autism but also because of their potential for early diagnosis and treatment.

It is important to keep in mind, however, that identification of abnormal brain structures must always be considered in a context of what may be a chain of abnormalities in which the identified structure is but a link. The brain is a highly complex organ characterized by intricate hierarchical functions. Thus knowing that the cerebellum is structurally abnormal or that brain volume is larger than normal does not mean that either of these is a "cause" of autism. We need to investigate what caused the cerebellar abnormality, what effects the cerebellar abnormalities might have on other brain structures, and what other abnormalities are in the chain. Most important, we must seek to understand the brain-behavioral links. That is, how do these neuroanatomical anomalies translate into behavior?

We must also appreciate that this highly complex area of study is definitely a "work in progress." What is now exciting state-of-the-art research may ultimately prove to be wrong. In ten or twenty years, we may be looking at this genetic and neurobiological work as ancient history—perhaps in the way we now view the old psychodynamic theory of the past. Yet these current debates and issues should be the engines that drive future work. If these leads are pursued systematically and with an appropriately critical eye, I think there is reason to be very hopeful that we are heading in the right direction.

Autism as an Extreme Version of the Male Brain

In a real blockbuster of a theory, Simon Baron-Cohen at the University of Cambridge has proposed a completely novel neurobiological theory of the etiology of autism,[18] based on his view that the capacity for empathy is the critical difference between the "male" and the "female" brain. He postulates that the natural wiring of the human brain is such that it is geared toward either the capacity for empathy or the capacity for systematizing. Female brains are biased toward empathizing; male brains are biased toward the systematic as well as biased against empathizing. Baron-Cohen defines empathy as the drive to identify another person's thoughts and emotions, and to respond to them with an appropriate emotion of one's own. Since empathy and social understanding are hallmark deficits in autism, Baron-Cohen suggests that autism represents the extreme version of the male brain—geared more toward systematizing (orderliness, mechanical ability, and the like) and very limited in empathic response to people.

How could this extreme "maleness" of the brain occur? Simon Baron-Cohen believes that testosterone is the biological basis of the prenatal development of autism; he proposes that for some reason some individuals receive excessive levels of testosterone in utero, and that this results in the extreme male brain. In support of this theory, Baron-Cohen and his colleagues report a series of studies indicating that levels of testosterone in utero correlate with toddlers' social behavior and language.[19]

But what about autistic girls? If high levels of testosterone are responsible for the development of an extreme male brain, and thus possibly autism, why are not all autistic individuals male? Baron-Cohen counters that all females are exposed to low levels of testosterone in utero, but since they start from a lower baseline than males, they require much higher levels of testosterone to be affected with the extreme male brain syndrome (and thus, supposedly, autism). This would account for the appearance of autism in girls and also for the fact that many fewer girls than boys are affected.

While this is certainly an interesting theory, and one that makes some intuitive sense, Baron-Cohen is the first to admit that proof of the theory must await hard evidence for a relationship between fetal testosterone and autism. However, some critics are already balking at the theory and fear that it may only serve to perpetuate gender stereotypes unnecessarily. Given the absence of scientific proof of the testosterone-autism link, they feel it is premature to consider the theory seriously. While Baron-Cohen readily accepts the "politically incorrect" appearance of his theory, he still stands behind it.

It is important to remember that most of these findings in the neurobiology of autism represent correlational relationships. That is, anatomical differences may correlate with behavioral features, but in most cases we cannot infer a causal relationship. For example, one might find right hemisphere dominance in an individual with impaired language skills, but it could be the case that the brain dominance is a result of the individual's history of language impairment, or the language impairment is a result of the brain dominance, or it may be that both events are unrelated to each other and are caused by yet a third factor. It is the identification and clarification of these brain-behavior relationships that will provide the most important information in this area.

It is obvious that many years of research will be required to fully understand the biology of autism. It is also clear that what will be found is not a unitary etiology but rather a more detailed understanding of the multiple and complex etiologies involved in the development of this complicated disorder. As is often the case when definitive answers have not yet been found, there is plenty of room for disagreement in this field. But, in contrast to the earlier days of the psychogenic hypothesis, it is reassuring to know that the present disputes are based in science and that cumulative research by skilled scientists will likely lead to some, although probably not complete, convergence of opinion.

Does this scientific direction mean an end to the controversies associated with the etiology of autism? Probably not. Autism has always proven to be a popular yet frustratingly elusive target. It is easy to look back over fifty years and see gaping holes in prior theories that only became apparent with the accumulation of new knowledge, and doubtless the same will be said in the future about our current perspectives on etiology. But as long as these perspectives are based on critical inquiry as opposed to uncritical conjecture, we should remain on the right track.

Additional Areas of Controversy

There is little doubt that there are many possible causes of autism, and almost all of these have their proponents. Genetics, neurobiological factors, hormonal factors, viral infections, metabolic factors, birth complications, environmental toxins, and other causes have been put forward as potential etiological villains. As we have seen, some of these have more scientific backing than others. At present, the effects of genetics, neurobiological factors, and some viral infections (for example, congenital rubella and tuberous sclerosis) have the most empirical support. Yet despite years of study, no birth complications, specific metabolic factors, or environmental toxins have been verified as being causally related to autism. Similarly, research to date has failed to link autism to specific immunological problems. Studies in this area have yielded contradictory or inconclusive results. Let's look at a few of the major controversies currently under debate in the area of autism etiology.

Does the MMR Vaccine Cause Autism?

In recent years one of the most hotly debated issues regarding a potential cause of autism spectrum disorders has involved the role of the measles, mumps, and rubella (MMR) vaccine. This immunization, introduced in the 1980s, combines the three vaccines into one injection and is given in two doses, the first administered at around 13 months and the second around 4–6 years of age. The overall effectiveness of this vaccination is clear: the United States, as well as many other countries around the world, has reported a substantial decrease in the occurrence of these extremely serious diseases. The significance of the control of these diseases is obvious. Measles has a very high fatality rate among children—mainly in underdeveloped countries, although there have been outbreaks in more recent years in industrialized nations. Mumps is relatively mild but can lead to serious complications, such as meningitis or encephalitis, which can result in disability or death. Congenital rubella is a known cause of blindness, deafness, and mental retardation. The development and implementation of the MMR vaccine program has been hailed as a monumentally successful program and is credited with saving literally millions of children from death or disability.

Controversy regarding the possible negative effects of the MMR vaccine and its potential role in the development of autism was stimulated by the report of an English gastroenterologist, Dr. Andrew Wakefield, at the Royal Free Hospital and School of Medicine in the United Kingdom.[20] From observations during their study, Wakefield and his colleagues suggested the possibility that the MMR vaccine led to intestinal abnormalities, which resulted in not only impaired intestinal function but also developmental regression in the 12 children reviewed. These effects were noted to occur within 24 hours to a few weeks after injection of the MMR vaccine. The developmental disorder reported was usually autism. Dr. Wakefield and his colleagues hypothesized a causal relationship between the MMR vaccine and autism.

Needless to say, this report received high-profile coverage and frightened many parents. Many who already had autistic children could look back at the fact that their child had received the vaccine right before the appearance of autistic symptoms. The timing was suspicious, and it could explain the rather sudden behavioral regression often reported in these youngsters (for example, rapid loss of acquired speech). It all made perfect sense. When the television program *60 Minutes* presented a report on the role of the MMR vaccine in autism, it showed the correspondent attending a conference of parents and asking them to raise their hand if they believed the MMR vaccine had caused their child's autism. Every hand in the room went up. The Wakefield report initiated a huge debate that continues to this day.

The Wakefield report has led to a significant drop in the number of children receiving the MMR inoculation. This is alarming to health officials, since the risk of epidemics of these once-common diseases poses a huge health risk to society. After all, these diseases are potentially fatal, and even if the MMR vaccine could be related to autism in some cases, autism is not fatal or communicable (although truly devastating nonetheless). Yet the opponents of MMR inoculation point out that they do not oppose vaccination against these diseases but rather oppose combining all three vaccines into one. They argue that perhaps the combination of the three vaccines too severely taxes an immature system or affects a child already organically predisposed to autism, and they suggest that the vaccines be separated and given perhaps one year apart. However, health experts counter that to do so would expose young children to significant risk because the delay in vaccination could leave the children vulnerable to the yet-unvaccinated diseases.

What do the scientific data tell us about the MMR vaccine and autism? Most studies argue against a link between the two. One of the most thorough evaluations was conducted by the United Kingdom Medical Research Council (MRC), which reviewed the findings of a number of studies, including Wakefield's, and concluded there was no association between the vaccine and autism.[21] Both the journal in which Wakefield's study appeared and one of Wakefield's coauthors have stated that the study was not specifically designed to investigate the relationship between the MMR vaccine and intestinal disorders or developmental disorders. In the absence of an experimental protocol geared to studying this question specifically, the results could not be considered conclusive. Another study identified all 473 individuals with autism in five districts of northeast London who were born between 1979 and 1998.[22] The researchers found no jump in the number of autism cases after introduction of the MMR vaccination program in 1988. If the MMR vaccine caused autism, one would expect to see a dramatic rise in cases when the vaccination program was initiated. Further, there was no difference in age at diagnosis between children vaccinated before or after 18 months of age and children who were never vaccinated. Thus the vaccine did not lead to earlier appearance of symptoms. Finally, the research indicated there was no developmental regression clustered around the time of vaccination. The first signs of autism were not more likely to occur within time periods following vaccination than during other periods. (In fact, as we have seen, studies using anatomical and behavioral measures have demonstrated abnormalities before one year of age.) A large study conducted in California looked retrospectively at MMR immunization coverage rates among children born between 1980 and 1994.[23] Although during this time period there was a substantial increase in the number of autism cases reported, there was not a concomitant increase in the rate of vaccination. All of these studies, in addition to others,[24] argue persuasively against a causal link between the MMR vaccine and autism.

Yet another recent study and its aftermath again illustrate the contentious nature of this issue.[25] This large study, conducted at the U.S. Government Centers for Disease Control and Prevention, concluded there was little evidence of a link between vaccines and developmental problems in a study of more than 140,000 children. These researchers analyzed data from three health maintenance organizations on children born between 1992 and 1999 and tracked them for several years in order to determine if any developmental disability was subsequently diagnosed. They looked for instances of autism, attention deficit disorders, stammering, and emotional disturbances. The researchers found no link between the vaccines and *any* disorder, including of course autism. Yet this study did nothing to quell the strong feelings of those believing in the link, and the minute the study appeared, critics began issuing charges of a "cover-up." Despite the facts of the case, the debate is likely to continue for a long time.

In another stunning development that serves to highlight the contentious nature of claims in this area, ten of the thirteen authors of Wakefield's original study that reported a possible link between the MMR vaccine and autism recently retracted the conclusions and renounced the study.[26] Their retraction followed the disclosure that Wakefield was being paid separately by lawyers for parents who alleged that the immunizations caused their children's autism. Some of the children in the lawsuit were also involved in the now widely discredited study.

The rather consistent finding against the MMR vaccine as causative in autism is shared by a number of very credible organizations, including the American Medical Association, the Institute of Medicine, USA, the World Health Organization, the American Academy of Pediatrics, the Population and Public Health Branch of Health Canada, and the Irish Department of Health and Children. Despite the weight of the evidence, and the importance of these organizations, the questions persist. It is interesting that even in light of the seemingly overwhelming evidence against MMR as a risk factor for autism, it seems no one is willing to completely shut the door on the possibility.

Although it appeared that the last nail in the coffin of the MMR-vaccine-causes-autism issue was the final report issued by the Institute of Medicine in 2004, it was not. This report, reflecting conclusions drawn from a panel of prominent scientists who reviewed national and international studies conducted since 2001, found no association between autism and vaccines. Moreover, the panel recommended that it was time for science to look elsewhere for the cause of autism.[27] Yet no sooner were these findings announced than they were subjected to criticism in terms of the "competence" of the panel and various suspicious motives. It is clear that we have not heard the end of this debate.

Does Mercury Cause Autism?

Closely related to the theory that childhood vaccines contribute to the development of autism is the view that a potential contributing factor for the development of the disorder is prenatal or postnatal exposure to heavy metals such as mercury. In fact, historically many vaccines contained thimerosal as a preservative (although this is no longer the case), and thimerosal consists of approximately 50 percent ethylmercury by weight. Certainly we know that mercury can have devastating effects on the developing brain. Proponents of the view that mercury is a causative agent in many cases of autism point to the striking similarities between symptoms of autism and those of mercury poisoning. These include social deficits, social withdrawal, failure to develop speech, speech comprehension deficits, sound sensitivity, poor performance on verbal IQ tests, mental retardation, and stereotyped movements such as arm flapping and rocking.

As noted earlier in the discussion of the MMR vaccine and its hypothesized role in the etiology of autism, another reason why mercury-containing vaccines became suspect is the coincidental timing of administration of the vaccine and onset of autistic symptoms. The vaccines are typically given to a child between 1 and 3 years of age, and this is often when the characteristics of autism appear. In fact, proponents of this theory point in particular to cases of regressive autism, where the child seems to be developing normally but then suddenly loses acquired skills and exhibits some of the unusual behaviors of the disorder. The skill loss and appearance of autistic behaviors seem to occur within a short time after vaccination. The fact that not all children who receive the vaccines become autistic is attributed to the fact that the effect only occurs when there is a genetic or some other predisposition to mercury sensitivity. Since even "normal" people are differentially sensitive to mercury, it makes sense that not all vaccinated children would be equally susceptible to developing autism.

To date, however, the scientific data do not support a connection between mercury or thimerosal and autism.[28] First, if mercury were associated with autism, one would expect to find elevated levels of mercury in autistic individuals, but there is no conclusive evidence of higher levels of mercury in these people. Second, as in the case of the MMR vaccine and autism, there does not seem to be a correlation between the tremendous rise in the number of autism cases and the relatively stable rate at which these vaccines are given. Third, the similarities between autism and mercury poisoning, while apparent, cannot be considered definitive. Many of the symptoms shared by the two conditions are also seen in other brain disorders such as mental retardation.

Once again, more critical attention is called for. While it may be possible to conclude that in general there is no link between autism and mercury, one cannot exclude the possibility that a small number of children may be affected. Of course one needs to determine whether the risk of autism is any higher than the known risk associated with any childhood vaccine. At present, this does not seem to be the case.

What Will Research on Etiology Contribute to Effective Treatments?

In recent years there has been some additional controversy involving the study of autism etiology. While everyone can agree that the study of etiology is crucial to our ultimate understanding of the disorder, some parents and professionals are concerned that the focus on etiology may have shifted too much attention (and resources) away from the development of effective treatments. To date, the research on etiological factors in autism has led to no substantial improvements in treatment. It must be acknowledged that even our ultimate identification of specific biological causes of the disorder (such as specific genes or neuroanatomical anomalies) will likely have no immediate treatment implications. Knowing the cause of a disorder does not necessarily mean that such knowledge will inform treatments. For example, although we have known the specific genetic basis of Down syndrome since 1959, this knowledge has not led to the development of any specific treatments for the disorder.

Similarly, since we do not yet know what to look for, etiological research has not yet led to a prenatal test for autism. Such a test (which does exist for Down syndrome) may someday allow for prenatal interventions that will prevent the expression of autism in the child. It is also possible that if autism is determined to be caused or exacerbated by very early environmental factors, these factors, once identified, could be altered or eliminated. Such is the case with phenylketonuria (PKU), which at one time was a major cause of mental retardation in children. A specific metabolic defect was identified in which the child's metabolism could not process the protein phenylalanine, which subsequently became a toxin in the brain. Today all newborns are tested for this defect and if it is found, the child is immediately placed on a phenylalanine-free diet to prevent subsequent mental retardation.

The reality is that we are still awaiting the contribution of etiological information that will allow us to detect prenatally, prevent, alter, or treat the course of autism. However, there is little reason to doubt these contributions will be forthcoming.

CHAPTER 5

Are There Core Deficits in Autism?

Does the autistic child have a "theory of mind?"

> —Simon Baron-Cohen, Alan M. Leslie, and Uta Frith, in *Cognition*
> (1985)

The theory-of-mind deficit in the majority of cases with autism is very severe. It has the potential to explain the social, communicative, and imaginative abnormalities that are diagnostic of the condition, because being able to reflect on one's own mental states (and those of others) would appear to be essential in all of these domains.

> —Simon Baron-Cohen and John Swettenham, in *Handbook of Autism
> and Pervasive Developmental Disorders* (1997)

Autism is a complex and heterogeneous disorder that should not be reduced to a single underlying cognitive impairment.

> —Helen Tager-Flusberg, in *The Development of Autism* (2001)

Given the severe and pervasive nature of autism, it has been tempting to try to identify the "core deficit," or the basic problem that may underlie all the features of the disorder. Identification of a central problem is an attractive prospect for several reasons. If a single core deficit could be found, it would likely assist in the discovery of the etiology of autism. If we could identify a particular brain structure or a single neuropsychological mechanism that has somehow gone awry, we would know where autism begins. Given this information, it might also be possible to prevent or "cure" the disorder if the core deficit was something we could identify from the very earliest stage (probably prenatally) and fix. Even if prevention or cure were not possible, focusing our treatments to target the core deficit might be expected to have a more profound impact on the course of autism.

Researchers have in fact worked very hard to try to identify the core or primary deficit in autism, but not surprisingly, the heterogeneous nature and complexity of the disorder have made the task frustratingly difficult. The sheer number and variety of proposed "primary deficits" illustrate how complicated the task is of identifying the core problem. Again, we have a fertile ground for arguments and conflicting opinions.

For a deficit to qualify as a "primary" or "core" deficit, four criteria must be met.[1] First, the deficit has to have *specificity,* meaning that the deficit is specific to autism and is not found in people with other disorders. Second, it has to show *universality,* meaning that all individuals with autism must have the deficit. Third, it has to show *persistence,* meaning that the deficit continues to affect the individual during the developmental process. Finally, the deficit must show *precedence,* meaning that it begins early in development. Precedence also suggests that this deficit is the beginning of what may be a long chain of related deficits; in other words, it is the first thing to go wrong and is associated with a cascade of further, but related, deficits down the line.

Because of the complex nature of autism, it is unlikely that a *single* core deficit will be found that explains all the features of the disorder. Such a core deficit would not only have to account for the major diagnostic symptoms of autism, including social impairment, communication impairment, and restricted interests, but would also have to explain ancillary autistic symptoms such as lack of pretend play, stereotyped/repetitive/perseverative behaviors, splinter skills, rote memory skills, and the like.

The focus on core deficits in autism can be broken down into four major areas of thinking and research: problems with cognition, problems with feelings and emotion, problems with attention and arousal, and problems with imitation.

Defective Cognitive Processes

Theory of Mind

This area of research includes theories that relate problems in thinking to the manifested syndrome of autism, particularly the way in which the individual thinks about his or her place in the social environment. The main theory in this area views the basic defect in autism as the inability to take the perspective of another person. In other words, the autistic person has difficulty understanding that another person has knowledge, beliefs, feelings, or intentions that are separate and perhaps different from his own. The ability to understand the different perspective of others is generally referred to as "Theory of Mind" (ToM), and this ability appears in normally developing children around the age of 1½ to 2 years. Prior to this age, typical children are very egocentric: they see events only from their own point of view and assume that others share this point of view. This egocentristic view declines as the child matures.

To test for ToM, Heinz Wimmer and Josef Perner developed an ingenious series of "false-belief" scenarios designed to measure a person's ability to distinguish between her own knowledge about reality and someone else's false belief about reality. These scenarios are acted out by an examiner, who uses two dolls.[2] A description of the most frequently reported task illustrates how these tests work. In the classic "Sally/Anne" task, the scenario involves two dolls, Sally and Anne. Sally puts a marble into a basket and then leaves the room. Anne comes into the room, plays with the marble, and then puts it in a box. Sally returns, and the examiner then asks the child who has observed this scenario where Sally will look for the marble. Normally developing children as young as 4 years of age will correctly say that Sally will look in the basket. That is, these children can correctly understand Sally's false belief even though the child knows that the marble is actually in the box. However, children with autism typically fail the test, saying that Sally will look in the box (where the child knows the marble is). Thus they seem to retain the egocentric point of view—they are unable to appreciate that another person's knowledge is different from their own. Moreover, ToM deficits may be specific to autism; children with mental retardation (such as those with Down syndrome) have been shown to pass the false-belief tests as easily as do typically developing children. Thus cognitive impairment per se cannot account for ToM deficits.

Interestingly, some individuals with autism are able to pass these "first-order" false-belief tests but may fail with "second-order" false-belief tasks. A second-order false-belief task, which is typically mastered by children of age 5 to 6, requires the child to track what one character mistakenly thinks about another person's belief. And even very high-functioning individuals with autism who can pass second-order ToM tasks exhibit difficulties in comprehending figurative language. According to the theory's proponents, this indicates remaining difficulties with ToM.

The fact that children with autism have difficulties in understanding the perspective, intentions, beliefs, and knowledge of others may explain why they seem to understand so little of their social environment. Imagine what it must be like to live in a world where you have no idea that people have different beliefs, desires, intentions, and knowledge than you do. Imagine how random and unpredictable their behavior would seem to you. Volkmar and his colleagues even suggest that this may help explain the often observed behavior of autistic children who treat other people as "objects."[3] Thus a child reaching for a cookie who stands on his mother's lap as if she were a chair may indeed have no conception that she is a thinking, feeling being who might not appreciate being treated as nothing but an object in the environment.

Proponents of the ToM hypothesis describe precursors to ToM that are apparent in autism. Alan Leslie believes that the ability to take the perspective of others is related to the ability to form temporary representations of reality,[4] such as when a child pretends a wooden block is a car. So the child essentially has two realities: he represents physical reality and also represents his own pretend attitude toward the proposition that "this block is a car." For a ToM task, the child needs to have two realities: where the marble is and where Sally thinks it is. This ability is made possible by postulated brain structures that allow for the development of a so-called "Theory of Mind Module," which is thought to emerge in typically developing children at around age 2. Leslie believes that dysfunction in the developing brain in children with autism prevents the emergence of this module and subsequently the ability to form representations. This view is supported by the fact that such representation is required for pretend play, a behavior notably absent in this population. While Leslie's points are well taken and make sense in terms of the behaviors one sees in autism, to date there have been no brain structures identified that would substantiate this theory.

Another often-reported precursor to deficits in ToM is deficits in joint attention. As noted earlier, joint attention is a first means of communication for children. It occurs when the child can respond to the gaze of another person and use his gaze to direct the attention of others. For example, a mother might establish eye contact with her child and then look at an object nearby. Beginning at the age of 8 to 9 months, a typical child will look over to where the mother is looking. At a slightly later age the child can control the attention of an adult, as when a child might look at his mother, then look at a cookie, and then look back at his mother. In this way, the child communicates to the mother his desire for a cookie and does so before he can use language. The ability to use gaze to engage in this sort of communication suggests that the child is aware of another person's gaze and has learned that this person has a different perspective (and therefore a different "mind"). Yet for children with autism, joint-attention behaviors are reported to be very limited or absent altogether. In a particularly ingenious study, Osterling and Dawson and their colleagues looked at home videos of children's first birthday parties.[5] Since almost everyone nowadays has a video camera and records such events, the researchers were able to acquire tapes of children who were subsequently diagnosed with autism, children who were subsequently diagnosed with mental retardation (but not autism), and children who were not diagnosed with any disability. They scored the tapes for the presence of the child's face-to-face interaction with parents and other children, response to his or her name being called, and following the pointing gestures of others. They found that the children later diagnosed with autism were significantly less likely to engage in these behaviors than either the children with retardation or the typical children. Thus by the age of one year, these children were clearly different in that they were less likely to use or initiate joint attention. Subsequent research has found deficits in this sort of social attention in autistic children as young as 9 and even 6 months of age.[6]

The research on joint attention in autism has produced a very robust finding: these children are definitely restricted in their use of this early form of communication. Interestingly, the deficit seems to follow a pattern that one can almost predict, given the nature of autism. That is, the children are reported to be less deficient in the use of joint attention to obtain something they want in the environment (*protoimperative* joint attention) than they are at using joint attention to merely engage another person socially or to share an experience (*protodeclarative* joint attention). This means that the child may indeed be able to get his mother's attention to obtain a cookie but is much less likely to want to get her attention to have her enjoy the sight of a fire engine. Further, autistic children are much less likely to look at others' faces for information.

Some proponents of the ToM hypothesis see a direct relation between deficits in joint attention and deficits in ToM. They view difficulties in joint attention as resulting from the lack of a neurological mechanism that detects eye direction in others and therefore allows for the understanding of people as goal-directed beings with their own feelings and perspectives.[7] The resulting difficulties in joint attention prevent the acquisition of pretense and thus ToM. Again, however, no neurological substrates of this proposed mechanism have yet been identified.

How well does the ToM theory meet the requirements of being a core deficit? The first issue is whether or not a deficit in ToM is *specific* to autism. Although the original research in this area seemed to indicate that ToM deficits were specific to autism in that children with retardation or other disorders did not fail false-belief tasks, more recent research has indicated that in fact nonautistic children and adolescents with mental retardation do fail such tests at a level higher than we might predict given their developmental level. Moreover, individuals with other impairments such as schizophrenia, blindness, deafness, and specific language disorders also have difficulties with ToM tasks.[8] This calls into question the specificity of ToM to autism.

The second issue is whether a ToM deficit is *universal* in that all individuals with autism exhibit these deficits. We know from the many studies of ToM that there are some individuals with autism who do indeed pass the false-belief tasks. Thus one could argue that the deficit is not universal. However, it might also be argued that the deficit in ToM may be universal at a key stage in development but not apparent at other stages (for example, some high-functioning people with autism may fail false-belief tasks at a younger age but pass them when they are older).

Third, do ToM deficits *persist,* continuing to affect the individual during the neurodevelopmental process? It appears that autistic individuals who exhibit difficulties with ToM tasks do retain those difficulties as well as other representational difficulties such as pretense.

The fourth requirement for a core deficit, the *primacy* of ToM deficits, is highly debatable—and debated. In fact, of the all the arguments presented in opposition to the Theory of Mind hypothesis, perhaps the strongest are those that contest the primacy of these deficits. The basic argument is that the ToM hypothesis cannot explain the appearance of autistic symptoms long before the emergence of representational ToM. Infants and very young children with autism already show abnormalities in social relating, joint attention, play, empathy, and imitation, long before the age of 4 years when the ToM develops. Therefore, not all deficits and abnormalities seen in autism represent difficulties in appreciating other people's minds.[9] Further complicating the picture is the fact that some theorists believe the social deficits in autism are primary and are the basis for the subsequent development of ToM deficits.

Thus, three out of four requirements for a core deficit have not been met. In addition, other problems with the ToM hypothesis have been pointed out. One is the fact that the ToM hypothesis, while providing a rather handy explanation for many of the social, language, and play deficits apparent in autistic children, does not provide a basis for other symptoms such as stereotyped behaviors, splinter skills, good rote memory, and insistence on sameness. Second, some researchers have argued that the observed difficulties with ToM tasks may be rooted in language deficits, and it is these language deficits that determine how the individuals understand the ToM tasks such as the false-belief scenarios. Third, some have speculated that other hypothesized cognitive difficulties such as executive function (discussed below) may be primary to, and responsible for, ToM performance in that shifting hypotheses and planning are involved. Finally, the cognitive tasks often used to measure ToM may be imprecise in that they really tap a variety of cognitive processes.

Central Coherence

Another view of a primary cognitive deficit in autism has been presented by Uta Frith and her colleagues, who posit that autistic children lack a *drive for central coherence*.[10] This is a drive that normally developing people have to integrate and organize environmental information in order to construct comprehensive interpretations of situations. They do so by reading the intentions of others through eye gaze, gestures, and other important contextual environmental cues. A failure to adequately consider contextual cues would explain the behavior of one of the children in Francesca Happé's research who, when shown a toy bed and asked to identify the rectangular object at the head of the bed, said "a piece of ravioli." Thus the child interpreted the rectangular object on a localized level and failed to consider the other features of the setting, where the context would have dictated a very different answer (pillow).[11]

Frith's conceptualization has several important advantages. It not only accounts for known specific deficits in autism including difficulties with joint attention and ToM, but it also provides an explanation for other significant features of the disorder such as insistence on sameness, repetitive and stereotyped behaviors, and restricted interests. These are behaviors that suggest reduced interest in, and shutting out of, contextual cues.

Frith and her colleagues, like other researchers who are hypothesizing social cognition as the primary deficit in autism, are attempting to identify specific neurological underpinnings that may account for a drive for "central coherence" and, more important, what may account for its failure to develop in this population. To date, such a neurological correlate has not been identified.

Executive Function

Another hypothesized primary cognitive deficit in autism is difficulty with what is called *executive function,* which involves planning strategies for obtaining goals. To successfully plan goal-directed behavior one needs to identify several courses of action, consider a number of factors, and ultimately decide on the best strategy to pursue. This process might also involve rejecting an option that may be more direct but has disadvantages that require a less direct option to be adopted. Flexibility and the ability to alter a course of action in light of contextual or changing conditions are hallmarks of executive function. Children with autism are known for having difficulties in the planning of such strategies, and researchers have speculated that executive function deficits may be responsible for the deficits in ToM.[12] One has to appreciate various options and versions of nonreality to have a ToM (including the reality of another's beliefs), and it is just this sort of difficulty that one sees in autism.

The executive function hypothesis does account for a number of features of autism, including ToM difficulties. It is also able to account for other autistic symptoms such as the individual's restricted range of interests and insistence on sameness, since these symptoms certainly indicate a lack of flexibility. This hypothesis also helps to explain the splinter skills frequently seen in autism in that such skills usually involve an over-focused, single-minded approach. However, the executive function hypothesis fails one of the tests of a primary deficit in that it does not appear to be specific to autism.

Executive function deficits are found in other disorders such as attention deficit disorder, Tourette syndrome, obsessive-compulsive disorder, and schizophrenia. Moreover, although researchers have implicated the prefrontal cortex of the brain as a potential biological basis for executive function deficit, to date this has not been proved.

Deficits in Emotional Processes

Affect

In his initial description of autism in 1943, Leo Kanner concluded that autistic children are born with an innate inability to form the usual, biologically provided emotional contact with people. In fact, the title of his historic article, "Autistic Disturbances of Affective Contact," suggests that he felt this was the central defect in autism. Often presented as evidence of this defect is the frequent observation that autistic children seem to respond to people as if they were pieces of furniture rather than living, feeling beings. In addition, their limited use of eye contact, their sometimes situationally-inappropriate affect, their emotional aloofness, and their lack of attachment all suggest that these children are not emotionally tuned in to the world around them and are truly detached from others. It is the opinion of some researchers that this basic lack of affective contact is a core deficit.

There are indeed some very interesting findings that support the idea that children with autism have basic and profound difficulties with perceiving and understanding the expressed affect of others as well as the affect associated with various situations. For example, one study compared autistic and nonautistic children in a sorting task where various photographs of people could be sorted on the basis of age, gender, emotional facial expression, or type of hat.[13] While the nonautistic children sorted the pictures on the basis of facial expression, the autistic children sorted on the basis of the hats. Further, when specifically instructed to sort the photographs on the basis of facial expressions, almost half of the autistic children could not do so. This is a rather sobering finding; it suggests that not only are autistic children disinclined to interpret facial expressions, but perhaps they are truly unable to do so. In a similar study, children with autism, children with mental retardation, and typical children were shown pictures of faces expressing sadness, happiness, fear, and anger and were asked to match the pictures with vocalizations of these emotions and then with gestures.[14] Unlike the typical and retarded children, who readily matched the facial expressions with the vocalizations, the autistic children fared poorly. However, on a control matching task involving animals and animal sounds, the autistic children performed as well as the other children.

Another manifestation of this difficulty with understanding the emotional states of others is the characteristic lack of empathy reported in these youngsters. In fact, a common question used when conducting a diagnostic evaluation for autism is to ask a parent about the child's reaction if the parent is sad, sick, or injured. Most often the parent will report that the child does not notice the parents' distress and does not try to comfort them—in stark contrast to the usual response of a typical child, who might be quite upset at a parent's distress and offer comments, hugs, and other expressions of comfort. I saw examples of this kind of behavior in videos from a study by Dr. Marian Sigman of UCLA, who compared the empathetic responses of children with autism, children with mental retardation, and typical children. In the study, an experimenter sat next to a child while playing with a toy. The experimenter pretended to hit her hand with a toy hammer, saying "Ouch!", holding her "injured" hand, and facially expressing distress. The different reactions of the children were striking. The typical children became very concerned and offered comfort to the experimenter. The children with retardation reacted to the experimenter's distress and showed concern, but were less sophisticated in expressing comfort. In contrast, most of the autistic children failed to react in any way to the experimenter's distress, and some actually reached over and took away the toy she had been playing with. It is interesting (and perhaps hopeful) that this deficit in empathy may be less pronounced in high-functioning children with autism. Other researchers looked at the reactions of high- and low-functioning autistic children and found that when an experimenter knocked his knee into a table, exclaimed "Ouch!", and showed a pained facial expression, the high-functioning children did in fact notice the distress but were deficient in responding. The low-functioning children, however, were profoundly impaired in both their attending to the distress and their response.[15]

Peter Hobson, a major proponent of this theory, believes that this innate deficit in the ability to both perceive and respond to the emotional responses of others prevents autistic individuals from engaging in the very social interactions necessary to develop social understanding and perspectives—and thus a theory of mind.[16] In his view, this emotional deficit precedes a ToM deficit.

Again, however, theories based in the idea of an affective disturbance being primary do not meet all the criteria for a core deficit. We know that affective responsiveness differs significantly in individuals of different functioning levels, and while affective deviance seems to have many features specific to the autism population, we do not yet know if it has precedence.

Deficits in Attention and Arousal

Some researchers, going back to an even earlier process than perception and interpretation, hold that the core deficit in autism can be traced to neurological arousal and attentional processes. Attentional deficits (and deviance) have been noted in the autism population for many years. In his 1943 study, Kanner noted that the children often appeared not to notice people in their environment. Yet while these children may seem oblivious to the comings and goings of people and may not react to their name being called, they may be intensely interested in looking at patterns in wallpaper or listening to the crinkle of a candy wrapper. This "apparent" sensory deficit suggests that while the children are not impaired in their ability to perceive sensory input, their attention to it is abnormal. In a series of studies,[17] my colleagues and I determined that many of these children were "overselective" in their attention—that is, when placed in a situation where they were called upon to respond to multiple cues at the same time, they might attend to only one of the cues. For example, in the initial study we taught autistic, retarded, and typical children to press a lever when we presented a compound stimulus made up of three individual components: a visual cue (red light), an auditory cue (white noise), and a tactile cue (light pressure on the leg). All of the children learned this discrimination task. We then tested to see which of the individual components the children had attended to (and learned). We did this by running test trials where only one of the components was presented (for example, only the red light). What we found was quite surprising to us. While the typical children had learned about each of the single cues and responded to each one when it was presented individually, the children with autism usually only learned about one cue. Thus they might respond when the red light was presented alone, but did not respond to the individual presentations of the noise or tactile cue. (The retarded children responded at a level between these two extremes.) Several subsequent studies demonstrated that this difficulty in responding to multiple cues extended to situations where there were only two cues and where the cues were in the same modality.

This finding was intriguing for a variety of reasons. First of all, it helped explain why autistic children have so much difficulty in learning new tasks. But it also appeared to account for some of the seemingly bizarre behaviors that we, and others, had frequently noticed. Often these involved social situations. For instance, one child's father reported that when he (the father) removed his eyeglasses, his son responded to him as if he were a stranger. Another child would become extremely agitated whenever her mother wore new shoes. A third child refused to allow his mother to wear new dresses. I remember one child with whom I had worked for months who suddenly did not recognize me after I cut my hair. My colleagues and I began to think that this overselective attention with a severely reduced focus might underlie some of the features of autism, including deficits in social responsiveness.

In one study that I found especially interesting, we tested this hypothesis by teaching autistic and typical children to discriminate between a female doll ("Barbie") and a male doll ("Ken").[18] The girl doll wore high-heeled shoes, socks, a skirt, a blouse, and a jacket. She also had blond plastic fiber hair, a fair complexion, and blue eyes. The boy doll wore oxford shoes, socks, trousers, a shirt, and a jacket. He had brown painted hair, an olive complexion, and brown eyes. In other words, there were several ways (multiple cues) to distinguish between these two dolls; they looked nothing alike. Once the children learned to point reliably to the boy or the girl doll, we systematically switched one item of clothing at a time (for example, the pants and the skirt) to see which of the many available cues they were using to make the distinction. We also had a test in which we switched the dolls' heads, leaving the dressed part of the doll unchanged. Confirming our hypothesis that overselective attention may play some role in the difficulties autistic children have in social responding and recognition, we found that the autistic children in this experiment responded on the basis of some idiosyncratic feature of the doll such as the shoes, the socks, the jacket, or the shirt. For example, autistic children might identify whichever doll was wearing the skirt as the "girl" doll, even if the skirt was on the doll that was male in all other respects. In contrast, the typical children responded on the basis of the head. Although one might argue that responding to dolls as social stimuli may not be the same as responding to real people, these findings are intriguing because they seem to mirror the reported difficulties children with autism have with social recognition and relationships. Consider, for example, a situation where an autistic child meets a man who is wearing a green shirt. If the only thing the child attends to is the green shirt, and the next time she meets the man he is wearing a red shirt, it is unlikely the child will identify him as the same person she met before. The same may be true of glasses, shoes, or dresses.

Why didn't the autistic children in our study use the heads (faces) when learning to discriminate between the dolls? One possibility is that they have learned that faces are composed of multiple features, and these features move and change as a person smiles, moves his eyebrows, and so on. Perhaps the complexity of the face provides too many cues for the child, and the changing of the features just adds to the complexity. Thus it is possible that these children have learned, through experience, to rely on features that do not change during an interaction—for example, a shirt.

While it is true that stimulus overselectivity is related to mental age (that is, it increases with the level of cognitive impairment), it is also true that these findings are consonant with other findings on abnormal attention. Courchesne and his colleagues have demonstrated that individuals with autism have difficulty shifting their attention rapidly between modalities.[19] This difficulty in shifting attention might in fact underlie the difficulties reported in the overselectivity studies, and it would also help to explain difficulties in joint attention. However, other populations show difficulties in shifting attention and yet they do not exhibit the social difficulties characteristic of autism. For example, children with Down syndrome or attention deficit hyperactivity disorder have trouble with attention shifting, but they are socially skilled and responsive. We may therefore conclude that overselectivity and difficulties in shifting attention do not appear to be specific to autism and thus fail a major requirement for a core deficit. Nonetheless, it is quite likely that deficits and deviance in attention (based on one mechanism or another) play an important role in the symptoms of autistic disorder. If a child is unable to attend in an effective and efficient manner, this would undoubtedly strongly influence how she can respond to the social as well as the nonsocial world.

Attention to the environment is intimately related to one's overall level of arousal, and some have speculated that the difficulties autistic children exhibit with attention are due to faulty arousal levels. Deviant arousal would even precede attention in the chain of events of a core deficit. Not surprisingly, just about every form of arousal level has been hypothesized to be responsible.

Early on, some researchers speculated that autistic children are chronically *underaroused* and thus do not respond as they should to the environment.[20] This view was proposed to account for the failure of these children to attend to many cues in the environment (particularly social cues), with the result that they do not learn about their physical and social environment. This theory also seeks to account for autistic children's stereotyped, self-stimulatory behavior, which is considered to be an attempt to achieve appropriate arousal levels by providing stimulation through rocking, humming, staring at lights, and other such behaviors.

Other theorists have posited that autistic children are chronically *overaroused*,[21] are unable to selectively attend to the myriad stimuli in their environment, and consequently find it necessary to reduce environmental stimulation by withdrawing from the highly complex social world. Because social situations provide too much arousal for the children, they learn to avoid them and retreat into their own familiar world. Moreover, for these children self-stimulation serves the purpose of blocking out the additional stimulation of the outside world.

To add to the contradictory views, there are also hypotheses suggesting that autistic individuals suffer from a condition in which they are *alternately* over- or underaroused and unable to modulate responsivity.[22] This alternation is seen as explaining why autistic children are so variable in their responses to a person, object, or situation at different times: the extent of their responding would depend on the level of their arousal at a given time. While each of these arousal theories has its proponents as well as some supportive data (particularly the overarousal hypothesis), the fact remains that research findings have failed to support unequivocally any of these theories.

Given the variable arousal levels represented in these theories, it is hard to conceptualize any one of them filling the requirements for a core deficit. Although they may show persistence in individuals and they may (if found to be consistently true) show precedence, deviant arousal levels are certainly not specific to autism, nor are they universal to the population. Yet the fact that researchers seem to regularly come back to arousal as a potential core deficit does suggest that someday arousal may be determined to be a much more significant factor than currently thought.

Problems with Imitation

A deficit in the ability to imitate others has also been proposed as a core deficit in autism. This hypothesis makes sense when one considers the major role of imitation in the development of typical children. Imitation of adults is one of the first behaviors observed in infants, and all through the course of development, imitation of modeled behaviors provides an important and extensive route for learning. Imagine how much less efficient learning would be if children could not rely on following the modeled actions of others.

The developmental literature is clear in demonstrating the relationship between imitation and social behaviors, communication, affect, play, and other fundamental behaviors in typically developing children. Given that some of these areas are precisely where we see severe deficits in individuals with autism (and, as we know, are diagnostic of the disorder), it is reasonable to speculate that difficulties in the ability to imitate would have the "downstream" effect of leading to difficulties in these areas.

Can difficulties in communication be the result of an imitation deficit? As noted earlier, the research on normal development suggests that imitation provides the foundation of communicative language. Thus one might assume that a disruption in early imitation would negatively affect the development of communication skills in people with autism, and there is indeed evidence for a connection between imitation and communication abilities in autism. One study showed that performance on a vocal imitation task by children with autism was highly correlated with spontaneous communication ability.[23] Another study, using a gestural imitation task, showed that relatively good imitators verbalized more to an adult than did poor imitators.[24] A longitudinal study showed a relationship between performance by autistic children on a task involving imitation of body movements (gestural imitation) and the development of expressive language six months later. Another study showed that good imitators had better receptive language skills.[25] Thus, there are grounds to argue for a relationship between imitation ability and communicative skills.

Of course, one must also take into account that many verbal autistic children are echolalic—that is, they repeat (imitate) the speech of others immediately or after a delay. Rogers and Pennington speculate that different brain mechanisms are involved in echolalia and gestural imitation, and this would explain the preserved imitation of speech despite impairment in gestural imitation.[26] But this theory does not explain why vocal imitation is also impaired in autism.

Is there a relationship between imitation ability and social understanding? This is an area that has received a lot of attention because of the proposals that imitation may provide an important basis for the development of a theory of mind.[27] According to this position, the very early reciprocal imitation between parent and infant is crucial because it allows the infant to perceive that the adult's behavior matches its own, and since the infant realizes its movements are intentional, it attributes intention to the adult's movements. This aids the developing child in realizing that other people have intentions and helps promote the understanding of other people as distinct from oneself. This, of course, is an important underpinning of social understanding and hence ToM. As attractive and logical as this hypothesis may be, the fact remains that links between imitation and social understanding in autism are extremely complicated and variable, and no research to date has shown that a child's failure to recognize that she is being imitated by others is associated with ToM deficits.

What about the relationship between imitation and play deficits in autism? Here there is little evidence to support the imitation hypothesis. We know that autistic children exhibit deficits in symbolic and functional play. However, we also know that although these children are deficient in spontaneous engagement in these behaviors, they can do so if placed in a highly structured environment or if prompted. Thus the connection between imitation ability per se and play skills, while well founded in research on typical development, has not been clarified in children with autism.

Researchers have also been interested in the relationship between imitation and deficits in affective expression in autism. We know that autistic individuals have difficulty in comprehending facial expressions, and in combining facial expressions with eye contact in a communicative manner; we also know they have difficulties with empathy. Again, the developmental literature has demonstrated a relationship between imitation and the development of a variety of affective behaviors. In fact, the ability to discriminate and imitate the emotional expressions of others is present in infants as young as 2 days old. There is also evidence that autistic children have specific deficits in affective imitation. For example, one study examined im-

itation of both facial expressions (emotional expression) and pantomime of an activity (nonemotional expression) in children with autism, as well as in children with retardation and typical children.
The autistic children performed more poorly than any of the other
groups of children. Moreover, their ability to imitate facial expressions was worse than their ability to imitate pantomime, which suggested to the researchers that the autistic children had a specific
deficit in the ability to express emotion.[28] But even though we know
that children with autism are impaired on imitation tasks requiring
affective information, we do not know whether the problem is with
imitation per se or with emotional expressions.

Let's consider whether imitation deficits pass the test for a core
deficit. First, are deficits in the ability to imitate specific to autism?
Imitation deficits in autism have been reported on a variety of
tasks, including body movements, symbolic and functional object
use (such as pretend and functional play), vocal expressions, and facial expressions. Individuals with autism display deficits in these areas when compared with typical children, children with mental retardation (but without autism), and children with other disorders.[29]
Although there is some variability in the findings, we may conclude
that these particular imitation deficits are specific to autism.

Second, are imitation deficits universal and persistent among the
autistic population? Here the research is more equivocal. While
there is evidence that both high- and low-functioning people with
autism exhibit imitation difficulties, there is also evidence that the
deficiencies in imitation skills may be reduced with age;[30] thus the
deficits are more likely to be found in infants and young children
than in older individuals. These findings cast doubt on the theory of
imitation problems as a core deficit in terms of both universality
and persistence.

Finally, can we make an argument for the precedence of an imitation deficit? Some argue in favor of precedence because it has been
well established that imitation plays a crucial role in the develop-

ment of communication, social, and cognitive behaviors and these are known difficulties in children with autism. However, since autism is seldom diagnosed prior to age 2 or 3, little is known about very early imitation in these children. Thus it is impossible to determine conclusively that imitation deficits both precede and cause subsequent impairments.

The idea of imitation as a primary deficit is an intriguing one and, as we have seen, it is one of considerable interest to researchers. As attractive and parsimonious as this hypothesis may be, the fact is that the results of research in this area are still quite contradictory, with conflicting claims, and thus it is premature to draw any firm conclusions. Although many studies support the fact that autistic children lack imitation skills, other studies find that they do have some skills in this area. Imitation of oral-facial movements and emotional expressions is likely to be more impaired than imitation of actions on objects or gestures. This variety of findings has led some researchers to conclude that imitation may not be a unitary phenomenon in autism, and that there may be differential effects depending on the type of imitation task and the specific movements being studied. It is also important to ask whether the observed deficits in imitation skills represent true deviance in ability or whether they may reflect merely a delay (as noted earlier, the problem seems to abate with age). In addition, we still do not know if the problem is related to difficulties in attention, memory, comprehending, or expressing the modeled action. Further complicating matters is the fact that research findings in this area are variable and inconsistent. Different methods of assessment, different control and comparison group selection, and different research designs make comparisons among studies difficult.

Where do we stand in terms of identifying a core or primary deficit in autism? Although we have several candidates, there is no clear winner. Perhaps it makes little sense to look for the core deficit in autism; instead, it may be more fruitful to consider a variety of deficits. Another issue involves the identification of important neuro-physiological underpinnings of these deficits. In the case of each of the deficits discussed above, proponents of these theories have proposed a number of very specific brain areas and pathways as the underpinnings. However, there have been no definitive studies showing a causal relationship between brain structure or function and a specific deficit. Most of the neurophysiological findings are correlational at best and completely hypothetical at worst. The hypothesized existence of a "Theory of Mind Module," for instance, far outstrips our ability to find one.

CHAPTER 6

Developing Treatments That Work

[The] behavior of severely disturbed autistic children was brought under the control of an arbitrary environment by techniques of operant reinforcement. It was possible to sustain substantial amounts of behavior, as well as to widen aspects of the children's behavioral repertoire. The experimental methods suggest objective techniques for controlling the current repertoire of the child, as well as means for developing new behaviors by which the child may deal with the environment.

> —Charles B. Ferster and Marian K. DeMyer, in *American Journal of Orthopsychiatry* (1962)

The training regime . . . its use of "unnatural" reinforcers, and the like may have been responsible for producing the very situation-specific, restricted verbal output which we observed in many of our children.

> —O. Ivar Lovaas, *The Autistic Child* (1977)

There is now a large body of empirical support for more contemporary behavioral approaches using naturalistic teaching methods that demonstrate the efficacy for teaching not only speech and language, but also communication.

> —National Research Council, *Educating Children with Autism* (2001)

Nowhere is controversy more evident in the field of autism than in the area of treatment. Here we even have controversies *within* controversies. The history of therapeutic intervention for this population is at once fascinating, depressing, and hopeful. It is fascinating because of the complex nature of the disorder and the convoluted evolution of the science of treatment. It is depressing in that progress has been frustratingly slow, and in some cases improvement has been minimal or even nonexistent. We still have no cure for autism. Yet there is reason to be hopeful: over the years we have made steady progress, and the future of children with autism is much brighter now than it was even a few years ago. There have certainly been missteps over the years, but it is in the nature of research that we learn from our failures and build upon our successes. In this chapter I will focus on the development of effective treatments.

Few people would argue with the statement that today the treatment of choice is that based on the behavioral model. In fact, behavioral treatment is the only treatment that has been empirically demonstrated to be effective for children with autism.[1] This means that there is a sound scientific foundation for the methods employed. The scientific basis for the behavioral model of intervention has allowed it to progress in a systematic and relatively swift manner. Indeed, the refinement and improvement of this treatment model over the past forty years have been most impressive.

The behavioral model of treatment involves the systematic application to human behavior of the psychological principles of learning. In its original form it is often referred to as "behavior modification" or "behavior therapy," although now there are variants to the treatment that go by different names. All forms of behavioral treatment are derived from the experimental analysis of behavior, which is the science devoted to understanding the laws by which the environment affects behavior. Identification of these laws allows for the prediction and control of behavior and thus for the application of these laws to change behavior. The study and application of these laws to socially significant problems (of which autism is certainly one) is referred to as *applied behavior analysis,* and we owe much to this field of science for the development of effective interventions for the autistic population.

History of Behavioral Treatment Approaches

To appreciate where we are today in the treatment of autistic children, it is worthwhile to look back at where it all began. The application of learning principles to autism was, and continues to be, facilitated by four basic events.

The first event was the colossal failure of treatments based on the early erroneous conceptualization of autism as a psychogenic disorder caused by parental psychopathology.[2] Treatment based upon this model did not involve treatment for the *child* as much as it involved treatment for the *parent,* usually the mother. Since the parent was seen as the reason for the child's disordered behavior, it was the parent who needed "help." The parents were typically subjected to psychodynamically oriented therapy, while the children were "protected" from the parents and placed in a program where surrogate parents provided care. As we shall see in more detail later in this book, treatment based upon the psychodynamic model has not been shown to be an effective intervention for children with autism. Suffice it to say that if treatment based on a psychodynamic model were at all effective, behavioral treatments would never have seen the light of day.

The second factor contributing to the use of learning principles to improve the behavior of autistic children was the simple fact that prior to behavioral intervention, effective treatments were nonexistent. Add to this the fact that many of these children engaged in seriously disruptive behaviors, and you have a pretty bleak picture. The sheer enormity of the problem and the severity of the behaviors led to many of these children being institutionalized before they reached adolescence. Schools and clinics had few programs that were effective in teaching autistic children, and fewer still had procedures in place that could deal with behaviors such as tantrums, severe self-injury, and disruptive self-stimulatory and compulsive behaviors. The parents, understandably, were ill equipped to handle the children at home; when the children grew too big to handle, parents had few places to turn and little choice but to place the child out of the home. Large state institutions were all too frequently the last resort and the result of a wrenching decision. Autistic children in these institutions lived on wards with many other children suffering from severe disabilities, and any individual treatment was minimal because of the large number of residents and the fact that the staff did not know how to help them. Given the dire state of treatment availability, it is possible that those working in the field were more willing to try something, anything, new that might help.

The behaviorists came into this treatment vacuum with sound principles that could be applied to any behavior, including the most severe. Behaviorists had already demonstrated that application of learning principles could lead to improvement in some of the most severely handicapped, institutionalized populations. One of the earliest demonstrations, in 1958, described the changes achieved in the behavior of a (unfortunately called) "vegetative idiot."[3] Other studies showed the effectiveness of behavioral treatment with institutionalized chronic schizophrenic people and with other profoundly affected populations. The behaviorists were not afraid to try their skills on a wide variety of patients.

Many of the early demonstrations of the use of behavioral interventions involved extremely disruptive behaviors. In 1969, for example, Lovaas and Simmons showed how the basic principles of learning theory could be used to control severe self-injury in autistic and retarded children.[4] The study participants were children who had been in physical restraints (for example, tied to a bed, placed in arm restraints) for much of their lives because of their self-abusive behavior. These children, like most children with self-injury, had failed to respond to any other form of treatment, and their future appeared to be grim. Assuming they survived years of self-abuse, these children would likely spend the rest of their lives in physical or chemical restraints (drug treatment). They would not go to school, play with other children, feed themselves, or enjoy even the most modest of pleasures. Because these children had failed to respond to other treatments and because their future was so bleak, these researchers got the chance to try behavioral intervention.

The effects of the behavioral interventions used by Lovaas and Simmons were dramatic. Although some of the specific methods used in that early study might not be used today (such as contingent localized electric shock), they did serve to demonstrate that the procedures could be effective and that the behaviors in fact could be changed. Moreover, studies such as this helped to demonstrate that behaviors like self-injury were not the result of psychodynamic causes such as self-punishment or lack of ego-differentiation. We now know these are learned behaviors that serve important functions in the child's environment, such as avoiding unpleasant situations or acquiring desired things such as attention or access to treats.

A third factor responsible for the use of behavioral interventions with this population was that the pervasive nature of the disorder and the specific deficits in what are typically deemed to be the most basic human functions (social attachment, communication) proved irresistible to scientists who were interested in understanding how these behaviors develop and relate to their environment. Developmental psychologists, neuroscientists, psycholinguists, and others were fascinated and challenged by the failure of autistic children to follow the normal developmental progression and to develop the foundation for the appearance of more complex skills. These children provided a way to study how basic behaviors relate to each other, and this information in turn shed light on normal development. For example, how does the appearance of social understanding interact with language acquisition? How do play and language development relate to each other? Since relating behavior to the environment is what behaviorists do best, the joining of the two areas was a natural development. Since almost every area of functioning is affected in autism, behavioral researchers interested in all aspects of behavior were similarly drawn to the field. It seemed there was something for everyone in autism treatment research, and everyone would benefit from the knowledge gained.

A fourth factor that continues to contribute to the acceptance and utilization of behavioral treatments is simply that there are still no other effective treatments that currently exist, or are even on the horizon. We do not have any pharmacological treatments for autism; there are no available genetic interventions; there are no nutritional, sensory-mediated, or other treatments that have been empirically validated as effective for many of these children. Perhaps in the future (the distant future when considering possible genetic interventions) such treatments may exist and prove to be beneficial, but at present this is not the case.

The final important factor in the acceptance of behavioral intervention (and the rejection of psychodynamically oriented treatments) was the tremendous effort and influence of groups organized by the parents of children with autism. Organizations such as the Autism Society of America became important and tireless advocates for the development of effective treatments. Since behavioral treatments were effective and also did not implicate them as causative agents, the parents were quick to accept and promote the interventions.

Major Strengths of the Behavioral Approach

The most important strength of the behavioral approach to the understanding and treatment of autism is that it is the product of many years of rigorous research that established the basic principles of behavior and the effectiveness of the specific procedures involved in successful treatment. Thus there is a sound, comprehensive foundation upon which current behavioral interventions are based.

A second strength, related to the first, is that continued progress in treatment development is assured because the behavioral approach is a self-critical, self-analytical approach that is constantly undergoing evaluation. Because of the emphases on detailed operational definitions of behavior, specific description of treatment procedures, and careful, objective assessment of treatment outcome, behavioral researchers and clinicians are in a position to look closely and critically at treatment effects. Thus a detailed picture emerges of where treatments are effective and, perhaps more important, where they are not. Treatment limitations can then be used to inform future directions of study aimed at increasing treatment effectiveness. Ultimately this allows for constant improvement and refinements to treatment.

A good example of this kind of evaluation is something I will discuss later when I talk about highly structured training for autistic children. Although the specifics of this approach were soundly based in the behavioral literature, subsequent assessment of treatment outcomes showed that there were some significant limitations to treatment effectiveness. The problem was "caught" because of evaluation of the treatment, and subsequent modifications to the behavioral treatment have ameliorated some of these difficulties.

A third strength is that because of the objectivity of measurement and the detailed description of procedures, the behavioral researcher or clinician knows exactly what was done in any particular case and can replicate the treatment effects. Since the treatment population is carefully described, as are the treated behaviors and procedures, others in the field are able to assess replicability for their cases. This replicability is crucial since it allows the field to develop as a directional whole, as opposed to an array of disparate parts. Put another way, it is what distinguishes a systematically developed treatment approach from a bag of tricks.

General Controversies Associated with the Behavioral Approach

The first controversy that arose with the behavioral approach to treatment was of course that it flew in the face of the existing theory and the "preferred" psychodynamic treatment. Unlike the followers of Bettelheim and other psychodynamic advocates who viewed autism as a specific "disease" caused by pathological parenting, behaviorists rejected the disease model and instead viewed autism as a behavioral syndrome characterized by a pattern of excesses and deficits. Examples of behavioral excesses include self-injury, self-stimulation, and echolalic speech, while examples of behavioral deficits include social deficits, language deficits, and deficits in play. Behaviorists viewed each of these excesses and deficits as related to the environment in specific and discoverable ways, and proposed that these relationships could be identified and treated through the application of the known technology of behavioral principles. With this perspective, it was possible to consider changing behaviors by manipulating environmental events.

The 1969 study by Lovaas and Simmons mentioned earlier provides an illustration of the differences in approach. Prior to this study, self-injury was often viewed as a form of self-punishment in which the children inflicted damage to themselves because of some psychodynamic motivation such as worthlessness or lack of ego differentiation (for example, they wished to punish their parents but had not yet differentiated their own ego from that of the parent, so they inflicted the punishment on themselves). The form of "treatment" based on this view was to provide the children with affection and reassurance. However, such treatment not only proved to be ineffective but typically led to an *increase,* rather than a decrease, in self-injury (as illustrated in another study by Lovaas and his colleagues).[5] Adopting the behavioral approach, Lovaas and Simmons viewed self-injurious behavior as an operant behavior (a behavior determined by its environmental consequences) and thus predicted that they could change the behavior by manipulating the environmental consequences. Accordingly, they speculated that the self-injury might be reinforced (rewarded) by its social consequences—that is, social attention—and that withdrawing social attention would lead to a reduction in the behavior. When they allowed two children who engaged in self-injury (for example, face slapping or head banging) to do so without providing any contingent attention, the children's rate of self-injury declined substantially. (It is important to point out that it was established at the outset that these children would not seriously injure themselves when exposed to this treatment.) Further, an operant behavior is one that can be reduced with the application of contingent punishment. Again, Lovaas and Simmons demonstrated that contingent punishment (in the form of a loud "no!" and a localized, painful but harmless, electric shock delivered by a handheld device) led to an immediate cessation of the behavior.

The impact of this study was substantial. This was one of the first demonstrations of behavioral intervention to treat an extremely serious, and often intractable, behavior that had not responded to any other form of treatment—certainly not psychodynamic treatment. Now many children who had spent their lives in pharmacological or physical restraints (and away from school or social events) could be freed from these restraints and could engage in educational and social activities. Indeed, Lovaas and Simmons described how one child, John, finally free of self-injury, was able to benefit from a treatment program previously unavailable to him because of his dangerous behavior and necessary physical restraints.

From today's perspective, more than thirty years later, the positive and negative aspects of this early study can be seen quite clearly. Although the specifics of the intervention strategies (for example, contingent electric shock) may seem extreme and unacceptable to-day, the fact remains that when this study was conducted, the lives of these children held little hope for the future. (Indeed, one of the children in this study had been tied down to a bed for so long that the tendons in his legs had atrophied to the point where he could not walk without assistance.) It is certainly true that later research has enabled us to deal with such challenging behaviors in more positive ways, but it is because of early studies like this one that we have been able to pursue treatment development. Other applications of behavioral principles have involved dealing with severe aggression, pica (ingestion of nonnutritive substances such as paper, dirt, rocks, or glass), tantrums, and other behaviors guaranteed to keep a child out of school, social groups, and possibly even his own home. In essence, these early studies demonstrated that the application of learning principles could lead to important behavior changes in children with autism. The significance of these demonstrations was nothing less than monumental. A whole new way to look at the treatment of autism was now available. And while over the years the specifics of the interventions may have changed, the basic principles have not.

Predictably, the psychodynamic establishment was horrified at this turn of events. Practitioners of the psychodynamic point of view predicted that punishing the children for their self-injury would worsen the behavior because the children would feel more worthless and deserving of self-punishment. Despite these dire predictions, the opposite proved to be the case. Several behavioral studies in which aversive procedures were employed reported that positive behavioral changes were accompanied by increases in positive affect and social behavior, such as increased eye contact and approaches toward others.

Significantly, many of the early demonstrations of the behavioral approach involved more positive target behaviors and procedures. In 1962 Ferster and DeMyer were among the first to demonstrate that autistic children could learn if the systematic application of operant discrimination learning techniques was employed.[6] These investigators demonstrated that the youngsters could indeed learn new behaviors under conditions where correct responses to a discrimination task (pressing a key) were followed by contingent applications of reinforcement (such as food, candy, or trinkets). Although the discrimination taught was simple and not very functional in terms of an academic curriculum or a social interaction, it did indicate that the children could learn—and this study was conducted in an atmosphere where many doubted the ability of autistic children to benefit from educational programs.

Later, other behavioral researchers built upon this early demonstration by greatly expanding both the repertoire of behavioral intervention procedures and the array of target behaviors. Thus we have seen the development and refinement of basic procedures such as positive reinforcement, negative reinforcement, and punishment but also other procedures such as prompting, stimulus fading, response shaping, chaining, antecedent stimulus control, and other techniques too numerous to be covered here.[7] While these techniques were at first applied to very simple behaviors (such as bar pressing), this application was soon expanded to more functional and complex behavioral repertoires including those associated with improving areas of behavioral deficit, such as language, social behavior, play skills, and academic tasks, and with decreasing behavioral excesses such as self-injury, tantrums, and self-stimulation.

Another major area of controversy associated with behavioral treatment involved the highly structured—some might say mechanical—nature of the treatment procedures. The particulars of the treatment strategies, reflecting their origin in experimental analysis, were precisely defined and applied. The treatments were very detailed and always grounded in sound behavioral principles. However, because these treatments were based in operant discrimination learning, a form of intervention based on studies with animals such as rats and pigeons, some people were offended by their use with children—and especially with handicapped children. The idea of teaching children as you might "train a dog" was a difficult concept for both clinicians and families. Of course, this public relations problem was not helped by the fact that the behavioral lexicon is geared toward the scientific; terms such as "control," "extinction," "punishment," "manipulation," "aversive control," and "negative reinforcement" did not endear the behavioral approach to the general public.

Many of these terms, of course, can be traced to B. F. Skinner, who was extremely influential in the identification of behavioral principles. In the 1930s Skinner was influenced by the physicist Percy Bridgeman and admired the way physics could demonstrate scientific principles so clearly and precisely. Wanting to foster a "science of behavior," Skinner emphasized the need for experimental manipulation and control in order to demonstrate scientific principles. Skinner borrowed terms from physics and other sciences as well as from fields such as classical conditioning and included them in the description of his behavioral technology. These terms thus came from basic science studies with animals and were applied unchanged to studies with people. Luckily, what behavioral intervention lacked in public relations flair, it had in effectiveness, and most consumers of behavioral treatment for children with autism, especially parents, soon came to embrace it. As one mother said, "When your child is smearing feces on the wall, you cannot afford to be picky about treatment names. You do what works." In fact, parents were some of the earliest and strongest advocates for behavioral treatment of autistic children.

Another criticism aimed at the first applications of behavioral treatment was that the treatment targets were simplistic. Since early behavioral strategies typically broke down complex behavioral repertoires into small components and taught the components separately, this comment was somewhat accurate. For example, language is a hugely complex behavior, and the early studies involved first teaching the children to imitate sounds and words, then associating words with objects, then teaching relational words such as prepositions, pronouns, and so on. This was followed by teaching sentences, and so on. Critics questioned whether children who learned in this manner really "understood" what they were saying. Did a child who was trained to say "I want a cookie" through operant conditioning really understand the meaning of all the words? Did she understand "want" as a general concept meaning desire? Did a child who was trained to give his mother a hug really "mean" it? Or were these children just robotically doing what they were taught? Of course to a behaviorist, the question was unimportant: if the child engaged in the behavior in a contextually appropriate manner, and if the child engaged in the behavior appropriately in a variety of situations, then that was all the proof one needed. Thus if the child correctly used "want" in relation to other (untrained) desired items, this allowed one to conclude that the child "understood" the concept. If the child hugged his mother in other contexts, similar to those in which typical children hugged their mothers, this could also be interpreted as proof that the child "meant" the hug. For a behaviorist, only those behaviors that could be directly observed were considered as proof. Trying to discern whether or not the child "understood" or "meant" anything would involve getting into the child's head, which was of course impossible.

No matter how many questions one had about the highly structured behavioral approach or the exact nature of what was learned, it was hard to deny that many of the children benefited greatly from the treatment. The literature is full of reports of successful implementation of behavioral treatment with a broad and comprehensive variety of target behaviors of children with autism. Moreover, since the principles of behavior are well known and easily taught to others, we have seen successful implementation of the treatment by a variety of treatment providers including teachers, parents, siblings, peers, and many others who come into contact with an autistic child.

Specific Controversies within the Behavioral Approach

Even among those who are staunch advocates of behavioral intervention strategies, there are, and have been, contentious issues sur-
rounding the specifics of the intervention techniques. Behavioral
intervention does not imply a specific form of treatment, and thus
several variations of the approach have been developed over the
years. Some of these variations are a direct result of identified
limitations to earlier forms of behavioral treatment, while others
are the result of theoretical or philosophical positions. What has
evolved is an extremely interesting set of treatment options—and
arguments.

Generalization of Treatment Effects

As noted earlier, the original forms of behavioral intervention to
teach new behavioral repertoires were based closely on the principles of discrimination learning that had been established after many
years of work in animal laboratories. Animals such as rats and pigeons were trained to perform easily quantifiable responses such as
pecking a lighted key or pressing a bar. The animals were rewarded
with bits of food, and the schedules of food delivery (schedules
of reinforcement) were carefully manipulated for desired response
patterns. Thus the specifics of very early autism intervention in
many ways matched the specifics of animal learning. In fact, the
Ferster and DeMyer study mentioned earlier involved teaching autistic children to press a lever for bits of food or candy, and the
schedules of reinforcement were manipulated. Despite the importance of this early demonstration, when reading this report today
one almost cringes at the similarity between the actions of these
children and the actions of laboratory animals.

More recent adaptations of behavioral techniques to the treatment of children with autism, while focusing on more elaborate
behavioral repertoires and functional curricula (for example, lan-

guage, social, and academic target behaviors), continue to adhere to a rather strict discrimination learning format. Typically the children are taught through a series of discrete teaching "trials" that include three components. First, an instruction or question is presented. This is called the discriminative stimulus (S^D) and is the antecedent stimulus that will come to control the child's behavior. In the early phases of training, this may be accompanied by an additional stimulus to guide the child's response (a "prompt"). The second component is the child's response (R), incorrect or correct, or perhaps lack of response. Third, depending on the child's behavior, a consequence is presented (S^R). These consequences take a variety of forms, and their nature is determined by the desired effect. If the teacher wishes to encourage the response because it is correct, a positive reinforcer such as food, praise, or access to a favored toy is presented. Similarly, the teacher may wish to discourage an incorrect response either by presenting a "punisher" (for example, saying "no" or frowning) or by not presenting any consequence for the behavior (that is, ignoring it).

The three main components of the discrete trial can thus be diagrammed like this:

$$S^D \rightarrow R \leftarrow S^R$$

Let's look at an example of teaching a child, Carolyn, to say her name. The question "What is your name?" is presented (the S^D). She either answers correctly (R) with "Carolyn" (or an approximation thereof), provides an incorrect response (such as "geegeegee"), or remains silent. The trainer then provides the appropriate consequence (S^R): a piece of cookie and praise for the correct response, "Carolyn"; a "no" for "geegeegee"; or no consequence for silence.

These three-part trials are presented in a series of successive blocks, and the child's progress is calculated by determining the percentage of correct responses within a block of 10 or 20 trials. This makes it apparent whether progress is or is not occurring. If inadequate progress is found, various things may be altered including the specifics of the instruction, the addition of prompts, the nature of the consequence, and so on. In addition, the target behavior may be broken down into smaller components to make the task easier.

The example given above is of course a very simple one; more extensive descriptions of this kind of training are available elsewhere.[8] My purpose here is to give the reader the flavor of the highly controlled structure of this treatment. This form of training is correctly referred to as "discrete trial training" (DTT),[9] and it revolutionized the treatment of children with autism. In fact, one can argue that the development and refinement of DTT provided the first real treatment regimen for teaching simple, and later more complex, skills to autistic children. Its contribution to the treatment of autism, particularly in the early 1960s and 1970s, cannot be overstated.

The highly structured, repetitive-practice nature of DTT is not limited to the three major components. There are also important rules regarding the specifics of stimulus presentation, timing, successive approximations of correct responses, and both the nature and schedule of consequences. For example, the instruction or question must be consistent across trials, and should be very brief and simple. Thus the child would be asked "What is your name?" in a consistent fashion across trials. Similarly, the consequences need to be consistent and maximally functional. Because autistic children are rather unlikely to respond to praise only, maximally functional reinforcers such as food are often used. Also specified are the number of incorrect responses allowed before a prompt is delivered, and so on. In other words, the rules for effective use of DTT are detailed and specific; adherence to these rules is very important for delivering the treatment effectively and for determining the specifics of needed alterations to the treatment if necessary.

DTT changed the world for autistic children, their families, and their treatment providers. After this treatment had been used for many years, however, some troubling trends emerged. Although the treatment was effective initially, limitations to the generalization of treatment effects became apparent. People noted that the positive effects of the treatment did not always hold up over time as well as one would hope (generalization over time), and the positive responses did not always appear in different settings or around different people (stimulus generalization). Further, the training itself was often not very efficient in that treatment effects seemed to be specific to the behaviors taught rather than spreading to other behaviors (response generalization). Thus many individual behaviors had to be taught if the treatment effects were to be demonstrated across other behaviors.

These limitations are perhaps best illustrated by examples. Looking at maintenance, or generalization over time, one study reported that after one year of intensive inpatient behavioral treatment by trained clinicians, most of the autistic children showed substantial progress. However, after the children were brought back for assessment between one and four years after treatment, many of the children had lost their treatment gains.[10] In other words, the treatment did not hold up. This was indeed discouraging.

Problems generalizing across stimuli (instructions and people) can be illustrated with additional examples. I was asked to consult on the case of a 5-year-old boy, Kenny, who had had many months of intensive DTT in his home. His mother proudly showed me a notebook containing descriptions of specific responses Kenny had learned. I noted that he had learned to say his address and decided to see how he would respond to me. After ensuring that he was paying attention, I asked, "Where do you live?" Kenny stared at me and said nothing. I repeated, "Kenny, where do you live?" Again nothing. After my sixth or seventh unsuccessful attempt to elicit his address, his mother tapped me on the shoulder and said, "You have to say 'What is your address?'" Apparently this latter phrase was the antecedent stimulus in Kenny's DTT training, and I was presenting a different antecedent by saying "Where do you live?" Obviously, this is a severe problem. The real world is too variable for a trained response to a specific stimulus. If the child will only respond to a very specific question or instruction, it is unlikely that the variable nature of the real world will come to control the behavior. As I explained to his mother, if Kenny became lost, a police officer might not ask the question in the specific way Kenny had been taught.

Another time we held a holiday party for families participating in our research program. There was a bowl of punch on the table, and one child, Freddy, wanted some. We knew Freddy's parents had taught him to appropriately request what he wanted, and thus we were surprised to see him grab a cup, wave it repeatedly over the punchbowl, and vocalize gibberish. He kept doing so until his mother, who had been out of sight in the kitchen, appeared and said, "Freddy, you say it right!" Freddy saw her and said, "Punch, please." It appeared that the presence of his mother was necessary for Freddy to use his speech appropriately; the behavior did not sufficiently generalize to other people in his environment.

The problem of failure to generalize across responses can be illustrated by a situation where a child has learned to walk across the street when the traffic signal is green and to wait when the signal is red. Yet this control may not be apparent when the child is riding a bicycle. In this case the go/wait discrimination must be taught separately for each of several modes of mobility (walking, riding, roller skating). Obviously, this is not a very efficient training regimen.

Robotic Responding

It has often been mentioned that autistic children who have been taught via DTT tend to sound "robotic." In a certain situation the child may always say the exact same thing, in the exact same way. This lack of vocal variation, coupled with the difficulty many of these children have with prosody (appropriate intonation, inflection, rhythm of speech, and the like) often makes their speech sound unnatural and abnormal, which may stigmatize the child further. Because of the highly structured nature of DTT and the reliance on strict rules regarding antecedent stimulation presentation (that is, short and consistent questions) and reinforcement of specific correct responses, it is easy to see how robotic responding may be inadvertently encouraged.

Lack of Spontaneity

It can be particularly frustrating to parents and clinicians that although the autistic child may have learned a rather impressive amount of language, social behaviors, play, and other skills through training, it is often difficult to get him to use his language spontaneously. I have heard many parents complain that even though their child can talk, they have to prompt or ask the child a question before the child speaks. For example, a child may be quite capable of describing what she did at school but will not volunteer the information. Instead, the parents have to ask "What did you do at school today?" or some other question to learn about the child's activities. Essentially, the problem boils down to the fact that there are too few environmental stimuli to cue speech. Some argue that this is another effect of DTT, since much emphasis is placed on training with trials that begin with specific antecedent stimuli.

Prompt Dependency

Another often reported limitation to the effectiveness of DTT is that sometimes the children remain reliant on prompts, or extra cues, to help them respond correctly. For example, in the early stages of training a child might be assisted in discriminating red versus blue blocks by means of the teacher pointing to the correct block on each trial when the stimulus "Point to the red/blue block" is presented. In well-conducted DTT, prompts are carefully and systematically reduced, or "faded," in order to gradually eliminate them so that the appropriate stimulus controls the behavior. In this instance, as the child continues the training, the teacher might fade the prompt by holding her finger further and further away from the blocks. The idea is to transfer control of the child's response from the prompt (the pointing) to the appropriate stimulus (the correct colored block). This type of prompt is commonly used for everyone, not just for children with autism. However, we know that problems with attention can lead to autistic children having severe difficulties in weaning themselves from the prompts, and the teaching literature is full of studies addressing issues of presenting and fading prompts.

Issues of Acceptability by Child and Clinician

One of the biggest problems reported with the highly structured and "mechanical" nature of traditional discrete trial training is the simple fact that often the children and the parent or clinician just do not like it. To be frank, it may not be enjoyable to either receive or present this sort of therapy.

Traditional discrete trial training typically involves requiring the child to sit in a chair, facing the therapist, and to do what the therapist is requesting. Despite the fact that the therapist is doing her best to encourage and motivate the child by offering favorite treats and toys, it is often the case that the child just does not enjoy the training. He may not want to stay in the chair; he may not be interested in the teaching task; he may want to be doing something else (perhaps *anything* else); he may find the task too difficult. These are the times when various escape and avoidance behaviors may occur, such as crying, screaming, throwing the task materials, attempts to leave the setting, and perhaps even aggression toward the therapist (for example, hitting, pinching, or biting). While a typical child may be able to say "I am tired," "I don't want to do this," "It is too hard for me," a child with a severe language impairment may not have any other means to communicate but a tantrum.

Similarly, therapists and parents may not enjoy using this sort of treatment either. They may find it a too highly structured and artificial way to interact with children. In addition, it is not an intuitive way to work with children; the specific procedures involved have to be taught until the therapist or parent sufficiently learns the principles. This can make the training a very labor-intensive affair, especially for parents who typically do not have a prior background in education. The fact that the treatment may not be enjoyable and may in fact be quite difficult to implement leads to a very serious problem: it may not be used. DTT can be a very effective form of treatment for most children with autism, but only if it is used.

Use of Aversives

Probably the number one complaint (and a major source of controversy) about the behavioral approach in general and DTT in particular is the use of aversive stimuli. Technically, an aversive stimulus is anything that someone does not like and will try to avoid. Such events can range from a disapproving frown or a soft "no" to a physically painful stimulus such as a spank.

As mentioned earlier, one of the reasons behavioral interventions came to be applied to children with autism was that these treatment procedures proved effective for serious behavior problems such as self-injury for which no existing treatments had proved effective. Some of the very early demonstrations of the application of behavior theory involved some dramatic uses of aversives. For example, the Lovaas and Simmons study used harmless yet painful localized electric shock to stop the self-injury of the children. Although the demonstration had quite an impact in terms of rapid cessation of severe self-injury, many people in both the professional and lay community had difficulty accepting the use of electric shock, which was delivered by a hand-held device which many labeled a "cattle prod." (It was not really a cattle prod but looked like a miniature version of one.) As horrified as some may have been by the application of painful shocks, others were led to its acceptance by the fact that in many cases the children's severe self-injury was far more painful and potentially lethal than the shock. Consider, for example, the little girl who had blinded herself because of self-injurious eye-gouging, or the boy who died from skull fractures after repeated escapes from restraints to beat his head against a metal bedframe. When I was a graduate student working on the children's ward of an institutional setting, I witnessed a young girl beating her face bloody against the faucet of a bathtub. If it had been available to me, I would not have hesitated for an instant to deliver a shock if it would have stopped her from what she was doing.

Other early applications of behavioral treatment also involved contingent aversives. Ivar Lovaas, a UCLA psychologist and a leader in the development of DTT, described the use of a loud "No!" and spanks as punishers for inappropriate behaviors such as self-stimulation, self-injury, and, in some instances, failure to respond during discrete trial sessions. In one rather unfortunate example, Lovaas is seen in an educational film using such an aversive.[11] In this instance he is trying to get a little girl, Pamela, to identify the color of a crayon he is holding in front of her face. Although she has demonstrated in the past that she knows the correct response, she persists in ignoring the question and engaging in bizarre self-stimulatory hand manipulations. After presenting the question a number of times, Lovaas loudly tells Pamela to pay attention and slaps her hard on the leg. This is indeed a dramatic moment—and it is followed immediately by Pamela stopping the hand movements and correctly naming the color of the crayon. I have seen this film many times, and this scene never fails to elicit a collective gasp from the audience.

The issue of aversives is a very complex one. On one hand, no one wants to cause a child pain. On the other hand, it is true that these demonstrations of punishment with aversives proved to be effective in dealing with some of the most severe and intractable autistic behaviors (such as self-stimulation and self-injury). The dilemma was whether to use punishment or whether to allow the child to engage in behaviors that (1) were dangerous, (2) were stigmatizing, or (3) would interfere with learning more appropriate ways to behave.

Another issue involves the fact that punishment can have the effect of being a reinforcer for the person who administers it. That is, given the fact that punishment leads to very rapid cessation of an undesirable behavior, it can be the case that the person providing the punishment finds it an easy and effective way to get an immediate effect and thus is more likely to choose that option on future occasions. This can be a particular concern when the punisher involves a physical aversive. The systematic application of punishment requires very careful implementation and a good understanding of the principles of learning. The people who have provided some of the best examples in the literature of the use of aversives are individuals with expertise in learning theory who have used the procedures correctly. People knowledgeable in the use of punishment know that it only serves to temporarily suppress behavior; to achieve a lasting suppressive effect, it is necessary to teach the child another, appropriate, response. Punishment just teaches what *not* to do, not *what* to do, so it is important to replace the undesirable behavior with a new, positive behavior. Unfortunately, in the past many individuals who were not well qualified were using aversives inappropriately and without the proper controls.

There is also the issue of what constitutes an aversive and is acceptable as a treatment. Most people consider an aversive as something rather strong, such as a shout, a spank, a localized electric shock, or the like. Yet by definition, an aversive stimulus is something people want to avoid. Thus there are some people in the field who consider even saying "no" or frowning to be an aversive stimulus and believe these should not be used in the treatment of autistic children. These individuals believe that even informative feedback like "no" is inappropriate. I cannot imagine a world where such feedback is not used, and I certainly would not want to try to stop a child from running into a busy street by saying "I would prefer that you not run into the street" or "Let's discuss some options." Ultimately, it seems that there are few adherents to either of the extreme ends of the punishment continuum.

Fortunately, much has changed over the years, It is rare today to see the use of physical aversives in the behavioral treatment of children with autism. In fact, the evolution of treatment for seriously challenging behaviors is one of the most interesting areas in the field. We now have a much more comprehensive and detailed understanding of the environmental determinants of these behaviors and their maintenance and can use this information to treat the children without aversives. Thus many behaviors that would have been treated with aversives a number of years ago are now effectively treated without such measures. This change reflects our increasing knowledge of relationships between behavior and the environment. It also reflects the strong emphasis on developing a technology of "positive behavioral support," as the following examples will show.

One recent strategy is the use of *antecedent stimulus control* to change behavior. If we can prevent or avoid the disruptive behavior in the first place, there would be no need to use aversives to suppress it. A good example of this strategy can be seen in a study conducted by Touchette, MacDonald, and Langer, who demonstrated how one could use antecedent events to control severe behavior problems.[12] Working in an institutional environment, they studied several individuals who engaged in severe aggression, self-injury, property destruction, and other challenging behaviors. Not surprisingly, they observed that these people did not always engage in these behaviors. In fact, there were times when the individuals behaved quite well. Touchette and his colleagues decided to investigate what was going on when the individuals were behaving well. They developed an assessment (a "scatter plot") in which an individual's day was broken down into small observational periods. For the assessment, the observer noted exactly what the individual was doing (ongoing activity such as eating, watching TV, and so on) and the level of disruptive behavior. Looking across the individual's day, the experimenters could identify a pattern showing that high rates of disruptive behavior occurred during certain activities (for example, demand situations, the presence of other residents) while the disruptive behavior occurred at a very low, or zero, rate during other activities (such as eating a meal, watching TV). The experimenters showed that *immediate* reduction of the problem behavior to zero rates could be accomplished by providing the environmental situations associated with zero rates and not presenting the situations associated with high rates of disruptive behavior. Thus the serious behavior could be controlled immediately by manipulating the environment in such a way that it did not provoke the behavior. One might object that someone cannot spend the entire day eating or watching TV. But this is a temporary situation; once the behavior is under control, it is important to gradually introduce the problem antecedents and events while teaching the individual to tolerate them. Thus one might provide positive reinforcement for tolerating greater and greater lengths of time with nonfavorite activities, or one might reward the individual for communicating his displeasure in a more appropriate manner.

Manipulating antecedents is one strategy that behavioral researchers and clinicians have developed to deal with behaviors that previously might have been treated using aversives. The application of *functional analysis* technology is another. Functional analysis involves identifying the environmental consequence that is maintaining a problem behavior. Once this is accomplished, the autistic individual can be taught another, more positive behavior to gain the same environmental consequence. In a very interesting demonstration, Carr and Durand showed how severe behavior problems such as aggression served as a form of communication.[13] They noted that if a nonverbal child was presented with instructional demands that were too difficult for her, the only way she could communicate that she was frustrated and needed help was to attack the teacher. This had the desired effect (from the child's standpoint) of having the teacher stop the demands and probably try to avoid presenting such demands in the future. Obviously, another form of communication would be preferable. Carr and Durand found that if they taught these children to say "Help me" by giving a manual sign, or to otherwise communicate the message, the children would engage in the more appropriate communication and did not attack the teacher. This "functional communication" training is now widely used to reduce behavioral problems that were once likely addressed through aversive stimuli.

Responses to Limitations of DTT

"DTT Lite"

While traditional discrete trial training continues to have a strong following, the limitations to its effectiveness have led others to move away from the highly structured nature of DTT to other forms of behavioral treatment that hold promise for addressing these limitations. There are two basic approaches that have been applied in an attempt to address some of the limitations of DTT while still retaining the emphasis on empirically driven principles of behavior.

One of these approaches is to retain the structured DTT format but to systematically address each of the areas found to be problematic. Thus the issues of generalization, spontaneity, robotic responding, and dependence on prompts have served as the foci for specific procedures designed for each area. In fact, there are several specific strategies available to the clinician that are designed to enhance stimulus and response generalization,[14] and these are incorporated in the improved versions of DTT. To enhance stimulus generalization, for example, the child is taught a behavior through the use of multiple stimuli ("exemplars") including task materials, settings, and people. For the child who would only say his address if presented with a specific form of question, this type of problem could be prevented if during the training the child was taught to say his address in response to a variety of questions, such as "What is your address?" "Where do you live?" "Where is your house?" and the like. It would also be helpful if during training a variety of people asked the child these questions and did so in a number of settings. Similarly, response generalization would be enhanced if during training the child were prompted and rewarded for using a variety of responses in association with an antecedent question or instruction. Thus when crossing a street a child might be taught the green-go, red-stop discriminations while walking, riding a bicycle, riding in a car, and so on. A child might also be taught when given an instruction that a number and variety of responses are appropriate. If asked "Which one is red?" the child could be taught that pointing to the red item, saying "This one," and handing the red item to the clinician are all correct. One can see how robotic responding would be reduced by the use of such training. The issue of maintenance of treatment effects (generalization over time) is addressed by all the strategies just described, since they make responding in the natural environment more likely and appropriate. Further, training people in the child's environment such as parents, siblings, and peers to use the treatment strategies also enhances maintenance. In this way, the child essentially remains in a treatment environment.

Problems of dependence on prompts and lack of spontaneity are likewise addressed specifically. Prompt strategies have become a technology in itself, and many specific strategies have been designed to assist in the removing of these aids. One such prompt-fading strategy, called "time delay," involves gradually increasing the time between when an instruction or question is presented and when the prompt is delivered. Thus when a child is asked "What is your name?" at first the therapist might immediately say "Denise" and reward the child for saying "Denise" right after the prompt. As the child progresses through the training, the therapist would gradually increase the time between "What is your name?" and the prompt, "Denise," until the child says her name *before* the prompt. At this point, it is apparent that the child is responding correctly to the question, independent of the prompt. While such prompting strategies have been helpful, some children still have great difficulty in weaning themselves from the prompts.

Lack of spontaneity is addressed by constructing the teaching situation in such a way that the child is rewarded for responding in the absence of a specific, planned antecedent question or instruction. Thus, for example, the child is taught to "comment" on her environment in response to an environmental cue. Instead of waiting for a parent to ask what she did at school, the child learns to talk about school without being asked.

Today the best DTT treatment programs incorporate these generalization-enhancing strategies, and as a result, many of the limitations noted with the more traditional DTT formats are avoided and the treatment overall is more effective. Incorporating these generalization-enhancing strategies also means that the training is less highly structured (hence my use of the term "DTT lite"). However, even though these improved treatment programs are less formally structured, the fact remains that they may still be rather difficult for nonprofessionals (such as parents or peers) to learn and implement, and a good deal of training is required for these nonprofessionals (as well as the professionals) to become effective treatment providers for autistic children.

Naturalistic Strategies

Another more recent approach to treatment that seeks to avoid the limitations of DTT involves moving away from the laboratory-based DTT style of training and toward more naturalistic strategies that allow the child with autism to learn behaviors in their usual context under more natural conditions. The idea behind the development of these naturalistic strategies stems from the view that the reported lack of generalization and maintenance of treatment may be directly related to the specificity and artificiality that characterize the traditional DTT approach. When skills are taught in a highly controlled and typically repetitive manner, the behaviors are unlikely to generalize to the natural environment where more variability is present in terms of antecedent stimuli, behavioral requirements, and consequences. It is argued that what is needed is a treatment approach that adheres to the proven principles of learning but more closely mimics the natural environment in terms of antecedents, the child's responses, and environmental consequences.

Interestingly, several similar naturalistic behavioral strategies were developed independently by different researchers in different laboratories across the country. This simultaneous development suggests that many in the field were becoming aware of the specific limitations of DTT. And the fact that the new strategies shared many of the same features suggests that they were on the right track. This reliability across treatment centers is rare, and it instills confidence in this approach.

Several naturalistic approaches have now been developed and empirically validated. They are referred to by various names, including "Pivotal Response Training,"[15] "Incidental Teaching,"[16] and "Milieu Training."[17] These procedures have in common the teaching of behaviors in the environment where they would naturally occur and the use of the same principles of behavior as DTT, but with natural contingencies. Training for the acquisition and generalization of new behaviors occurs simultaneously and in the natural environment. This contrasts with DTT, where often the training takes place in the highly structured format of a teaching environment (classroom or home), and then the teaching is moved to the natural environment for generalization training.

A brief description of one of these naturalistic teaching strategies, Pivotal Response Training (PRT), will illustrate how naturalistic strategies work and how they differ from DTT. One area of difference can be seen in the *nature of the training stimuli* used. Let us say we wish to teach the child the concept of color. We could teach "yellow" by using highly structured teaching involving yellow cards, yellow blocks, and so on. Indeed, this is probably how it would be done using DTT techniques. However, the color concept can also be taught in a format that involves the natural contexts in which colors are found. Thus one may walk through a park and teach that a car is yellow, a bench is yellow, a leaf may be yellow, and so on. Because the yellow stimuli are observed in naturally occurring circumstances, generalization of the concept is more likely to occur without specific training for generalization.

Another difference between early (and, to some extent, current) DTT programs and naturalistic strategies such as PRT is the *nature of the consequences* used in training. Autistic children are notorious for being difficult to motivate. While other children may be highly motivated to receive social praise, a hug, a kiss, or a hair-tussle, autistic youngsters typically are unmoved by such signs of approval and affection—which is not surprising, given that social unresponsiveness is a hallmark feature of the disorder. Because of this difficulty, early behavioral interventions with these children employed consequences that *were* motivating to the children, including positive reinforcers such as food, drinks, and access to favored toys. Such consequences are still widely used in DTT training programs. However, since the "real world" typically does not provide such consequences, it is not surprising that behavioral gains are not generalized or maintained well with this sort of training. No one is walking around giving us pieces of candy or sips of a soft drink for being social or talking as we go about our daily lives. Rather, our social skills and speech are maintained by the natural consequences directly associated with our behavior. If I want a book at the library and say to the librarian "I want this book," it is not because I expect, or want, him to say "Good talking" and give me a piece of candy. I want the book, and it is the delivery of the book that maintains my speech in this context.

Similarly, naturalistic teaching strategies for children with autism employ consequences that are directly related to the child's behavior so that these natural consequences will maintain the behavior and assist in its generalization. These types of consequences are called "direct" reinforcers and are distinguished from "indirect" reinforcers which are unrelated to the response (for example, receiving food for saying "car"). For instance, if I am teaching the child using a toy car she has chosen, I know that the car is a direct reinforcer for her speech. If she says she wants to "roll" the car, then the consequence (reinforcer) for saying "roll" is being allowed to roll the car. Rolling the car when she says "roll" is a much more natural consequence than a piece of candy and saying "Good talking." This direct reinforcement is how typical children learn to use language in their environment. When one considers that most of us acquire and use generalized language because of the direct effect on the environment, it seems reasonable that direct reinforcement would lead to enhanced generalization. (Of course, it is important to point out that food can be a direct reinforcer. If the child were talking about the food, then access to the food would be a direct reinforcer. Thus the child might say he wants "the big cookie" or "the red apple" for access to that item.)

Another approach used in PRT to increase motivation to learn is to give the child a *choice* about the nature of the teaching interaction. It is common in DTT procedures for the therapist to decide what skill will be addressed, what training stimuli will be used, and what the available consequences will be. In naturalistic strategies such as PRT, the child is allowed to make these choices. When the child is given a choice, it is reasonable to expect higher motivation than if the therapist made all of these decisions. After all, everyone would be more motivated to participate in a conversation or other activity of our own choosing as opposed to one imposed by someone else. If we present a variety of toys, edibles, and similar things to the child and ask her to choose one, we can be fairly confident that the child is interested in (that is, is motivated for) the chosen item. This means that the child is likely to be willing, perhaps even eager, to work for that item and that the item is a powerful reinforcer.

Another difference between DTT and naturalistic strategies such as PRT is the *nature of the response* required for a reward. Typically in DTT a specified response is designated as correct, and only that response, or responses at least as good as a previous response ("shaping"), are reinforced. This can lead to frustration on the part of the child because, unless the training is conducted very carefully, the child will make many errors. Under such conditions it is not unlikely that the child will give up and stop responding, or perhaps have a tantrum. In fact, some have noted the similarity between the phenomenon of "learned helplessness" seen in animal studies[18] and the lack of motivation to respond seen in many children with autism. Learned helplessness is noted when animals come to believe that their behavior is unrelated to what happens to them, and under such circumstances the animal ceases to respond and even seems unable to subsequently learn an appropriate response. Therefore it is imperative for the autistic child to learn immediately and frequently that his behavior controls his environment and what happens to him. PRT addresses this need by providing reinforcement not just for correct responses or even near-correct responses, but instead for any reasonable attempt to respond. This means that the child obtains access to the relevant (direct) reinforcer for *trying*, not just for correct responding. If trying is reinforced, we will get more trying, and with more trying there are more opportunities for teaching. Further, since trying is rewarded, the child obtains a high frequency of reinforcement and thus the overall level of reward, and related motivation, is high.

PRT also involves *turn-taking*, where the child and the therapist engage in a more natural "give-and-take" interaction than is typically found in DTT training programs. Thus the therapist may take a toy car the child has chosen to play with and say "I am going to make the car go fast" while rapidly moving the car across the floor, then give the car to the child and ask "What are you going to do with the car?" and so on. Alternation of responding serves both to allow for the modeling of a variety of appropriate responses by the therapist and to engage the child in the type of give-and-take discourse that characterizes social interactions. Moreover, such interactions allow the child to learn that a particular object or activity may be associated with a variety of actions and characteristics, which encourages generalization.

It is important to emphasize how the teaching environment is structured in naturalistic strategies. The setting is carefully arranged to encourage and promote language, play, and other activities that may be naturally rewarding to the child. Yet the learning challenges allow for instruction. For example, highly desirable toys are placed out of reach (so the child has to use language request them), brightly colored toys are made available (if teaching colors is a goal), and lids are placed tightly on containers of preferred toys (so the child learns to request help). It is also important to point out that while naturalistic strategies do not involve the "drill" type of repetitive trials that one finds in DTT, many trials may be presented in a short period of time, but in a more naturalistic manner. For example, the turns in turn-taking may be short, or the child may have to request a cookie several times because only part of the cookie is given each time.

Table 6.1 Comparison of Discrete Trial and Naturalistic Treatment Procedures

Discrete Trial	Naturalistic
Teaching format	
Highly structured sessions, paced by teacher, who initiates teaching trials by providing occasions (discrete trials) for the child to respond that are separated by a specified interval.	Loosely structured sessions are paced by the child, who initiates trials under free-operant conditions by attending to stimuli or expressing a particular want.
Directness of instructions and setting	
Direct instruction conducted with teacher and child seated for discrete-trial episodes with distractions minimized.	Indirect instruction conducted with teacher and child in various places and positions in the presence of a variety of stimuli; e.g., a play setting.
Stimuli preceding response opportunities	
Antecedent stimuli are teacher-selected and presented until the child reaches criterion.	Antecedent stimuli are child-selected and therefore can vary from episode to episode.
Targeted response	
Same response targeted for several successive trials.	No particular order of target responses within a session.
Prompt strategies	
Prompts remain constant for particular target responses.	Prompts vary according to the child's initiating responses.
Reinforcers	
Indirect and functionally unrelated to target responses. Relatively invariant across trials.	Direct and functionally related to target responses. Variant across teaching episodes.
Criteria for presentation of reinforcer	
Reinforcer presentations for correct response or successive approximations (shaping).	Liberal shaping whereby attempts to respond are positively reinforced.

Source: Adapted from Table 1 in Dennis J. Delprato, "Comparisons of Discrete-Trial and Normalized Behavioral Language Intervention for Young Children with Autism," *Journal of Autism and Developmental Disorders* (2001).

These types of interactions and the natural variability they introduce reduce the likelihood that the child will associate very specific responses to particular stimuli. The stimuli, the responses, and the nature of consequences vary greatly, and this serves to reduce the generalization problems that may be associated with DTT. Further, as with DTT, naturalistic strategies can be used to teach a variety of behaviors in addition to language. While most of these strategies began with language training, they have since been used very successfully to teach play, social skills, and academic behaviors.

The major differences between highly structured discrete trial training and more naturalistic strategies are summarized in Table 6.1.

Advantages of Naturalistic Strategies

There are several advantages associated with the use of naturalistic strategies that make them more attractive than highly structured discrete trial training. The most important advantage is the documented effectiveness of the naturalistic strategies and their superiority in terms of increased generalization of treatment effects. Such strategies have been empirically documented to not only be effective, but to ameliorate several of the specific limitations that are often associated with the more highly structured approaches.

Another advantage of naturalistic strategies is that they may be more "user-friendly" in terms of acceptability by lay practitioners such as parents. Parents seem to enjoy using the naturalistic strategies more than they do the highly structured DTT. To illustrate, in one study naive observers (university undergraduates) were shown videotape clips of parents working with their child and using either PRT or DTT.[19] The observers were asked to rate with a Likert scale the degree to which the parents appeared to be happy, interested, and enthusiastic while working with their children. The results showed that the parents implementing PRT were rated as significantly more positive in their affect than were parents using DTT. Another study found that family/home interactions of parents who had been trained in PRT were rated by naive observers as more positive than were the family/home interactions of parents who had been trained in DTT.[20] Moreover, parental stress has been shown to be lower with naturalistic strategies than with DTT.[21]

A related advantage is that naturalistic strategies more readily lend themselves to use by parents and teachers in naturally occurring situations. Whereas DTT teaching typically involves setting up a structured teaching situation (such as two chairs and a table, with specific materials for the planned teaching session), naturalistic strategies can be used—indeed are best used—in natural situations. Although a parent can teach a child to discriminate colors using blocks in a structured DTT situation, the parent can teach the same thing while sorting laundry or planting flowers. The latter situations also involve colors but occur naturally in the child's environment, which should enhance the generalization of the training. To maximize teaching in natural settings, parents learn to use naturally occurring opportunities for teaching. For example, if a parent sees a child reaching for an apple on a table, this suggests that the child has "chosen" the apple and would be motivated to gain access to the apple. The parent could put her hand on the apple, ask the child "What do you want?" (or a question appropriate for the child's language level), and then allow the child to take the apple if a reasonable attempt is made.

Yet another important positive feature of naturalistic strategies is the fact that such teaching appears to be more enjoyable for the children. Again, this contention is supported not only by anecdotal observation but by research. Koegel and his colleagues found that autistic children who were being taught through naturalistic strategies versus DTT were rated as having more positive affect than children being taught through DTT.[22] Further, when the number of escape and avoidance behaviors such as crying and attempts to leave the teaching situation were recorded, there were significantly fewer such behaviors during the naturalistic teaching. This suggests the children found the naturalistic teaching to be more "fun" and less aversive than the DTT teaching. Therefore, teachers using naturalistic strategies are much less likely to have to resort to aversives in the training in order to control disruptive behaviors, because the children are less likely to be disruptive to begin with.

Of course, these naturalistic teaching strategies are not without critics; some have argued that the body of substantiating research is still inadequate to conclude that such treatments are generally superior to the more highly structured treatments. Thus, as with almost everything else in the field of autism, the debate about which form of behavioral treatment is "best" endures, and it bedevils parents, clinicians, teachers, and researchers alike. Not only do the different sides in this debate differ on which treatment is better, they also disagree on how far each treatment can take the child with autism. However, as we shall see in the next chapter, other treatment debates have taken center stage, and the whole issue of the "best" behavioral treatment has been questioned.

CHAPTER 7

Are Other Treatments Effective?

If investigators cannot demonstrate that applying the treatment protocol and only application of the treatment protocol is associated with meaningful improvements in the behaviors being taught, then further resources need not be expended. Is this minimal requirement too much to ask?

—Howard Goldstein, in *Journal of Autism and Developmental Disorders* (2000)

We cannot afford to listen to wishful thinkers or fanciful theorists and assume that their claims of effective treatments are true. Our mantra should be "Show me the data."

—Howard Goldstein, in *Journal of Autism and Developmental Disorders* (2000)

In this chapter I will discuss treatments that have been advocated for autistic children but have not been fully supported by experimental evidence, as were the behavioral interventions described in the previous chapter. This does not necessarily mean that these additional treatments are ineffective, but rather that when they are held to the standard of scientific evidence, their efficacy has not been proven. In some instances this is because the requisite research has not yet been conducted to validate their effectiveness. In other cases the supporting data are in the form of descriptive reports or chart reviews rather than controlled studies. In yet other instances, research has been conducted but the results are inconclusive or inconsistent, or the research is flawed to the extent that no firm conclusions may be drawn at this time. It is also important to note that for some of these treatments, individual responsiveness is quite variable, so that while some children may benefit, many or most may not.

Another reason why these additional treatments may be hard to evaluate is that they are frequently applied as part of a comprehensive package of treatments received by the child, and thus if a child improves, it is difficult to discern the relative contributions of any single treatment. For example, if a youngster is receiving intensive one-on-one discrete trial treatment, daily doses of megavitamins, auditory integration training, and a casein-free diet, one cannot say that the child's improvement (if any) was due to any one of these treatments. In addition, we have to look at the effects of maturation, especially in the case of very young children. Yet another problem in the evaluation of many of these treatments is that often a child's improvement is determined by parental or clinician report, and such reports may be inadvertently colored by the individual's understandable desire to see improvement.

It is also important to mention that most of these treatments are benign because they are not detrimental to the child (the few exceptions are noted below). However, even if there is no *direct* harm, one can argue that the child is *indirectly* harmed in terms of time lost and effort wasted on an ineffective treatment. A child spending time in an ineffective treatment is losing time she could be spending in an effective treatment. The same goes for the parents, who likewise spend time and effort. But perhaps the main cost to parents is the ultimate disappointment when a treatment fails. Of course, there is also a literal cost to the parents, since many of these treatments are quite expensive. Obviously both kinds of cost can be very painful for the parents.

All of these factors contribute to the highly charged and emotional debates engendered by these treatments. People on all sides are passionate about their positions. Hopeful, vulnerable, and even desperate parents are eager for something that can help their child, and they vigorously defend what they believe may be an effective, or even miraculous, treatment. Scientists and clinicians are more likely to be skeptical and pragmatic. They do not want to see time, money, and hope invested in wild-goose chases. These confrontations are even more likely when both sides can cite findings and reports to support their positions. Unfortunately, this is generally the case for most of the treatments described below.

The parents are put in a difficult position when it comes to considering all the currently available treatments, both proven and unproven. Wanting the best for their child means that they may worry about entering her in the wrong program, and so they may hesitate to begin any program. This approach has the risk of losing valuable time, especially in the case of very young children, since we know that early intervention is important. On the other hand, some parents adopt the approach of entering their child into every program they possibly can so they will be sure not to miss the "right" one—an approach that has various risks of its own. The child might be involved in so many programs that any amount of time spent in a truly effective program would be minimal. The multiple treatment regimens might be overwhelming and exhausting for the child, thereby limiting the effectiveness of all of the programs. In addition, involvement in multiple treatments usually makes it impossible to determine which of the many treatments (if any) is truly helping. And of course this approach is a major drain on the family in terms of time and money.

My point here is not to be a naysayer for all treatments that do not have the blessing of strong scientific validation. However, I believe it is absolutely essential for parents and clinicians to have sufficient knowledge to make informed decisions about treatments. Of course, a major part of this information should come from objective evaluation of an intervention by researchers who can conduct controlled studies and who are not emotionally or financially invested in a particular form of treatment. If the facts are out there, then the consumers of treatment will not be as easily influenced by hyperbole, anecdotal testimonials, or peer pressure. This maximizes the likelihood that the children will receive the most efficacious of the available treatments.

I will first consider treatments that are widely used and that are likely effective yet lack the strong scientific validation that behavioral treatments have been given. Next I will look at treatments that are less likely to be effective, at least for the majority of children with autism.

Treatments Likely to Be Effective

There are several forms of treatment which are similar in many aspects to the empirically supported treatments but which to date have not been put to the empirical test, or else the findings of such tests have proven inconclusive. These are educationally based treatments that share features of both highly structured and naturalistic behavioral strategies.

Floor Time

> This approach has had a noticeable effect on children's prognoses and progress. Many children diagnosed as having autistic spectrum disorders have become warmly related and joyful—characteristics thought to run counter to the very definition of autism. (S. I. Greenspan and S. Wieder, 1998)[1]

> However, there was a major confounding element in use of a comparison group: their parents had been dissatisfied with their previous interven-

tion. Ratings were also not blind to intervention status. (National Research Council, 2001)[2]

BACKGROUND AND RATIONALE Floor Time (based on the Developmental, Individual Difference, Relationship-based, or D.I.R., model) is a treatment that involves an interactive developmental approach to working with children with autism and other developmental disorders. Developed by Stanley Greenspan and Serena Wieder, this approach views autism as a biological disorder in which sensory processing difficulties work to prevent the normal development of social, communicative, and cognitive skills. These processing difficulties may include problems with auditory understanding, sensory modulation, and motor planning. The primary goal of the intervention (Floor Time) is to help the child work around his sensory processing difficulties so as to reestablish affective contact with important people in his life.

For Greenspan and Wieder, the critical engine driving development is social relationships, and they believe the brain and mind simply do not develop without the nurturing of human relationships. Because of this perspective, the treatment focuses on socially interactive relationships as the basis of the Floor Time intervention.

Greenspan and Wieder identify six "functional emotional skills" that are seen as fundamental to normal development.[3] These include (1) the dual ability to take an interest in the sights, sounds, and sensations of the world and to calm oneself; (2) the ability to engage in relationships with other people; (3) the ability to engage in two-way communication; (4) the ability to create complex gestures, to string together a series of actions into an elaborate and deliberate problem-solving sequence; (5) the ability to create ideas; and (6) the ability to build bridges between ideas to make them reality-based and logical. The goal of Floor Time is to help the autistic child climb the "developmental ladder" and achieve these milestones.

This approach emphasizes following the normal developmental

sequence when working on specific milestones even if it seems strange to be working on a very early milestone for a child who is chronologically ahead of where that milestone would fall for a typical child. It is important to begin at the child's current level and to bring her up through the milestones in the normal developmental sequence. Thus language, social engagement, and play are targeted as the child proceeds through the developmental process. Greenspan and Wieder's approach thus differs from a typical behavioral approach, which might emphasize these behaviors because they are important treatment goals in general but not necessarily because the child is at the appropriate developmental stage. Moreover, a straight behavioral intervention might begin by working on eliminating disruptive behaviors, since this approach views the control of such behaviors to be a prerequisite for working on any other skills. Using a developmental approach, Floor Time works to alleviate these behaviors as part of the ongoing developmentally-based curriculum.

THE TREATMENT Floor Time is broken down into three parts. First, the parents engage in Floor Time with their child to create the sorts of emotional experiences considered important to the mastery of the six milestones. Here the child learns the rewarding features of social relations and feels safe and confident enough to move on. Second, Floor Time is implemented by speech, occupational, and physical therapists, educators, and/or psychotherapists. These professionals use specialized Floor Time techniques to help the child meet specific challenges and to facilitate development. Third, parents work on their own responses and styles of relating with regard to different milestones. This works to create a family pattern that supports emotional and intellectual growth in all members of the family.

Floor Time is a very descriptive label: the treatment involves working with the child on the floor in a series of 20–30 minute sessions usually held several times a day. The treatment is very child-directed in that it is the adult's job to follow the child's lead in engaging in activities, maintaining attention and encouragement. The goal is to promote positive social and emotional interactions, leading the child to want to continue the interaction. During these interactions the child will open and close "circles of communication" with the adult; these include the child's lead and the adult's response. These circles of communication are seen as the vehicle by which the child advances through the milestones. Along the way, the adult is careful to maintain the child's attention and positive affect while presenting specific small challenges designed to move the child forward along the milestones. Some of these challenges may be a bit intrusive. For example, if the child is playing with a toy train and does not seem to be interested in doing so in an interactive manner with the adult, the adult may take another toy train and block the child's path, thus encouraging a reaction by the child (another circle of communication).

Ideally, these interactions will successfully guide the child through the developmental milestones and move the child from a position of social isolation and lack of communication to a position where the child is socially and emotionally involved and has learned to communicate. Problem-solving skills, creation of novel ideas, and logical thinking are all important treatment goals.

DOES IT WORK?   Greenspan and Wieder have reported a descriptive chart review study of 200 children which they say suggests the effectiveness of the technique.[4] However, judgment must be reserved because of methodological limitations such as the lack of experimental controls, the absence of post-treatment tests, and the lack of description of the specific treatment protocols used. While Floor Time has not been systematically and independently validated, it does share important features with other forms of treatment that have received empirical validation. If one looks at the specific procedures involved in Floor Time, it is clear that it resembles several naturalistic behavioral treatments such as Pivotal Response Training (PRT). As described in the previous chapter, PRT involves child choice, turn-taking, frequent variation of tasks, contingent reinforcement (for example, the reaction of the therapist), and maintaining positive motivation. In fact, I have watched tapes of adults using Floor Time and have been struck by how much it looks like PRT. Thus, although the theoretical foundation of Floor Time is completely different from that of PRT and other overtly behavioral strategies, its implementation (and therefore probably effect on the child) is very similar. However, while PRT and other behavioral interventions have been subjected to substantial empirical validation, Floor Time has not yet undergone such validation. Although I suspect it might do well under such scrutiny, we cannot say for sure as yet.

There are a few issues of concern with Floor Time. One is the fact that Greenspan and Wieder say it is important to work on the child's milestones in sequential order, beginning with the child's current level, before moving to more advanced skills. The earlier skills are a base necessary for generalization and maintenance of higher-level skills. Greenspan and Wieder believe that while it is tempting to work instead on language skills, color recognition, or some other age-appropriate behavior, such an approach is not likely to be very effective. Although this position certainly makes logical sense, there are many years of treatment research demonstrating that working on such "higher-level" skills may indeed be effective. This is not to say that very low-functioning children will not benefit from targeting more basic skills, but the fact remains that behavioral intervention has shown that treatment targets may not necessarily be "developmentally appropriate" in the sense that they must be addressed in the order in which they occur in normal development.

Another concern I have is that Greenspan and Wieder criticize the highly structured type of behavioral intervention by saying that treatment approaches that do not put the child into spontaneous, joyful relationship patterns may "intensify rather than remediate the difficulty."[5] While I would agree that the highly structured behavioral approach may not be as effective as the more naturalistic approaches, I would be surprised if it could be shown to make the children *worse*. There has been no empirical demonstration that the children's difficulties are intensified by a highly structured approach.

TEACCH

Nowhere have we found another program which matches TEACCH's emphasis on the strengths and the abilities—not the weakness—of disabled persons. Nowhere else have we seen an agency match the success TEACCH has in helping handicap[ped] persons develop their potential. (G. B. Mesibov, 1997)[6]

Program evaluation information on the TEACCH model has included consumer satisfaction data from parents, trainees, and replication sites, as well as objective assessment of parent teaching skills, and child progress. . . . There have been a number of studies describing progress in follow-up samples of young children who received services at TEACCH, and substantial IQ score gains have been commonly reported for nonverbal children who were diagnosed at early ages. However, these studies are not direct evaluations of treatment outcomes. (National Research Council, 2001)[7]

BACKGROUND AND RATIONALE The Program for the Treatment and Education of Autistic and Related Communication Handicapped Children (TEACCH) in North Carolina has been the largest and most influential state agency program dedicated to children with autism and other developmental disorders. It was founded in 1971 by Dr. Eric Schopler at the University of North Carolina at Chapel Hill. What distinguishes TEACCH from most other treatments for autism is the comprehensive, community-based nature of the program. Collaboration is key to the program, which seeks to coordinate all services for the autistic child and the family. Parents, special education teachers, speech pathologists, social workers, and other professionals form a team dedicated to working together to help the autistic child achieve the best possible outcome. The program was originally developed in part to counter the prevailing psychogenic theory of autism. Whereas the psychodynamic point of view "blamed" the parents for causing the disorder and excluded them from the treatment, TEACCH sought not only to include the parents but to make them a critical part of the child's treatment program.

The TEACCH approach posits that autism is an organically based disorder and one that is irreversible. Because of this view, the goal of the educational and therapeutic efforts is not specifically for the child to become "normal." Rather, the goal of the treatment is to play to the child's strengths, to develop these strengths through structured teaching, and to foster independence, in order to allow the child to fit as well as possible into society as an adult. This is accomplished by combining a variety of specific treatment strategies including basic operant training such as DTT, as well as naturalistic behavioral strategies and augmentative strategies such as picture exchange.

Because the perspective of TEACCH is that autistic children have basic difficulties with cognitive processing, especially auditory processing, the main focus of the specific treatment strategies tends to be highly structured and visual in nature. Many of the specific training strategies rely heavily on visual stimulus control techniques.

THE TREATMENT There are five main principles guiding the TEACCH treatment philosophy. These include (1) utilizing the child's strengths to "build a bridge" between the autistic child's world and that of the typical child; (2) ongoing assessment of the child's abilities as a means of optimizing opportunities for independence and maximizing success; (3) providing a carefully arranged environmental structure to assist the child in understanding meaning; (4) viewing challenging behaviors such as noncompliance as indicating that the child does not understand what he or she is to do; (5) involving the parents as crucial collaborators on the interdisciplinary team.[8]

As noted, TEACCH uses a variety of specific treatment strategies. The program philosophy emphasizes that because of the central deficit in autism, the children require a highly structured environment and task-analyzed goals (goals that have been carefully parsed into their constituent parts) in order to learn. Accordingly, the child's learning environment in the classroom is one with a high degree of organization and structure. This "structured teaching" is very individualized; after careful and ongoing assessment, each child is provided with a tailored set of educational tasks. These tasks are typically completed at individual workstations within the classroom, where the child is given a set of tasks such as sorting colored blocks, placing items in specific categories such as animals versus vegetables, completing puzzles, or folding letters to place in envelopes. Most of these tasks are visually oriented. To foster independence, the child is presented with a visual schedule composed of pictures depicting the specific tasks to be completed within the session. The picture schedule allows the child to complete one task and then to know what to do for the next task, and so on. This predictable, structured environment is one in which the child can proceed at her own pace, experience success, and learn independence, all in a positive setting. This environment makes learning more enjoyable, and thus disruptive behaviors are reduced.

An important feature of TEACCH is that all venues of the child's treatment are coordinated. Thus the parents are trained in the same procedures used in the classroom, speech therapy, and any other community services the child is receiving. Frequent interaction among these service providers is seen as a major strength, allowing for generalization of the child's skills across environments. The aim of the TEACCH program is to continue with the comprehensive and coordinated program throughout the child's life span.

DOES IT WORK? As with Floor Time, the TEACCH program comprises several specific interventions that have been empirically validated as effective. Discrete trial training, naturalistic behavioral strategies, picture schedules, and parent training have all met the test of objective evaluation. Assuming these techniques are employed in the correct manner, there is no reason to believe they would not be effective. Moreover, TEACCH was one of the first comprehensive programs to emphasize individualization of treatment. The use of multiple treatment strategies, ongoing assessment, and the inclusion of the parents in determining specific needs of the child and family all serve to meet the needs of each individual child. It seems that in some ways TEACCH was ahead of its time.

However, as with Floor Time, there is a paucity of data supporting the efficacy of the comprehensive TEACCH program (although TEACCH enjoys a broader research basis than does Floor Time). This is one of those cases where a popular program that is very widely used and disseminated (through training workshops and other venues) still lags a bit when it comes to empirical validation. This is why I can only say that TEACCH "most probably" is effective. Without independent and rigorous studies, one cannot be more definitive at this time. Of course this does not mean that TEACCH would not be found to be very effective, only that it has not yet been subjected to the scrutiny required to determine its effectiveness. Almost all of the published studies on TEACCH have been conducted by the TEACCH developers rather than by independent researchers, and much of the material in the outcome evaluations consists of parent or teacher reports and consumer satisfaction data. While these published studies have reported positive outcomes, most suffer from rather serious methodological flaws that preclude unambiguous interpretation of results. Moreover, one of the main findings, reported by Schopler, Mesibov, and Baker,[9] is a long-term finding that when institutionalization rates in North Carolina are compared across the years (with almost every autistic child in North Carolina being involved in TEACCH), the rate of institutionalization has dropped dramatically. Several researchers have discounted this finding, since changes in government policies (such as the closure of institutions) and other factors may have acted to reduce the institutionalization rate, independent of any effects of TEACCH. However, one well-designed study has provided support for the use of the TEACCH model with young autistic children.[10]

One of the problems with independent research on the TEACCH model is that the model involves almost all state resources in North Carolina. Hence one of the most impressive features of TEACCH, the coordination and collaboration of almost all child and family services, is also what would make it almost impossible for anyone to replicate the model for an independent research evaluation. Yet even when evaluating specific components of the model, most of the developers' studies utilize satisfaction questionnaires and anecdotal information as opposed to "hard" data on specific child behaviors.

Another concern about the TEACCH model is that the children are typically placed in special education classrooms with other developmentally disabled children. This is in line with the TEACCH philosophy that normalcy, per se, is not the goal of the program, given that autism is a disorder with an irreversible central deficit. However, placement in such a classroom may deprive the child of opportunities to interact with typically developing children and perhaps adopt more "normal" modes of functioning.

Treatments Less Likely to Be Effective

In this section I discuss treatments that do not enjoy strong scientific support, nor do they share any of the features of empirically validated treatments (as do Floor Time and TEACCH). Essentially, these are treatments that when put to a rigorous test lead to in-conclusive results and/or seem to be effective with only a sub-population of individuals with autism.

Sensory-Based Treatments

Auditory Integration Training (AIT)

> Auditory integration therapy (AIT), however counterintuitive it may be, can and often does produce significant improvement. (S. M. Edelson and B. Rimland, 2003)[11]

> Probably because AIT lacks a plausible rationale and is counterintuitive, it has become the target of skepticism and of negatively biased research. . . . There is a place for skepticism, but there is also a place for safe, non-intrusive, short-term and relatively inexpensive therapies with reasonably good track records. (S. M. Edelson and B. Rimland, 2001)[12]

> In summary, auditory integration therapy has received more balanced in-vestigation than has any other sensory approach to intervention, but in general studies have not supported either its theoretical basis or the spe-cificity of its effectiveness. (National Research Council, 2001)[13]

> Auditory integration therapy does not meet scientific standards for efficacy that would justify its practice. (Policy statement of the American Speech-Language-Hearing Association, 2003)[14]

BACKGROUND AND RATIONALE   Auditory integration training (AIT) is one of a number of different treatments that have as a basis the frequently cited sensory abnormalities in autism. Research has shown that while sensory processing abnormalities are not specific to autism, nor do they characterize all autistic individuals, they are relatively common in this population. As noted earlier in the book, individuals with autism have frequently been reported to have a high degree of auditory sensitivity; they may become quite agitated by certain sounds such as crying babies, vacuum cleaners, and sirens. Conversely, they are often reported to be hyposensitive to other sounds, such as their name being called. The term "apparent sensory deficit" is used to describe the fact that autistic children are able to hear; they just do not respond to particular sounds. Further, while the hyper- and hyposensitivity to sound may be consistent with some stimuli, other times it is quite variable. The frequent observation that these children may respond in an unusual manner to auditory stimuli together with the finding that sensory processing abnormalities seem to be correlated with higher levels of repetitive and stereotypical behaviors has led some to believe this is an important relationship that may be useful for treatment. Yet from this rather minor relationship, an extensive theory has evolved. The proponents of AIT have proposed that treating the sensory abnormalities in autism should facilitate a child's acquisition of communication and social skills, as well as leading to a reduction in autistic symptoms. Thus, by implication, reducing the abnormal auditory sensitivities in these children should lead to widespread behavioral improvements.

THE TREATMENT   AIT was developed by Dr. Guy Berard, an otolaryngologist in Annecy, France. While Berard originally developed his treatment to ameliorate disorders of the auditory system such as hearing loss or distortion, he determined that difficulties in hearing and auditory processing were likely to lead to behavioral and learning disorders. Since disturbances in auditory processing are often noted in cases of autism, it made sense that since AIT was designed to treat auditory disorders, the treatment might help in cases of autism. In fact, Berard considers autistic symptoms to be largely an avoidance reaction stemming from oversensitivity to sounds. Thus the goal of AIT is to "normalize" the hearing of the affected individual who is likely hyper- or hyposensitive to certain aspects of sound.

When embarking on an AIT regimen, the clinician first obtains an audiogram of the child. An audiogram is a graphic representation of a person's sensitivity to different sound wave frequencies (Hz) against decibels (dB). Using the child's individual audiogram, the clinician employs a specialized piece of equipment to prepare music recordings to be used in the treatment. The music used for AIT typically consists of CD recordings of popular or classical tracks chosen for their wide frequency range.

The music is presented to the child through headphones in such a way that at first it is modulated, which means that high and low frequencies are emphasized randomly. Then the music is filtered so that it does not contain those frequencies to which the child is known to be hypersensitive. Over a period of sessions, usually twenty half-hour sessions distributed over 10 to 20 days, the music is systematically altered to "teach" the child how to listen. Proponents of AIT suggest that the method works because the music can "massage" the middle ear (hair cells in the cochlea), reduce hypersensitivity to particular frequencies, and generally improve auditory processing. This in turn, they claim, translates into improved attention, arousal, language, and social skills, along with a reduction in autistic symptoms.

Interestingly, the proponents of AIT claim that the treatment is effective even for those autistic children (probably the majority) for whom a valid audiogram is not obtainable and thus specific frequency sensitivities cannot be determined. These children are presented with only the modulated version of the music and, according to AIT proponents, this also leads to positive changes.

DOES IT WORK? As one might expect, the effectiveness of AIT is a hotly debated and emotional issue where proponents and skeptics have each taken firm positions. AIT is one of the most heavily researched of the "alternative" treatments for autism. The literature abounds with testimonials from parents and others, and there is even a book describing a case where a child was "cured" with

AIT.[15] However, the fact is that AIT has not fared very well when subjected to scientific scrutiny. The proponents of AIT cite many studies that suggest the effectiveness of AIT in terms of improving autistic symptoms and reducing behavior problems, but the majority of such investigations suffer from serious problems in methodology and interpretation. Sometimes the researchers have depended on parental reports and/or have failed to include appropriate experimental controls; sometimes the effects of concurrent treatments and/or maturation cannot be ruled out.

Another significant problem is that there has never been any scientific substantiation of the underlying rationale for AIT. AIT treatment is supposed to change the child's auditory processing and "normalize" auditory sensitivity; yet the studies have not demonstrated this effect. Moreover, there is no scientific evidence for the mechanism by which AIT is purported to work. That is, we have no evidence that the presentation of digitally modulated or filtered music does anything to "massage" the inner ear or affect the brain. Of course, we also do not know that, even if the inner ear or brain were "massaged," we would see any effects on behavior. In other words, most of the various causal relations that are presented have not been confirmed.

Most of the well-controlled investigations that have been conducted on AIT have not found clinically significant treatment effects. For example, in one study the researchers randomly assigned 40 autistic children to an AIT training group and 40 to a control group which heard unmodified music over headphones.[16] The parents and teachers of the children were "blind" in that they did not know the group assignment of the children. After the treatment, the researchers found that children in *both* groups improved on measures of autism severity and cognitive abilities as well as showing improved responsiveness to auditory stimuli, and some of these improvements were maintained over 12 months. The fact that both groups showed improvement to the same extent indicates that AIT per se was not responsible for the behavioral gains. Several other well-controlled studies have reported no treatment effect for AIT. In addition, some studies suggest that any initial reported effects are transient.

My own experience with parents who have tried AIT treatment for their child with autism suggests that while the parents often report some initial effect, they find that the effects do not last. This leads me to believe either that any positive change is temporary, or that the initial reported effects might have been due to expectation on the part of the parent. A careful review of the scientific evidence has led both the National Research Council and the American Speech-Language-Hearing Association to conclude that AIT is not supported either in its effectiveness or in its theoretical basis. Given that the treatment usually runs several hundreds or thousands of dollars, parents should definitely consider these issues.

Sensory Integration Therapy (SIT)

The three treatment approaches outlined above (AIT, SIT, vision training) complement one another. Autistic individuals often become more attentive and more motivated to learn soon after their biomedical and sensory problems are treated. A child may do well with only one of these approaches, but the combination can lead to amazing results, and even recovery for some children. (S. M. Edelson, 2003)[17]

Sensory integration, as the name suggests, is supposed to provide ways in which the child will develop better modulated sensory responses, and as a result (and here's the leap of faith) should become more social and communicative. (B. Siegel, 1996)[18]

BACKGROUND AND RATIONALE Based on a model similar to AIT, sensory integration therapy (SIT) is a form of treatment developed by an occupational therapist, Jean Ayres,[19] who emphasized the importance of the relationship between sensory experiences and motor and behavioral performance. SIT emphasizes neurological processing of sensory information as the foundation for the learning of higher-level skills. It has been noted that many children with autism exhibit abnormal sensory responses and motor difficulties such as hyper- and hypo-responsiveness to certain stimuli, dislike of being touched, attenuated response to pain, engaging in repetitive movements, sniffing objects, and obsession with particular sensory experiences (for example, fascination with spinning objects). It is this unusual responsiveness that leads to the hypothesis that these behaviors are manifestations of abnormal sensory integrative processes occurring in subcortical regions of the brain. Not surprisingly, these problems interfere with the child's interaction with the environment and thus his ability to utilize environmental experiences for learning. The goal of SIT is to improve the somatosensory and vestibular functions of the brain by providing controlled sensory experiences that re-educate the sensory processing system. In turn, this should lead to improved learning and a reduction in the behavioral symptoms of autism.

THE TREATMENT   Unlike auditory integration training, SIT is not so much a single treatment approach but rather a variety of interventions, all aimed at retraining the child's sensory processing. There are many specific variations of SIT, but all share the same general focus, which is to provide the child with controlled sensory experiences. For improvement of vestibular functions, the child might be put into a suspended, swinging, or spinning chair, given "deep pressure" massage, or fitted with a weighted vest. For improvement in tactile tolerance, the child's arm might be brushed with a soft brush. To improve visual function, the child might be fitted with special lenses or presented with colored lights. Usually the treatment is conducted in a controlled one-on-one situation where the child is actively engaged in a play activity. The SIT therapist (usually an occupational therapist) presents the child with "just right" demands (at a level that gently challenges); as the child demonstrates tolerance of the experiences and improvement in motor and sensory responding, the demands are progressively increased, requiring more and more sophisticated responses. The treatment is typically delivered one to three times per week in one-hour sessions, although this can vary depending on the preferences of the practitioner. The treatment is continued for several months or even years.

DOES IT WORK? Again, many of the positive reports of SIT are anecdotal reports by parents. For example, one parent describes her child's treatment like this: "Augie lay on a special table in a dark room for half an hour, twice a day. The table moved in a circular motion, either from side to side, or head to foot. While he was on the table, Mary put earphones on him for AIT. While this was going on, a light box above Augie's head showed him colored lights, one color at a time, slow(ly) pulsing from bright to dim and back to bright. Mary gave him glow-in-the-dark toys to play with so he would not be bored or sleepy, and Gary and I massaged him and encouraged him."[20] Obviously there was a lot going on for this child; usually the treatment is more focused on a single modality. The mother reports that following this treatment Augie became more interested in climbing play structures, riding a bicycle, and being with animals. All of these behaviors were new. Can these reported improvements be attributed to SIT? It is impossible to say. This child was simultaneously receiving other forms of treatment, which is not uncommon for autistic children since the parents understandably and appropriately were seeking a comprehensive program. But reports of this nature can easily encourage others to view SIT as effective.

When subjected to scientific scrutiny, however, SIT's effectiveness is not substantiated. Actually there is relatively little research on these treatments, one reason being that there is no single SIT approach. Some of the studies that have been conducted report posi-

tive results in terms of the children's awareness, social responsiveness, and communication skills, but most of these studies have
serious methodological flaws that make interpretation difficult. In a
comprehensive review of research in the area,[21] the existing studies
were faulted not only for methodological flaws but also for a failure
to demonstrate the supposed relation between a given type of sensory experience and behavioral changes. As with AIT, there have
been no convincing demonstrations that the behavioral changes reported are associated with any neurological changes, as proposed
by the underlying rationale for the intervention.

Pharmacological and Nutritional Treatments

Several proposed treatments for autism have involved various pharmacological agents or nutritional changes. The treatments listed
here represent some of those that have had the most attention and
publicity—and have been the most controversial. However, this list
is by no means exhaustive. It seems that new proposed drugs, nutritional supplements, and diets are coming up almost daily.

Secretin

The day he had his first secretin infusion, he started telling us when he
needed to poop, which he hadn't been doing. His ESD teacher and ABA
therapists began to report progress on emotional issues: more "appropriate happiness" and more "shared affect." His language seemed to blos-
som, and his fine motor skills really picked up. (parent of child with autism, quoted in S. M. Edelson and B. Rimland, 2003)[22]

Secretin-treated children did not differ from placebo-treated children.
(National Research Council, 2001)[23]

Given the weight of published findings, however, including the data we
present here, it appears unlikely that secretin offers any clinical benefit to
the majority of children with autism. (J. Coplan and colleagues, 2003)[24]

BACKGROUND AND RATIONALE   As has often been the case with autism treatments, a research report and the ensuing widespread media attention raised the hopes of many that another potential magic bullet might have been found. Specifically, in 1998 Karoly Horvath reported that a gastrointestinal peptide hormone called secretin may show benefit in improving the symptoms of children with autism and PDD who also exhibited diarrhea.[25] Secretin is a hormone used in the diagnosis of certain gastrointestinal and pancreatic disorders. Horvath infused three autistic children with porcine secretin for the purpose of diagnosing pancreatic function in an attempt to account for these children's problems with diarrhea. He reported that after secretin infusion, the children exhibited rather significant improvements in social and language behaviors. Shortly thereafter a mother, Victoria Beck, reported in an article in the *Ladies' Home Journal* that after her autistic son had received secretin for gastrointestinal diagnosis, his behavior improved dramatically.[26] This mother's story was picked up by other magazine articles and television reports, complete with dramatic before-and-after films of the child. Soon parents across the country were seeking secretin infusion treatments for their autistic children, and Web sites popped up all over the Internet promoting secretin as a treatment for autism.

Several mechanisms have been proposed for how secretin might affect the central nervous system and autistic symptomatology. One main rationale depends on the assumption that children with autism are more likely to have gastrointestinal disorders than are nonautistic children (but of course there is no strong consensus on this). The idea is that there is an association between secretin receptors in the intestine and receptors found in the hippocampus of the brain, and this association has a negative effect. Since the neurological basis of autism is still relatively unknown and undoubtedly complex, it is impossible to disprove the association at this time. However, any potential detrimental effect on the central nervous system resulting from this association makes it at least possible that social, communication, and other behaviors would be affected.

THE TREATMENT   The sudden and emphatic demand by parents for secretin treatments for their children proved to be a complicated situation. Many physicians would not provide the infusions because such a use of secretin was an "off label" use, meaning that secretin had been approved for use as a diagnostic tool but not for use as a treatment for autism or any other condition. Yet some physicians were willing to use the secretin infusions as a treatment for autistic children.

Typically the child receives porcine or human synthetic secretin by intravenous infusion. Often there is only a single infusion, but sometimes there are multiple infusions distributed over time.

DOES IT WORK?   There has been quite a lot of research on secretin, and the bottom line is that secretin does not seem to have any significant effect on the behaviors of children with autism spectrum disorders. Many of the reports, particularly the early studies, were uncontrolled case studies or anecdotal reports. Many children receiving secretin are also receiving other forms of treatment at the same time. This of course makes determining the effect of the secretin alone impossible. However, when secretin treatment is subjected to appropriately controlled, methodologically rigorous study, the evidence does not support secretin as a treatment for autism. As is the case with other "unproven" treatments, the findings of control-group, double-blind studies generally show that neither the secretin-treated children nor the placebo-treated children show improvement or, on the other hand, that both groups show improvement. In either case, it is impossible to attribute any specific effects to the secretin per se. Further, one study demonstrated that if the parents were blind to whether their child was receiving a placebo or secretin, they were unable to distinguish the difference.[27]

This study is of particular interest because while scientific investigations have failed to show much of an effect, it is possible that the effects of secretin are more subtle and thus more apparent to parents than others. However, this study found that this was not the case.

Vitamins

> However, despite the remarkably consistent findings in the research on the use of vitamin B6 in the treatment of autism, and despite its being immeasurably safer than any of the drugs used for autistic children, there are at present very few practitioners who use it or advocate its use in the treatment of autism. (B. Rimland, 2003)[28]

> Due to the small number of studies, the methodological quality of studies, and small sample sizes, no recommendation can be advanced regarding the use of B6-Mg as a treatment for autism. (C. Nye and A. Brice, 2003)[29]

BACKGROUND AND RATIONALE   There have been many reports that children with autism have a metabolic disorder resulting in gastrointestinal problems. In fact, it has been suggested that approximately 25 percent of autistic children have chronic diarrhea and 25 percent have constipation. Yet there continues to be lively debate regarding how universal or specific this proposed metabolic disorder may be, and whether it is acquired or genetic. It has been proposed that these children suffer from a "leaky gut," meaning that their gastrointestinal tract is abnormally permeable. One effect of the "leaky gut" is that the condition depletes beneficial bacteria, with the result that fewer vitamins are produced. According to some, this means that more vitamins are required than are normally provided by the diet; hence the need for larger-than-normal doses of vitamins.

While megadoses of various vitamins have been advocated, by far the most frequently proposed and studied is Vitamin B6 (pyridoxine), often supplemented by magnesium. Vitamin B6 is important for the digestion of proteins, and magnesium is a mineral that plays a role in building bones, maintaining nerve and muscle cells, and enhancing the function of several enzymes in the body.

THE TREATMENT   In early work with vitamin B6, it was reported that many autistic children showed improvement in attention, reduced social withdrawal, decreases in stereotyped behavior, and increases in language. However, it was noted that withdrawal symptoms occurred upon cessation of the vitamin, mostly involving an increase in irritability. In later studies, magnesium was added and seemed to both prolong the positive effects of the vitamin B6 and reduce the negative side effects.

The regimen for megavitamin treatment has not been consistent. Dosages of vitamin B6 in different studies have varied considerably, from as little as 30 milligrams per day to over 3,000 milligrams (the U.S. recommended daily allotment is between 1 and 2 milligrams per day). Dosages of magnesium have varied as well, ranging from about 350 to 500 milligrams per day (the U.S. recommended daily allotment is between 80 and 400 milligrams).

DOES IT WORK?   On the basis of the many studies that have been conducted with this vitamin regimen, there is some reason to believe that a small subgroup of individuals with autism may indeed show some benefit. In fact, some studies, including ones with appropriate double-blind experimental designs, have indicated that as many as 30 to 50 percent of the study participants show improvement.[30] However, no one claims that this treatment is a cure for autism or that it should replace other therapies. Moreover, there are other studies that have not shown this benefit, and few studies have assessed the long-term effects of megavitamins.[31]

Methodology is of course crucial to evaluating the veracity of the claims of any treatment, and vitamin treatment is no different.

There have been several methodological challenges to vitamin studies. First is the fact that in many of these studies the data supporting the efficacy of the treatment are provided by parents, teachers, or staff members who are not blind to the treatment versus placebo status of the child and who also may be predisposed to expect positive effects. Second, the wide variation in dosages, age of research participants, and behaviors measured makes it very difficult to compare the results of several studies to determine a firm recommendation for the use of this treatment regimen. Finally, the vitamin regimen is often administered jointly with other forms of treatment, so that it is impossible to determine the relative contribution of each treatment to any observed improvement.

There is also a strong opinion by some in the field (such as Bernard Rimland, one of the main advocates of megavitamin treatment) that the medical field is vehemently opposed to this form of nonmedical intervention. These individuals feel that the medical community is using its influence to discount the positive-outcome studies and discourage the use of vitamins as a treatment option for autism. On the other side, people in the medical community may point to the megavitamin treatment regimen as another off-the-wall, wishful-thinking form of treatment that has not really met the scientific test of effectiveness. As one can imagine, at times these accusations and counteraccusations are quite rancorous.

The bottom line is that it is probably true that vitamin B6, with or without magnesium, is helpful for some individuals with autism. However, we cannot say at present which individuals will benefit and which will not. Nor can we say that the majority of individuals will benefit, or that the benefits are long-lasting.

There are other factors to consider before beginning a megavitamin treatment. While it is understandable that parents would consider using high doses of vitamins before they would consider other biological treatments such as potent drugs, the fact remains that vitamins, particularly in such large doses, are not necessarily benign. There are reports of withdrawal symptoms such as an increase in irritability when vitamin B6 is discontinued. It is also known that high doses of vitamin B6 can lead to muscle weakness and numbness. High doses of magnesium are associated with abnormal slowing of the heartbeat and weakened reflexes. Other side effects have been reported, including nausea, excitability, and more severe disruptive behavior. Although these side effects are typically reversible and have not been reported in individuals with autism per se, they are important to consider.

Obviously the debate, and the acrimony, about megavitamin treatment for autism will continue for some time—at least until more studies are conducted. But what will likely be the outcome of these studies is the familiar one: there will be variability in the response to this treatment, and until we can determine which individuals will or will not benefit, it will remain a hit-or-miss proposition.

Special Diets

There are many excellent scientific studies showing that B6/magnesium as well as the GFCF [gluten-free casein-free] diet are effective. (B. Rimland, 2003)[32]

Based on this review [New York State Department of Health, 1999], it was concluded that there are no known advantages associated with the use of special elimination diets for children with autism. (T. L. Whitman, 2004)[33]

BACKGROUND AND RATIONALE   As noted earlier, it has been reported that individuals with autism have gastrointestinal problems such as a "leaky gut." The result of this overly permeable tract membrane is that digestion products of foods such as gluten (present, for example, in bread) and cow's milk pass through the membrane into the blood, causing antigenic responses and interfering with the functioning of the central nervous system. This could lead to some of the behavioral problems associated with autism. In fact, some have viewed this gastrointestinal phenomenon as potentially of great importance in the etiology of autism.[34]

The special diet most often promoted in the treatment of autism is one that is low in casein and/or gluten. Gluten is a protein found in wheat or barley, and casein is the major protein in found in milk. This diet is thought to be beneficial because it removes proteins which produce toxic peptides that are typically absorbed via the leaky gut. Removal of these proteins is predicted to reduce autistic symptomatology.

THE TREATMENT   This treatment involves placing the autistic child on a diet low in gluten and/or casein. This means that foods containing gluten such as wheat, barley, rye, oats, or their derivatives should be avoided. Eliminating or reducing casein involves avoiding milk and other dairy products. This is a difficult dietary regimen to implement; it requires that the parents be involved in everything the child eats—at home, at school, at restaurants, and everywhere else that may provide access to food. A further difficulty is that many of these children have highly restricted food preferences to begin with, and the addition of even more restrictions may leave very little in the way of available foods for the child.

DOES IT WORK?   As with vitamin treatment regimens, the case for the effectiveness of these special diets remains controversial. The controversy involves not only the effectiveness of the treatment but also the strength of the underlying rationale upon which it is based.

The case for the presence of gastrointestinal abnormality is open to debate. While several studies have suggested that significant and widespread gastrointestinal pathology may characterize at least a subpopulation of autistic individuals, it may be the case that the pathology is not central to the etiology of the disorder but rather is a secondary consequence of autism. (Here again we see the difference between a correlational and a causal relationship.) Other studies have failed to find that gastrointestinal disorders are more frequent in individuals with autism than in control populations.[35] In general, the results of these various studies lead to the conclusion that there is not a strong association between autism and gastrointestinal abnormality, although there may be such an association in a small minority of cases.

Those advocating the use of these special diets cite studies suggesting that improvements in behavior follow the implementation of such diets. Although much of the supporting literature here consists of case studies and anecdotal reports, two studies involving a large number of autistic participants reported improvement of social, cognitive, and communication skills.[36]

However, even some of those who report positive effects of these diets acknowledge problems that prevent us from drawing firm conclusions. First, there is the issue of the confounding effect of other simultaneous treatments that the child may be receiving. Moreover, it is difficult to conduct double-blind placebo studies with diets. Even more important is the fact that these diets, now quite popular in the lay press, are often implemented with little or no monitoring by medical professionals. Nutritional monitoring is essential to ensure that these children receive diets that are safe and nutritionally sound over time.

Medications

There are currently no medications that effectively treat the core symptoms of autism, but there are medications that can reduce problematic symptoms and some that play critical roles in severe, even life-threatening situations, such as self-injurious behavior. (National Research Council, 2001)[37]

BACKGROUND AND RATIONALE   Since autism is now known to be a biological disorder, many believe that certain pharmacological agents may be useful in treatment. While this may make intuitive sense, the situation has turned out to be quite complicated. (One need only look at the situation with secretin and the past unfortunate history with fenfluramine to see that what might initially seem like a promising lead can turn into a dead end.) It is certainly not the case that autism is caused by a single biological factor; rather, it appears that the severity and expression of autism are determined by a very complex and interactive set of influences. Further, the heterogeneity that one finds in the diagnostic category of autism suggests that different biological factors are affecting different individuals. Even in the highly unlikely event that a single biological basis for autism were found, this would not mean that we would have a biological treatment to correct the problem. No biological "cure" is on the horizon. However, certain pharmacological agents have been used to target specific symptoms of autism.

THE TREATMENT   A variety of drugs are administered to individuals with autism. The medications most commonly applied and studied include agents intended to alter various neurochemical systems, such as the dopamine system, serotonin, and neuropeptides.

DOES IT WORK?   Despite anecdotal reports of dramatic improvement in specific symptoms of autism and major improvements in intelligence with the use of various medications, well-controlled replication studies almost always fail to support these reports. The bottom line is that while several of the behavioral symptoms of autism may indeed respond positively to various pharmacological agents, no medications have proven effective in treating the core symptoms of the disorder (basic deficits in social interaction and communication).[38] Yet there is no doubt that symptomatic relief in some of the behaviors often exhibited by children and adults with autism may be very important in improving the lives of these individuals and those around them. Moreover, it is undoubtedly the case that reductions in behaviors such as stereotypies, hyperactivity, and aggression make it more likely that the individual will be able to benefit from other forms of treatment and to remain in the home and community.

One area of intense interest is the dopamine system and whether or not changes in this system affect behavioral changes. Drugs that block dopamine have been shown to have some positive effect on hyperactivity and stereotypical behavior. In contrast, drugs that enhance the effect of dopamine exacerbate autistic symptoms. Specific drugs in the dopamine agonist category include haloperidol, chlorpromazine, and thioridazine. Such medications have proven effective in treating agitation, hyperactivity, aggression, withdrawal, self-stimulation, motor and vocal tics, and affect liability. However, as expected, they have not been shown to be effective in reducing the core deficits of autism. In addition, some rather serious side effects of these drugs have been reported, which include sedation and various movement disorders (dystonia and tardive dyskinesia). Newer versions of these drugs such as risperidone, however, have been shown to have the same beneficial effects but with fewer and less severe side effects.

As noted earlier in the book, there have been reports that children with autism have elevated levels of serotonin (a neurotransmitter). Several studies have suggested that serotonin reuptake inhibitors (SSRIs) such as fluoxetine may be helpful in the reduction of repetitive behaviors, aggression, and perhaps self-injury. Again, however, not all studies support this conclusion, and those studies that do report positive results on these symptoms do not show significant changes in the core symptoms of the disorder.

Yet another area receiving attention is the idea that autistic symptoms are at least partly attributable to overactivity in the endogenous opiod system. As discussed earlier, investigators who subscribe to this theory focus on the idea of a metabolic disorder (leaky gut); they propose that neurotransmission is negatively affected by the excessive peptides and opiod activity that result from certain foods, particularly those containing gluten and casein. Support for this theory comes from some early studies suggesting that opiate antagonists (such as naltrexone) might reduce self-injurious behavior in autism. However, more recent and well-controlled investigations have not supported the effectiveness of naltrexone on self-injury, and the opiod theory of autistic symptomatology remains speculative at this point.

Research into the actions of various pharmacological agents has been difficult for a number of reasons. First, there is the large variability in expression of the disorder that we call autism. This means that children who are mute, have high levels of stereotypical behavior, are severely cognitively impaired, and so on, may be included in treatment groups that also contain verbal children who engage in almost no stereotypical behavior and are not cognitively impaired. Analyses are often conducted in a manner that precludes looking at individual responsivity to the drugs. Further, these drugs may have differential effects depending on the developmental level of the individual. This heterogeneity in groups also poses a significant problem in the selection of outcome assessments, since it is difficult to determine assessments that would be reliable and valid for all subjects in these studies.

A second problem is that most drug studies are of short duration and do not include adequate follow-up over time, so the long-term effects of the medications are not assessed. A third problem is that to date we have no good animal models of autism. Such models would allow for hypothesis-driven research into the effects of various drugs. A final problem involves the ability to draw firm conclusions regarding the effects of the drugs per se. That is, it is difficult if not impossible to determine whether positive effects of drugs are due to the direct action of the drug as opposed to an indirect action. For example, a positive effect might be noted if a drug reduces hyperactivity and increases attention so that the individual can benefit more from an educational program. Thus one has to be very careful when considering the effectiveness of these various medications.

It should be clear that there is no shortage of potentially effective treatment options for individuals with autism. Yet in the absence of controlled research necessary to draw unambiguous conclusions regarding effectiveness, we are not in a position to fully support any of the treatments described in this chapter. While it is possible to predict which treatments are most likely to survive the test of experimental validation (for example, Floor Time, TEACCH), the effectiveness of these treatments, and their relative effectiveness in relation to other treatments, must remain in question. It is the task of future research to answer these questions and make additional treatments available to this population.

CHAPTER 8

Miracle Cures or Bogus Treatments?

You may feel I've conveyed a sense of negativism about many alternative treatments. If this seems so, it's because I've seen too many parents invest time, money, and hope in treatments that they eventually give up on in cynical dismay. I also worry that time spent pursuing unproven treatments is time that is lost. This is especially a concern in the early years, when intervention is so critical.

—Bryna Siegel, *The World of the Autistic Child* (1996)

In this chapter I look at some purportedly effective treatments for autism that are in fact clearly *in*effective. Bryna Siegel calls treatments like these "think twice" treatments,[1] and I believe she is being too kind. These are "treatments" that both parents and professionals should regard with caution because they have not been found to be effective in treating autism. While some of them (for example, riding horses) are relatively benign in that they do not cause harm, others are more actively detrimental.

As we have seen, it is often the case that the development and dissemination of these treatments are initiated by an anecdotal report, followed by media coverage and the enthusiasm of hopeful parents and clinicians. The lack of an identified cure for autism makes some of these "miraculous" treatments seem all the more attractive. Another factor that should be kept in mind is the "placebo effect" of questionable treatments. This occurs when expectations and hopes lead to perceptions that treatments are resulting in improvements even though they are not. There may also be pressure to perceive changes when one has invested a good deal of time and money in a treatment program.

Facilitated Communication

Perhaps Prometheus' gift of fire to mankind provides the most fitting metaphor for the advent of Facilitated Communication in the worlds of people without speech. (A. M. Donnellan, 1993)[2]

A little suggestion and a little distraction go a long way. (J. Randi, 1993)[3]

The obvious interpretation is that they have a neurologically based problem of expression; in other words, their difficulty with communication appears to be one of praxis rather than cognition. (D. Biklen, 1993)[4]

There is no empirical evidence that there is a strong relationship between apraxia and autism . . . In fact, superior fine-motor skills are often associated with autistic disorder. (G. Green and H. Shane, 1994)[5]

Research tests could intrude upon and upset the communication process. (D. Biklen, 2004, Web site)[6]

That's like saying all pigs can fly but they can only fly when we're not looking. (Morley Safer, *60 Minutes,* 1994)[7]

Perhaps it is best to begin with an example of what can go terribly wrong with unproven treatments. Facilitated Communication (FC) is a prime example of a highly touted, widely adopted, but ultimately bogus treatment for people with autism. It provides an important lesson about the devastating effects that can result when emotions, testimonials, and unbridled belief serve to impede or delay the all-important objective, critical evaluation of a treatment.

There has been nothing in the history of autism treatment to rival the FC phenomenon, which began in the early 1990s and continued for almost ten years. Somewhat surprisingly, FC still has some adherents today.

BACKGROUND AND RATIONALE Facilitated Communication is an augmentative communication system first developed in Australia by Rosemary Crossley, a teacher who worked with children suffering from cerebral palsy in a Melbourne institution in the 1970s. Crossley suspected that some of these children were much more capable than previously thought, but that their physical disabilities prevented them from using normal vocal or manual modes of communication. Perhaps if their physical impairments could be circumvented through an augmentative communication system, the children would be able to exhibit their "true" level of capability. She developed a system where the child was presented with a keyboard, typewriter, or other form of letter display and then provided with physical assistance (in the form of holding their hand or elbow, touching their shoulder, and so on), allowing them to point to letters on the display. Using this technique, the children would pick out the letters needed for spelling out messages. With this "facilitation," these children apparently were able to express themselves in some quite sophisticated messages. Thus it seemed that children who had been trapped in uncooperative bodies could now communicate with the outside world.

Douglas Biklen, a special education professor at Syracuse University, was intrigued by Crossley's work and became convinced that FC could be effective for individuals with autism. He brought FC to the United States, where it caught on and spread like wildfire. Biklen reported that children he observed using FC could engage in communications that were conceptually sophisticated, highly literate, emotionally perceptive, socially skilled, and sometimes purposely humorous. The individuals using FC came up with messages that were grammatically, semantically, and conceptually far more sophisticated than would be expected given the literacy and cognitive levels these individuals had displayed on prior assessments of intellectual ability. In short, they displayed skills that far exceeded their expected level of literacy and overall competence. Children who had been labeled severely retarded and autistic were now telling their parents that they loved them. They were making their wishes known, from the mundane "I want ice cream" to the profound "I want society to accept us for who we are and not to judge us."

According to Biklen, most autistic individuals (and others with severe communication disabilities) are not necessarily severely cognitively impaired. Rather, their intellect may be unimpaired but their ability to communicate by usual means is impeded by difficulties in motor expression, that is, a motor praxis problem. The assistance provided by the facilitator enables the person with autism to communicate despite motor impairment because the hand is steadied, preventing the intrusion of unwanted movements. Further, the facilitation assistance gets around what Biklen calls the "word finding" problems of autism since the facilitator can prevent errors and help the facilitated partner find the correct words to express what he or she means to communicate. The fact that these mute or minimally verbal children can express themselves by using correct, often complex words and grammar is attributed by Biklen to the individual's exposure to written and spoken language from television, movies, family, school, and the like; they apparently learn the complexities and subtleties of linguistic communication without the benefit of formal training.

THE TREATMENT FC is conducted with a "facilitator" (a normally functioning adult, typically a teacher or parent) who assists the student in pointing to, or typing, letters on a computer keyboard, typewriter, or other letter display. In the early stages of FC the facilitator holds the student's hand with the finger extended in a pointing position over the letter display and assists the student first in pointing to or touching a letter, then in withdrawing the hand in preparation for pointing to the next letter, and so on. The facilitator's job is to ensure that the student only points to one letter at a time and also to prevent errors by withdrawing the student's hand before an error occurs. As the student becomes more proficient in pointing to/touching the letters, the facilitator reduces the amount of assistance by holding only the wrist, then maybe the elbow or the sleeve, and then by touching the shoulder. The goal is for the student eventually to be able to type independently with no physical contact from the facilitator.

As one can understand, FC was immediately embraced by many parents and clinicians. This form of treatment enjoyed tremendous popularity with parents and teachers of autistic individuals largely because it "showed" that these individuals were much more intelligent and perceptive than anyone had believed. With the use of FC, it appeared that even those individuals who tested in the severely retarded and/or severely autistic range could communicate with others, express deep emotions, write poetry, compose essays, engage in philosophical discussions, declare political affiliations, and advocate for better treatment and resources for people with disabilities. They were much more literate, mathematically skilled, insightful, perceptive, and socially aware than all the professionals had suspected. FC seemed to be the "silver bullet" that parents, teachers, and clinicians had hoped and dreamed of for so many years. Now the minds of these severely handicapped people could be opened to us, and communication was possible. For many this completely changed the typical conceptualization of autism. According to the proponents of FC, people with autism were not cognitively impaired, or unable to communicate, or even socially uninvolved.

Imagine the tremendous impact of this new treatment. One television show, ABC's *Prime Time Live,* called FC "a miracle."[8] Joyful parents believed that their hopes and dreams for their child had finally come true. Enthusiastic teachers found that their charges were now attaining unexpected levels of literacy and competence. Conferences and training workshops in FC proliferated, and Syracuse University established the Facilitated Communication Institute, headed by Biklen, to further promote FC. Parents and teachers from all over the country were caught up in this intoxicating movement. Many of them became major and even rabid advocates, fiercely defending FC against critics who doubted its efficacy.

DOES IT WORK? No. FC is truly unusual in that it enjoyed tremendous popularity and widespread use *before* it was ever put to the scrutiny applied to other new treatments. It is amazing to recall that thousands of autistic and other language-impaired individuals were being "facilitated," new schools were established, training workshops were conducted, and parents were eagerly learning how to facilitate with their children—all without any objective validation of this treatment. Many existing classroom programs tossed out most of their old curricula so they could use FC. This blind acceptance and use of a new treatment is akin to widespread use of a brand-new vaccine or drug before it has passed rigorous testing and approval by the FDA.

The popular media had a field day. Numerous television programs, newspaper stories, and magazine articles touted the new miracle that was allowing autistic children to escape the prison of their autism. Children who had been considered severely autistic and/or retarded were now being placed in chronologically age-appropriate classrooms with typical children. Children who were not toilet-trained and could not speak or communicate in any way other than FC were placed in algebra and literature classes.

Was all of this too good to be true? Absolutely. In fact, it turns out that not only is FC not a valid means of communication, but it has been associated with major tragedies in the lives of families with children who were treated with this method.

When FC first came to the attention of researchers in the field of autism, it was viewed with extreme skepticism. To those of us who had conducted treatment research for many years and who had a strong background in the study of autism and its characteristics, the whole thing just did not make sense. I remember receiving a large number of phone calls from parents, teachers, and other researchers asking me if I thought there was anything to this treatment. I said that I could not imagine it would work, but since I had seen no research on the treatment, I could not categorically rule it out. Yet it took some time for the research to get under way. This was due in part to the fact that any scientist or clinician who expressed doubt about FC was subject to angry and persistent harassment from FC proponents, including those parents and teachers who strongly advocated the approach. These people did not want to hear anything negative.

When FC was finally put to the test, it failed miserably. It took little time for the first studies to discover what was happening, and the house of cards began to collapse. These studies found that it was not the student who was communicating; it was in fact the facilitator.[9] The authorship of the messages that had been attributed to the autistic individuals was now placed in doubt.

There are two main types of studies that have been used to determine the authorship of facilitated messages. One of these involves a situation where the facilitator and the autistic student are shown the same versus different pictures. Then, using FC, the student is asked to type out the name of the picture. When both student and facilitator are shown the *same* picture, the student typically types the correct response. Yet when the facilitator and the student are shown *different* pictures and each cannot see the picture presented to the other, the student typically types out the name of the picture the *facilitator* has seen. Thus it is apparent that the facilitator, not the student, is providing the response. In another type of test, called the "message passing" test, the student is taken outside the presence of the facilitator and presented with some information such as a picture of an object or the name of a pet. The facilitator does not have access to this information. Then the child is returned to the facilitator and is asked to indicate what he has seen or heard. Almost invariably, the student is unable to provide the information. Thus in the many studies conducted so far on FC, the findings indicate that the communications come not from the student but from the facilitator. In the few studies that have claimed success with FC, the methodological limitations are so severe as to make any conclusions ambiguous at best.[10] In fact, some have labeled Facilitated Communication the "cold fusion" of social services.

One of the most bizarre claims made by FC proponents was that autistic individuals communicating via FC could read the minds of their facilitators. It was even claimed by a professional in the autism field that the success of FC indicated these autistic people had a "well-developed sixth sense that allows them both to understand what others think, feel, or know, and to transmit their own thoughts to other nonverbal acquaintances, and sometimes to their facilitators."[11] In fact, in a published book, this author and a colleague provide an example of such a telepathic situation: "A young man we know told his facilitator what her high school nickname was, and that she had mourned a deceased relative who had been a musician. He was correct in every detail, including the instrument her uncle played, and her feelings about him."[12] While some FC adherents might wish to look at this situation as showing that the young man was reading the mind of the facilitator, I believe this strongly supports the idea that it was in fact the facilitator who was authoring the message. It seems far more likely to me that the facilitator knew the information communicated in the message than that the young man was reading her mind.

When confronted with the scientific evidence indicating the facilitator's authorship of communications, Douglas Biklen countered that FC was likely to fail such tests because in order for the facilitation to work, the student and facilitator must share a feeling of trust. Testing FC means that the trust is being questioned (with what Biklen calls "confrontational testing"), and this is upsetting to the student. Under these confrontational situations, the student will not communicate. Thus, Biklen claimed, FC will not work if it is tested—a position that prompted the sarcastic comment by *60 Minutes* correspondent Morley Safer quoted earlier. Saying that a treatment cannot be tested should raise a huge red flag, since every other form of treatment, whether medical or behavioral, must stand up to the scrutiny of objective validation. Biklen and other FC proponents also claim that under "artificial" test situations the student becomes anxious and unable to communicate. However, these arguments carry little weight when one considers that the students seem to be perfectly content while using FC during the testing process, and the tests are stopped if the student appears to be at all upset. Moreover, Biklen and others frequently exhibit students using FC in front of audiences of hundreds of people. It is likely that if anxiety produces failure, then failure would surely occur in those situations.

There are also theoretical and conceptual issues associated with FC that do not hold up to scrutiny. How can it be that individuals who have shown themselves to be so cognitively and linguistically impaired are able to produce messages with correct word spelling, grammar, abstract concepts, and factual information that is far above their assumed ability? FC proponents refer to this aspect of FC communications as "unexpected literacy" and claim that these individuals pick up the language from their environment. Yet often these communications are far above the level of what would be produced by *typical* children of the same age. Why is it that these autistic children should be able to learn from their environment much faster than their typical peers? Shouldn't we expect a child who can produce essays and poetry via FC to be able to label a tree?

Further, two of the tenets upon which FC is based have not been substantiated. First, Biklen points to the "motor praxis" problems of autistic individuals as the reason they require facilitation to communicate. However, such motor praxis problems have never been associated with autism. In addition, Biklen describes the "word finding" difficulties of this population. Again, word finding difficulties, per se, have never been associated with autism.

Another issue is that observation of facilitated interactions often shows that the individual being "facilitated" does not even look at the letter display. How can the child type coherent messages without looking at the keyboard or first anchoring her hand on specific keys? Even a skilled professional typist cannot do this. It is also interesting to observe that when the child may be looking elsewhere, the facilitator is watching the keyboard intently. In fact, it has also been demonstrated that if the facilitator cannot see the keyboard, the autistic individual cannot communicate. This is of course another indication that the facilitator is the one producing the messages.

It is important to point out that facilitators are not evil people who are trying to pull a fast one. Rather, it appears they are unaware that they are in fact the ones generating the communications. When confronted with the evidence (which often means demonstrating their own role in the facilitated message), most express surprise and even shock. They truly seem to believe that they are just a conduit for the child's communication. What is less clear is why these facilitators produce the messages. Some have stated that they believe there is pressure to be successful, and that FC training workshops emphasize success and the need to assume the student has unexpected literacy skills. Some have even referred to the "cult" mentality of the training programs.

Unfortunately, it took some time for the debunking of FC to have an impact on its use. Despite the research results, parents and teachers stuck by FC and defended it fiercely against the research that so clearly demonstrated it was not what it claimed to be. (In fact, I can remember wanting to send some of my graduate students to an FC workshop to learn more about the process. However, we were told that "no researchers" were allowed at the workshop.) These parents and teachers had invested their hopes and dreams in this treatment and were convinced that it worked, at least for their children. Finally calmer and more reasoned attitudes prevailed, but not before FC had caused a tremendous amount of damage.

THE DARK SIDE OF FACILITATED COMMUNICATION   Dr. Howard Shane of Children's Hospital and Harvard Medical School tallied up the serious negative consequences of Facilitated Communication, exposing what he calls the "dark side" of FC.[13] FC may be bogus, but it is definitely not benign. Probably the most serious adverse effect of FC is that it resulted in many cases of false accusations of physical and sexual abuse. Almost as soon as FC became widely accepted as a "genuine" means of communication for individuals with serious cognitive and communicative disabilities, there arose reports of abuse that were communicated by these individuals via FC. These accusations were chilling and resulted in many instances of children being removed from their homes and family members being jailed and charged with serious crimes. Although many courts demanded demonstrations of the validity of FC (which, of course, it failed), and charges were eventually dropped in the vast majority of cases, the fact remains that families were torn apart, financially ruined, and emotionally devastated.

We know that the facilitators were the ones putting the words in the mouths of these individuals. But why would they do that? We do not know for sure, and even the facilitators who eventually realized that they had in fact generated the messages do not know. Many have been truly devastated by the fact that their own behavior may have led to some of the family tragedies resulting from messages they "facilitated." One possibility is that there was a certain expectation factor. It is widely recognized that individuals with severe disabilities are more prone to being abused than typically functioning individuals. Perhaps the facilitators had learned this and were almost expecting this information. Whatever the reasons may be, many former facilitators involved in these false abuse cases have to live with the guilt over the misery their behavior, though unintended, caused.

There are a number of other serious negative effects of FC. First, one must consider that autistic or other communicatively impaired children are being deprived of an appropriate and effective education if they are spending their time "facilitating," particularly if they are doing so in a classroom that is ill-suited to their needs. These children do not have the time to waste. Moreover, it is almost certain that the student will experience failure in a variety of ways in these inappropriate educational environments. Second, vast financial and labor resources have been diverted from other, more appropriate, programs to pay for providing FC. Third, some students with severe disabilities have been allowed, via FC, to make important "decisions" concerning their educational programs, medical treatment, and living arrangements. In many cases these decisions have been inappropriate. A final negative effect, perhaps one of the most serious, is the dashed hopes of the parents and families who had such a large emotional investment in FC.

It is only fair to mention that FC procedures, such as gradually withdrawn physical support, have been effective in teaching some individuals independent typing skills. While this has allowed these people to communicate, they do so at their expected level of cognitive and literacy ability.

I have included a rather extensive discussion of FC in order to show the widespread negative effects that a bogus, unproven treatment can have. While FC may be one of the most egregious of such treatments, there are other forms of treatment that to date lack critical validation.

Rapid Prompting

Another purported treatment currently experiencing popularity is the "Rapid Prompting Method" (RPM). Many have noted that this treatment shares some of the features of FC in that the autistic child communicates via writing or typing and demonstrates unexpected levels of literacy. The treatment method was developed by Soma Mukhopadhyay to teach her son, Tito, to communicate. RPM involves constant work with the child. The therapist spends almost all of the child's waking moments working with the child—prompting, prodding, talking, and teaching. The child is never allowed to engage in self-stimulatory behavior or any other inappropriate behavior.

The reported results of RPM are all anecdotal and involve few cases. The reports describe communications that are far more sophisticated than anyone might have expected from such severely autistic children. To date, there are no scientifically derived data to support the treatment's effectiveness. However, unlike FC, this treatment may in fact have some effectiveness, although I suspect that any positive effects there might be would be due to what is essentially a form of intensive behavioral training. But claims that the treatment is "miraculous" or "new" are indeed unwarranted.

Psychotherapies

Psychodynamic Treatment

The many fascinating stories in the book [*Love Is Not Enough*] invariably have happy endings: the child is helped, the source of the trouble is located. But surely there must have been some failures, some kids who just didn't respond to treatment, or else shifted their symptoms to new hideouts as the Mounties closed in. It would be refreshing to hear about the big ones that got away, and perhaps instructive as well . . . It might have been something even more useful if its author had risen above, or sunk below, the foible of omnipotence. (Dwight Macdonald in a review of Bettelheim's book, quoted in R. Pollak, 1997)[14]

Psychotherapy with autistic children of the kind designed to provide insight has not proved effective and in the light of our knowledge about autism is unlikely to do so. (National Institute of Mental Health, 1975)[15]

In view of these problems, the continuing use of psychoanalysis as a treatment for autism is dismaying, and, like the experience with Facilitated Communication, it demonstrates how unreliable subjective opinions promoted by some professionals can be. (T. Smith, 1996)[16]

BACKGROUND AND RATIONALE   As discussed earlier in this book, the first form of "treatment" for children with autism was based on a psychodynamic model. This kind of treatment began in the 1940s when autism was first identified as a specific diagnostic entity. In the 1940s and 1950s, and even into the 1960s, the psychodynamic model was essentially the only form of treatment available for these children. The popularity of the psychodynamic model reflects the prevailing psychological theory of the time rather than any demonstrated effectiveness.

Psychodynamic treatment is based on the conceptualization that autism is the result of the child's withdrawal from an environment that is seen as hostile, threatening, and dangerous. Because of parental psychopathology (particularly on the part of the mother), the child's normal frustrations and normal minor episodes of withdrawal are misinterpreted by the parent as rejection. This leads to an extreme negative reaction by the parent. Rather than responding to these normal withdrawals with supporting behaviors such as cuddling and feeding, these mothers respond with hostility and rejection. These responses in turn are interpreted by the child as dangerous and even as potentially fatal (that is, the parent wishes the child were dead). Because of this fear of a threatening environment, the child withdraws into what Bettelheim called a "chronic autistic disease"—or the "empty fortress" of autism. This involves an arrest in ego development, since the child's libidinal energies are spent in defending against the hostile environment.[17]

THE TREATMENT   There are two forms of treatment based on this model: the first is for the child and the second for the parents. As noted earlier, the main proponent of the psychodynamic approach to the treatment of autism was Bruno Bettelheim, who headed the Sonia Shankman Orthogenic School at the University of Chicago. Bettelheim pointed out that in most institutions the basic approach is to encourage the child to see the world as it really is, which is precisely what the autistic child is incapable of doing. Instead, he proposed, what is needed is to create for the child a world completely different from the threatening one which he has abandoned in despair, and one which he can enter exactly as he is.

The treatment involves removing the child from the home environment and from the parents, who are deemed responsible for the autistic withdrawal; the child is placed in a residential setting with "surrogate" parents who provide the supportive, accepting environment which the child has been deprived of in the original home. These surrogate parents (that is, the therapists) provide a setting within which the child is allowed to express feelings and engage in activities with absolutely no fear of the frustration and pressures that characterized the home environment. The child is encouraged to gradually reach out for experiences and to develop a strong concept of self and of the world. All of the child's attempts to reach out and grow are met with love, acceptance, and patience. Behaviors associated with withdrawing into autism, such as aggression, tantrums, and the like, are also met with love and acceptance. In addition, such attempts by the child to reach out are met with a reciprocal response from the therapist, which serves to show the child that her behavior has an effect on others. Thus the child's sense of her own power, lost in the early days with the natural parents, is revived. Such a step is considered essential to the development of autonomy.

As an example of the importance of autonomy and how it is encouraged in this form of treatment, consider Bettelheim's description of one of his patients, "Laurie." This child's withdrawal included the refusal of food. On one occasion, Laurie showed independence by reaching for, and eating, a piece of chocolate. After this, her therapist attempted to feed her another piece of chocolate, an act greeted by Laurie with a bite on the therapist's hand. This was interpreted by Bettelheim as a positive sign because it indicated Laurie's newly asserted independence. The behavior was considered very encouraging and was readily accepted as appropriate.

Treatment based on the psychodynamic model is not well described in terms of specific procedures. Rather, the children are encouraged through a variety of means to engage in any behavior to express their growing autonomy. For example, the child would probably not be toilet-trained since this would impose the will of others and might involve potentially frustrating limits. Thus the therapist might encourage the child to eliminate at random times and in random locations.

As treatment continues, and the child's expressions of autonomy are met with acceptance, love, and understanding, he gains a sense of selfness. Other procedures such as tactile and kinesthetic stimulation are used to further encourage growth and the recognition of the presence of nonthreatening others. This leads the child to a sense of trust in people and the environment—a sense very different from the one that originally sent the child into his autistic state. There is no longer any need for the child to defend himself against reality.

Treatment for the parents consists of psychoanalysis aimed at identifying the underlying psychopathology that led to the parents' rejection of their child. The goal is for the parents to gain insight into the underlying unconscious and intrapsychic conflicts that have crippled their parenting of the child. To achieve this the parents are placed in intensive psychoanalysis, often for a prolonged period of time.

DOES IT WORK? There is no objective, empirical evidence that treatment based on a psychodynamic model is effective for children with autism. Bettelheim, as the main proponent and practitioner of this form of treatment, never provided any hard data to support his claims that the children improved. Rather, he documented his treatment effectiveness by providing dramatic case histories of some of his patients. Looking at these cases now, it is apparent that many of the children Bettelheim treated would not receive a diagnosis of autism today. For example, he described some children with advanced delusional systems. One such child, "Joey the Mechanical Boy," had an elaborate delusional system in which he viewed himself as a machine. While such delusional systems are frequently found in children with schizophrenia, they are not characteristic of autism. Schizophrenic children may be more likely to benefit from psychodynamic, language-based treatment. Others have challenged Bettelheim's claims of significant improvement in light of his use of selection criteria in admitting children into his program.

Many arguments have been presented that criticize the use of treatments based on the psychodynamic approach. First and foremost among these criticisms is that these treatments are based on an erroneous theoretical assumption. The view that parents are the cause of autism has been thoroughly and repeatedly discounted. Moreover, there is no evidence that these children have been exposed to the types of negative conditions that psychoanalysts consider important in the development of autism.

Second, attempts to empirically evaluate treatments based on this approach have not supported its effectiveness. The very nature of psychodynamic treatment, with its inferential terminology (for example, use of terms such as "ego" and "libidinal tendencies") and its lack of precision in describing procedures, precludes putting the theory to an empirical test. Indeed, systematic evaluation has been impeded by the failure of Bettelheim and other adherents to specify in any detail what is involved in the treatment and how it is to be implemented. Further, descriptions of outcome and evaluation criteria are similarly lacking. Despite these impediments to evaluation, some have nonetheless tried, but these evaluations have failed to demonstrate that this treatment model is effective for children with autism. In fact, as early as 1975 a report by the National Institute of Mental Health summarized the results of many years of research and concluded that this form of therapy has not proved to be effective for this population.[18]

Another serious problem with this treatment approach and the theory on which it is based is the needless blaming of the parents for their child's disorder. Such a cruel and misguided idea has caused immeasurable pain to parents who already have to cope with the difficulties of raising a child with a profound disability. Another problem is that the permissive, noncontingent environment provided to the children in psychodynamic treatments may be counterproductive. The acceptance and even encouragement of inappropriate behaviors, such as aggression or ritualistic behavior, may have the effect of rewarding such behaviors. A further problem is that the exclusion of parents from the treatment process is counterproductive, since parents can be such an effective and important resource in treating autism.

Despite the lack of empirical validation and all the other problems associated with psychodynamic treatment, there are still adherents of this approach. They are in the minority, however, and psychodynamic treatment is not considered to be a main treatment approach for autism today.

Holding Therapy

BACKGROUND AND RATIONALE Another treatment based on psychodynamic theory was developed by Dr. Martha Welch, a child psychiatrist from New York, as described in her book, *Holding Time*.[19] An additional theoretical foundation for Holding Therapy was the ethological perspective of Nobel Laureate Niko Tinbergen, who emphasized the symbiotic relationship between mother and child and believed that autism represents a failure in this relationship. Despite the fact that the psychogenic theory of autism had long been refuted, both Tinbergen and Welch proposed that children with autism fail to "bond" with their parents and consequently retreat into their autistic world. This view is very like the more traditional (and outmoded) psychodynamic theory advocated by Bettelheim and others in that the child's retreat into his autistic world is thought to be caused by adverse influences in the early social environment. This withdrawal from human contact is seen as the manifestation of the child's social rejection. Welch posits that autism represents a disturbed attachment to the parent, especially the mother, and that the child's lack of responsiveness and active withdrawal are the child's ways of defending against the ruptured bond with the mother. Using intense physical contact, the mother can break through the withdrawal and create strong emotional ties with the child.

THE TREATMENT Based on these theoretical underpinnings, Holding Therapy involves forcing the child to abandon his social withdrawal and to accept the warm, social contact of the mother. To accomplish this, the parent (usually the mother) places the child in a very tight embrace and maintains the embrace until the child stops struggling, is calm, and engages in eye contact with the parent. Since it is quite likely that the child will not enjoy being restrained in a social embrace, it is common for the child to react by crying and struggling. However difficult it may be, the parent must continue the "holding" until the child complies. Some forms of holding therapy also call for the parent to shout to the child that the parent loves her but that she must come out of the autistic aloneness.

Holding Therapy sessions are typically conducted for 20 to 45 minutes, but of course the length of time is mainly dependent upon the child's behavior. The faster the child settles down and complies, the shorter will be the sessions. Practitioners of Holding Therapy note that the sessions tend to get shorter as the treatment continues since the child learns that he can escape the holding by complying.

DOES IT WORK? It is extremely unlikely that Holding Therapy is effective with autistic children. While proponents of the treatment have reported some cases of children who have improved, these reports are largely anecdotal. There have been no empirically sound studies documenting the effectiveness of the treatment. Moreover, this is not a benign treatment. I have a vivid recollection of witnessing a Holding Therapy session (also sometimes called "rage reduction") when I was a graduate student. This session was conducted in a university clinic to show the staff and students how the treatment worked. A mother came in for the session with her 5-year-old autistic son. The child was very unhappy to start with, which was understandable in light of the unfamiliar situation and all the people standing around. The psychologist conducting the demonstration instructed the mother to hold the child face-to-face with her, very tightly, and not to release her grip until told to do so. Not surprisingly, the child began screaming loudly, crying, and struggling violently. It was excruciating to watch the panicked child and the equally panicked mother go through this exercise. Finally the mother's strength (and probably her will) gave out, and the session was terminated before the child complied. I was not alone in my reaction to this "treatment," and it was never again conducted or demonstrated at the clinic. It was pretty quickly dismissed as not only useless, but overly cruel as well.

Advocates of Holding Therapy cite instances of its effectiveness, but in those cases where an effect is seen it is likely that behavioral principles, as opposed to psychodynamic principles, were responsible. There are two behavioral principles that might explain any treatment effects of Holding Therapy. From a respondent conditioning point of view, one could argue that a contact-sensitive child might learn to tolerate physical contact as a result of desensitization. That is, the child would become "used" to the contact so that it no longer bothered him. From an operant point of view, one could consider the successful use of Holding Therapy as an instance of negative reinforcement, where the child learns that he can escape a negative situation by complying. However, even if Holding Therapy were effective as a kind of behavioral conditioning, it would certainly never be advocated by a behaviorally-oriented clinician. The use of such an aversive procedure is not only unnecessary (because other treatments are available) but also ethically abhorrent.

Holding Therapy made a bit of a splash in the 1980s when it first became somewhat popular. However, it is infrequently used today in the United States, although it continues to be popular in Europe.

Options Therapy

BACKGROUND AND RATIONALE   "Options" Therapy has its roots in the experience of one family. Barry and Samahria Kaufman concluded that they essentially cured their severely autistic son, Raun, by providing individualized loving care for most of his waking hours. They wrote about their son and their experiences in a book, *Son-Rise,* published in 1976.[20] The book gave detailed descriptions of their intensive interaction with their son. The basis for the treatment is the idea that rather than trying to force the autistic child to join our world, the parent should join the child's world as a way of building a bridge between the two worlds. Once this is accomplished, the child now has the encouragement to abandon his autistic world and to cross the bridge and come into our world.

The Kaufmans are convinced that this intervention transformed their mute, withdrawn child with an IQ of under 30 into a "highly verbal, socially interactive youngster with a near-genius IQ."[21] In fact, Raun went on to graduate from college and became the director of an education center for children.

THE TREATMENT   The central idea of Options Therapy is for the parent to join the autistic child's world. This is accomplished by essentially following the child's lead and doing what the child does. Joining in the child's repetitive and stereotyped behavior is seen as the "key to unlocking the mystery of these behaviors."[22] It is also seen as facilitating eye contact, social development, and the inclusion of others in play. The treatment encourages parents to utilize the child's own motivation to enhance learning, using a high-energy, positive interaction style, and being completely nonjudgmental about the child's behavior. No demands are placed on the child.

In the course of this treatment, the parent spends most of the child's waking hours in one-on-one, high-intensity interaction with the child in a small room. The parent imitates everything the child does, including engaging in self-stimulatory behavior. There are no judgments, no redirecting; the parent just mirrors the child's actions until the child realizes that the parent is there and that their behaviors are similar. The parent is taught to expect a breakthrough where the child will note the connection between himself and the parent and will emerge to cross the bridge to the parent's world.

DOES IT WORK?   Probably not. Again we have a treatment that has not been put to the test, so there are no scientifically valid data to support the Kaufmans' claims of effectiveness. While the Kaufmans' Web site states that the treatment leads to "dramatic improvement in all areas of learning, development, communication, and skill acquisition," there is not one shred of hard evidence to support this claim. There are, of course, the usual anecdotes and testimonials which, as we have seen, are of questionable value in evaluating the effectiveness of a treatment.

In addition to the lack of empirical validation for Options Therapy, there are other troubling features of the program. One problem is that, given what we know about autism and its treatment, the program just does not make sense. As Siegel points out, just mirroring the child's actions is not likely to lead to proper forward development.[23] Typical children grow and develop because the social environment not only mirrors the child but expands and extends the behaviors to help the child progress to more complex and interactive behaviors.

Another question involves the original case of Raun and his "cure" with this approach. Doubts have arisen about Raun's true condition, and there has been speculation that in fact he was never autistic.[24] Since we have no objective verification of his diagnosis, it is difficult to attribute his later success in life to this treatment. Of course, it may be that he *was* autistic and that this treatment indeed did help him. But, as we have already seen, just because a treatment *may* have helped one child, this does not necessarily mean it will help other autistic children.

Another rather serious problem with this treatment approach was brought home to me shortly after the book *Son-Rise* was made into a network TV movie. The movie depicted the treatment and showed how Raun was helped by his parents who spent hour upon hour, every day, sitting in a room mimicking Raun's actions. When the parents could not be there, they arranged for friends to come to their home and work with Raun. The TV show was barely over before my phone began ringing off the hook. Was it true? Was it a miracle? The most upsetting calls came from parents who had neither the time nor the money to provide this treatment. It was obvious that the Kaufmans had the ability to spend a great deal of time at home to be with their son—a luxury not all families have, especially if both parents work. Some of the parents who called me were in tears because they felt they were "dooming" their child, since there was no way for them to provide the treatment. Moreover, the TV movie depicted other forms of treatment such as behavioral interventions as punishing and cruel, while the Kaufmans' treatment was shown to be loving and effective. In fact, the Autism Society of America was so alarmed by the content of the movie (which had been prescreened for them) that they attempted to prevent the network from airing the movie.

In addition to the questionable claims of the Options approach, one must also consider the large expense of this treatment. The "beginning course" involves the parents coming to the Options center for a week, without their child. This costs $2000 per parent (plus travel expenses). The intensive program involves both the parents and the child and costs $11,500 for one week. This can be a significant drawback for many families, especially considering that the treatment has not been proven to be effective.

Animal Therapies

BACKGROUND AND RATIONALE   There have been a number of treatments for autism based on interaction with animals. These include riding horses, swimming with dolphins, interacting with dogs or cats, and otherwise bringing autistic children into contact with animals. The use of animals with autistic children is not a new concept; it follows a long-standing tradition of work involving the use of animals to treat individuals with disabilities. The theory behind the treatment for autism is that while these children have difficulty dealing with humans, they may find it easier to interact with animals, which are nonjudgmental and nondemanding. The confidence these children gain from relating to animals should then carry over to human interactions.

THE TREATMENT   It is a stretch to call these sessions "treatments"; essentially they involve interacting with the animals in a format appropriate for the specific species. Working with horses, probably the most common of these treatments, involves having the child come close to the horse, pet the animal, and eventually learn to ride. Following this the child may learn to care for the horse, thus learning some of the responsibility of caring for another being.

The dolphin treatment is somewhat more difficult, since dolphins are rarely as tame and predictable as domesticated horses. Moreover, the dolphin treatment involves not only the animal, but water. Luckily, many children with autism enjoy being in the water and swimming, and these children are considered ideal candidates for swimming in an enclosed area with dolphins. The children in some cases may pet the dolphins while they are swimming with them.

Working with dogs, cats, or other animals is not as common as a treatment for autism, or at least this does not get as much attention as the treatment involving horses and dolphins. However, the idea is the same: interaction with an accepting, nonjudgmental partner.

DOES IT WORK? Not surprisingly, there is no evidence to support the effectiveness of any of these "treatments" involving animals. No one has really subjected these treatments to a well-controlled test. Fortunately, very few of the providers of these treatments claim that they are curing autism. Yet many of these practitioners do make claims that go far beyond what they can prove. Thus we hear of autistic children becoming more social, more aware of their surroundings, and more communicative as a result of sessions with animals. Some reports talk about major "breakthroughs" which, although heartwarming, are typically unsubstantiated.

In the end, the question of whether riding horses or swimming with dolphins constitutes an effective treatment for autism is not terribly important. This is undoubtedly why no major research projects have been directed at the question. In contrast to the situation with treatments like Facilitated Communication, few people advocate pet therapy as anything more than a pleasant adjunct to whatever other treatments the child is receiving. That is, any child might enjoy and benefit from interacting with animals, and why shouldn't autistic children have the same opportunities as other children? Basically, the view is that "it can't hurt." However, as with other treatments discussed here, the cost may be a significant factor. Playing with dolphins is definitely not cheap.

The treatments discussed in this chapter are only a few of the better-known bogus treatments for autism. I could have included many more, since almost every day brings another dubious "treatment" to light. Many of these are highly touted and get their 15 minutes of fame in the media, but they ultimately and mercifully fade away. We must hope that they fade away before serious damage is done. Some of these treatments are almost humorous; some might make logical sense; some seem geared only toward making money for those providing them. But it is always a case of buyer and user beware. If a treatment sounds too miraculous to be true, if the supporting "evidence" is essentially testimonials, if there is no supporting research to back the purported effectiveness, then my advice is to hold onto your wallet and walk away. We should have no tolerance for these bogus "treatments." Certainly children with autism and their families deserve better.

CHAPTER 9

Early Intervention, "Recovery," and "Best" Treatment

Follow-up data from an intensive, long-term experimental treatment group ($n = 19$) showed that 47 percent achieved normal intellectual and educational functioning, with normal-range IQ scores and successful first grade performance in public schools. . . . These data promise a major reduction in the emotional hardships of families with autistic children.

—O. Ivar Lovaas, in *Journal of Consulting and Clinical Psychology* (1987)

Based on these issues, the most conservative conclusion to be drawn is that it is not possible to determine the effects of this [Lovaas EIP] intervention.

—Eric Schopler, Andrew Short, and Gary Mesibov, in *Journal of Consulting and Clinical Psychology* (1989)

The claims have given rise to controversy, sometimes heated, but existing empirical evidence does not provide a resolution. There are reasons for being cautious about the acceptance of these strong claims (if only because of the uncertainties of diagnosis in very young children and because the claims of "cure" run counter

to both clinical experience and what might be expected from prevailing theories).

—Michael Rutter, in *Journal of Autism and Developmental Disorders*
(1996)

Although the path has not always been smooth, the development of
empirically proven treatments such as those described in Chapter 6
has had an enormous impact on the lives of autistic individuals and
those who care for, and about, them. Of course, we could not expect that there would be consensus about treatment approaches,
and in the late 1980s there arose what has probably been the most
controversial of all issues regarding the treatment of autism: Can
the intensive application of behavioral treatments during the first
few years of a child's life lead to recovery from autism? The arguments over this issue have been impassioned, emotional, and acrimonious, and the stakes are extremely high.

Is "Recovery" from Autism Possible?

The issue of "recovery" from autism was instigated by a published
report by Ivar Lovaas, a psychologist at UCLA, in 1987.[1] In this
study three groups of very young autistic children (under 41 months
of age at the start of treatment) served as subjects. One group, the
experimental group ($n = 19$), received on average more than 40
hours per week of one-on-one discrete trial training (DTT) treatment delivered by trained student therapists in the children's home,
school, and community. This treatment also included the systematic
application of physical aversives for some of the children. In addition, the parents were taught to work with their children as part of
the intensive treatment. A second group of children, Control Group
1 ($n = 19$), received the same treatment but at a lesser intensity
(fewer than 10 hours per week) and without the application of

aversives. A third group, Control Group 2 ($n = 21$), did not receive any behavioral treatment. After two years the groups were evaluated. The results were quite impressive: 47 percent of the children receiving the intensive treatment achieved "normal functioning," defined by IQ scores in the normal range and successful passage through first grade in a regular public school classroom, and 43 percent of this group showed substantial progress, although not to the level of "normal" functioning. Thus fully 90 percent of the children receiving the intensive early intervention were reported to have very positive outcomes. In contrast, the outcome for the children in the control groups was poor: only one child in Control Group 2 and no children in Control Group 1 achieved the criteria designated in the study as "normal functioning." Moreover, the children in the experimental (high intensity) group were followed up at between 9 and 19 years of age, and it was reported that they maintained their gains in IQ and that their adaptive behavior and personality functioning (as reported by their parents) were normal.[2]

This study was truly a bombshell. Parents, teachers, clinicians, and others in the autism community could barely contain their enthusiasm. Essentially the message was that many of these children could be "cured," and this was certainly a far cry from the doom-and-gloom prognosis most commonly associated with the diagnosis of autism. However, while parents and clinicians rejoiced over the findings, many in the scientific community were far less impressed. Immediately after its publication, the Lovaas "cure study" (as many called it) came under very close scrutiny and criticism. While no one doubted that DTT was an effective treatment for these children or that treatment at such an early age would be beneficial, the extent of the improvement of the children in the Lovaas Early Intervention Project (EIP) study and the lofty claims of "normal" functioning were greeted with much skepticism by researchers. In particular, several concerns were raised regarding methodology and interpretation.[3]

Probably the most serious concern was the fact that the children who participated in the research study were not randomly assigned to the treatment groups. The children were assigned in matched pairs to the two treatment groups based on the availability of trained student therapists and on the geographic proximity of the families to UCLA. Failure to randomly assign subjects to groups is a major problem and one that violates the scientific integrity of an experimental design. Since there were systematic differences (staff availability and distance from UCLA) between the two groups, in addition to the intensity of the intervention, one cannot say for certain that it was the treatment variable per se that accounted for the group differences in outcome.

Another major concern was the definition of "normal" functioning. Lovaas used normal-range IQ scores and successful performance in first grade as the measures of normal functioning. However, many were quick to point out that a child could exhibit autistic behaviors such as social deficits, compulsive behaviors, and restricted interests yet still have a normal IQ and remain in a regular first-grade classroom. (In fact, anyone who has observed a regular first-grade class can attest to the wide variety of children in attendance.) Although Lovaas stated that the teachers described these children as "indistinguishable" from their normal peers, no data were presented to support this claim. Moreover, using parental reports to assess adaptive functioning and absence of psychopathology is inadequate. While parental reports are important, it is essential to include other assessments that can corroborate these reports. After all, the parents were not naive regarding their child's participation in the research, and their reports may have unintentionally been based on their knowledge of this participation or on what they knew the researchers wanted to hear.

There were additional concerns involving methodology. Many researchers have argued that the children in the Lovaas study were in fact not representative of the population of children with autism.

The study had very specific inclusion criteria, including a rather unusual metric of mental age ("prorated mental age," which calculated the child's mental age as a function of his chronological age at the time of test administration) and different levels of acceptable chronological age based on the presence or absence of echolalic speech. Using these criteria, Lovaas reported that he excluded 15 percent of the children referred to the UCLA clinic. In contrast, Schopler and his colleagues reported that if they used the same criteria, they would exclude approximately 57 percent of the children referred to their program.[4] It is largely recognized that the children receiving treatment in the EIP study were higher-functioning than most children with autism and in fact might be expected to have a better treatment prognosis. Whatever the specific level of exclusion may be, the point is that by excluding a percentage of referred children, one is not sampling the true population of autism. Thus, the generality of these findings to other children across the autism spectrum is not known. Further, the children in the high-intensity treatment group were about 6 months younger than the children in the lower-intensity group. This fact alone causes concern, since it may be this age difference that accounted for the differential outcome between the two groups.

Others have criticized the Lovaas study for using different tests of cognitive functioning at different points in the research. The children were assessed at post-treatment and follow-up with different instruments than were used at pre-treatment. Since the assessments were not consistent across time, comparisons across these time points are uninterpretable, and this seriously weakens any conclusions that might be drawn. In addition, it was reported that the standardized tests were not administered in the same manner at pre-treatment and at follow-up. Again, the lack of consistency across time points makes it difficult to draw any conclusions.

Another problem that has serious implications for the practicality, availability, and feasibility of this early intensive intervention is the fact that Lovaas and his colleagues emphasize that in order to effectively implement the treatment, therapists require extensive training, including hands-on supervision by highly trained personnel. They also say that such training may take six months to a year to complete. This being the case, one wonders how likely it is that any particular family would be able to obtain this treatment, and whether common early intervention programs could implement the program with fidelity. In fact, it is of great concern to many that the "Lovaas" treatment may only be available from a very few sources.[5] Of course, there is the additional issue of who will pay for this training.

Perhaps the most serious reservation about the conclusions of the Lovaas study is the fact that no one has been able to repeat these optimistic results. Until others who are not associated with the Lovaas group and who have no vested interest in the study outcome can replicate these results, one must be very cautious. Although there have been attempts to replicate the Lovaas study, these have not completely reproduced the variables from the original study (for example, they have involved different parameters of the treatment or a different population of children with autism), and none have reported the extremely impressive gains reported by Lovaas.[6] Moreover, if it turned out that Lovaas's results were valid but could only be obtained by his own program, we would have to be concerned about the practical issue of availability of the treatment. Any treatment that is only effective if implemented by one investigator in one program is certainly not one that will be widely available.

Not surprisingly, Lovaas and his colleagues immediately and vehemently countered these criticisms from the scientific community with arguments of their own, and other researchers, in turn, countered these. In fact, these arguments are still going on and are unlikely to end any time soon. This adversarial exchange has at times been very acrimonious and has not always reflected well on the professional community.

Still, when all is said and done, the fact that many of the children in the Lovaas study made substantial improvement cannot be denied. In fact, Lovaas and his colleagues have provided follow-up reports on the children who participated in the original study, and these reports suggest that the gains the children made held up over time.[7] Many of these children were reported to be "indistinguishable" from typical young adults. While this does not negate the scientific criticisms of the research (and indeed there are more critiques of the follow-up reports), it is an indication that many autistic children can achieve substantial gains with this treatment, and that these gains may be maintained.

As might be expected, there are many positive and many negative effects of the Lovaas study, and almost no one is on the fence in terms of opinion. On the positive side, this work cemented the place of behavioral interventions for the autistic population. Although behavioral interventions were the treatment of choice before the Lovaas study, the extraordinary claims of the study certainly brought it to the forefront in the field of autism. A few years after the Lovaas study appeared, a first-hand account was published by the parent of a child who achieved normal functioning through the early intensive intervention program, and this had an additional important impact on the autism community.[8] Indeed, the original Lovaas report resulted in a blitz of media attention, and even today, nearly two decades later, one continues to see media accounts describing intensive early intervention and its potential to bring about "recovery" in autistic children.

Another positive, and related, effect of the Lovaas study was that it made many people realize that not all autistic children necessarily have a gloomy prognosis. This of course gave many people, especially parents, real hope and encouraged them to pressure schools to provide better services to their children. I will discuss the issue of education in more detail in Chapter 10.

The Lovaas study and the debate over early intervention DTT

treatment have had negative effects as well. Perhaps the most serious negative effect is the fact that hearing the hopeful results of the "cure" study has led almost all parents of autistic children to actively seek the treatment. After all, a 47 percent "normalcy" rate is certain to get people's attention. However, even for the children who do very well, we do not have sufficient information about important treatment factors such as optimal age for beginning the treatment, optimal length of treatment, how we can predict which children will show the most treatment benefit, and how long we should continue the treatment before we decide that a particular child is not benefiting. Sometimes parents or schools are told that if a child is not showing improvement with the 20, 30, or 40 hours per week of one-on-one training, then more hours must be needed. Yet one could argue that if the treatment is not working for a child at this intensity, then it is unlikely the treatment will ever work for this child. Providing more hours of an ineffective treatment is certainly not the answer. Moreover, we are talking about very young children who will be receiving this treatment, and we must think about what level of intensity is excessive for these children. If a child is not going to benefit from the treatment, it is important to determine this as soon as possible and provide an alternative treatment.

It appears that some people are so fixated on the 47 percent "cure" figure that they do not appreciate the fact that 53 percent of the children did *not* attain "normal functioning." Obviously, early intervention with this treatment did not have the same outcome for all the children, and we need to find effective treatments for those children who do not have a positive outcome. Moreover, there has been so much emphasis on identifying and treating these very young children that parents of older children with autism find that fewer programs emphasize treatment for their youngsters. As one frustrated mother put it, "My kid is only five years old and he is over the hill? Something is very wrong here."

Another problem with these intensive early intervention programs is the huge cost involved—upwards of $60,000 a year. Of course, no one would argue that an expenditure of $60,000 or even more would be worth it if an autistic child could be brought to recovery. This could even be considered a bargain, given that the cost of providing services for an individual with autism has been estimated to be $5 million over the lifetime of that individual.[9] In an effort to cure their child, some families have mortgaged their homes, taken on extra jobs, and depleted their life's savings. Unfortunately, for many of these parents such sacrifices have not been rewarded by major improvement in their child. As noted above, the majority of the children do not make the kinds of advances that Lovaas and his colleagues reported, and it is often not until months or years have passed and many dollars have been spent that this becomes apparent. The disappointment and resentment felt by families in this situation are considerable.

It has also been a problem that many parents, in an understandable effort to help their children, have taken up the cause for the early intervention DTT treatment to the extent that other effective behavioral treatments may not be considered. This is also true to some extent within the scientific community. Some researchers advocate the effectiveness of DTT and tout studies showing its positive results. Others expound on the virtues of naturalistic strategies and cite studies to support the effectiveness of these treatments. While the Lovaas study is often brought up to support the superiority of DTT treatment, it is important to keep in mind that since the Lovaas study was not a *comparison* of DTT against any other treatment, one cannot use this study to claim DTT is superior to any other form of treatment. The Lovaas study compared different "dosages" of DTT with a no-treatment control group, and it showed that more DTT was better than less DTT and this was better than no DTT at all. Essentially, this just demonstrates that more of an effective treatment is better than less of an effective treatment. Yet even this position is not without controversy. For example, the results of one study suggested that 21 hours per week of DTT training was as effective as 32 hours per week.[10]

It is important to note that effective early intervention has also been successfully accomplished using naturalistic behavioral strategies. One of the most important implementation strategies is for this treatment to be provided in "integrated" toddler and preschool environments.[11] In these settings (to be discussed in more detail later) autistic and typical children are grouped together, and naturalistic behavioral strategies are implemented with all of the children. The autistic youngsters seem to benefit greatly from the "normalized" interactions and from the presence of the typical children. This situation is in stark contrast to segregated classroom settings or intensive in-home, one-on-one training situations where the child with autism is essentially isolated from typical children. Given that one of the main goals is for autistic children to learn to interact in the natural environment, and the natural environment for young children includes other young children, this approach makes good sense. Moreover, such approaches have received empirical support for their effectiveness.[12]

Which is better, DTT or naturalistic strategies? As noted earlier in the book, it appears that naturalistic strategies have the advantages of increased generalization of treatment effects and being more "user friendly" in terms of positive reactions by the child and therapist. Focusing on language outcome, a review of existing studies concluded that naturalistic teaching strategies were generally superior to the highly structured, repetitive-practice DTT as prescribed by Lovaas and other advocates.[13] Yet as we have seen, the early-intervention intensive DTT results are impressive as well. It is clear that early intensive intervention has the potential to bring about major improvements in many of the children.

Of course, the idea that intensive treatment early in development might lead to more substantive and enduring improvement than later treatment is not surprising. We all know that early treatment of almost any disease or disorder is considered to be extremely important, and treatments that are delivered "too late" may be of minimal or no benefit. In the area of autism, one can point to two main benefits of early intervention.

First, autism may be seen as a progressive disorder in that early deficits in social responsiveness and communication have a seriously negative effect on the development of subsequent important behaviors. A child who is not socially engaged and does not learn to communicate effectively is at a definite disadvantage in learning more complex and subtle social and communicative skills. Moreover, perseverative and ritualistic behaviors not only interfere with learning appropriate behavior but also serve to stigmatize the child and thus affect how the child's social world responds to her. If we can intervene early, we may be able to avoid many of the subsequent problems that we typically see as the child gets older.

Second, given the widely accepted concept of "plasticity" of the developing brain, it is certainly possible that early intervention may have an effect on how the child's brain develops. We know that early in brain development there is a period when brain cells develop and "migrate" to specific locations within the brain. The result is a differentiation of brain functioning where specific areas develop and assume their assigned duties. This makes the normal brain quite specialized and efficient. After a certain amount of time, however, brain functioning becomes more "set" and resistant to change. After this time it is much more difficult, if not impossible, to effect changes in brain functioning. Because the prenatal and early postnatal periods of maximal brain change are influenced by both genetic and environmental factors, it is possible that altering the child's environment through intensive early intervention programs may allow us to positively affect the development of the brain in order to minimize the expression of autism or, in ideal situations, prevent its appearance altogether. Although to date no research has shown directly that this is possible, such modification of brain functioning during a critical early period of brain development has some support from animal research.[14]

Which Behavioral Treatment Is Best?

In arguments about the superiority of one treatment over another, one extremely important point is typically overlooked: no single treatment can claim to be substantially effective for all children with autism. In fact, no single form of treatment can claim to be very effective (defined as truly substantial clinical improvement) for more than 50 to 70 percent of children with autism. Therefore, arguments claiming that one form of behavioral treatment is the "best" are essentially meaningless. The fact that there is such variability in treatment outcome tells us that other factors aside from the choice of treatment are important in determining treatment effectiveness. In order to reduce this variability and maximize the number of children who will significantly benefit from behavioral treatment, it is becoming increasingly apparent that we must understand what these variables are and how they interact with treatment. This understanding would allow us to specifically tailor the treatment for each child. The question should be which behavioral treatment is better for *which* child, under *which* conditions, and at *which* point in time?

In exploring the question of which variables might be important for individualizing treatment, it is apparent that certain child variables, family variables, and treatment variables all have significance. For example, we know that a child's age, level of cognitive impairment, and language ability are important predictors of outcome. In fact, each of these factors has been empirically demonstrated to be important. Thus Lovaas and others concede that the intensive early intervention of their studies may not be effective with children who are very low-functioning in terms of level of cognitive deficit. Other characteristics of the child such as specific behaviors or deficits may be important as well.

Similarly, family variables such as parental depression or stress are likely to affect how a family tolerates and implements treatments. Families in which the parents are highly stressed and/or depressed may not be good candidates for a parent training program; the additional effort involved in directly providing a new treatment to their child might turn out to be just one more pressure on parents who are already overwhelmed. In a case such as this it might be wise for a trained clinician to work with the child initially, until the parents are better able to handle the training themselves. Indeed, it may be the case that the major stressor for the parents is the disruptive behavior of their autistic child, and the efforts of a clinician may reduce this behavior and thus eliminate a main contributor to the stress.

Family cultural variables are also important. Different cultures may value certain skills over others and thus may wish to focus on teaching these skills. For example, some cultures emphasize early independence more than others, and this affects the extent to which the child is expected to dress herself or eat independently at an early age. Further, certain types of treatments may be more acceptable to families of different cultures, and this affects the extent to which the family would actually use the treatment. Many years ago in Germany I was involved in teaching the parents of autistic children how to set up structured behavioral programs for their children. I quickly learned that this would be an uphill battle. Although the German parents were very dedicated and polite, they resisted the training. I discovered that they considered the highly structured treatment to be too "mechanistic" and "impersonal." Yet this was the very same training that was so readily embraced by most American families with whom I worked.

There is no doubt that treatment variables are extremely important. Some of these have been discussed earlier: the issues of the "dosage" of treatment (how much treatment is necessary to achieve maximum benefit) and length (at what point in the treatment process does one decide that a treatment is unlikely to be very effective and should be terminated in favor of an alternative). Treatment variables are also important because they interact with teaching specific behaviors. For example, while one may wish to use naturalistic teaching procedures, sometimes there are behaviors that are not amenable to such training. Toilet training is a behavior that may not be "chosen" by the child and may not be intrinsically (directly) reinforcing. For such behaviors, the more highly structured behavioral approach may be more effective.

Ideally, we will someday understand enough about each of these important variables to truly tailor treatment to a specific child to maximize individual benefit. Research on developing individualized treatments is still in its infancy, and much work remains to be done. A study that Michelle Sherer and I conducted recently, focusing on child variables, illustrates how this process might work.[15] We looked at pre-treatment videotapes of 40 children who subsequently received Pivotal Response Training (PRT, the naturalistic behavioral program discussed in Chapter 6). We knew which of these children had made substantial progress in treatment and which children made minimal or no progress. By looking at the different tapes, we identified a profile of behavioral characteristics that differentiated the two groups of children—the treatment "responders" versus the treatment "nonresponders."

In comparison to the children who did not respond well to treatment, the treatment responders were the children who exhibited the following behaviors in the pre-treatment tapes: an interest in toys, low rates of social avoidance (thus they were more likely to look at people and accept or seek physical contact), high rates of social approach behavior (such as looking at people, sitting near an adult, giving an adult a toy), high rates of verbal self-stimulatory behavior (such as vocalizing sounds), and low rates of nonverbal self-stimulatory behavior (such as rocking, flapping arms). Thus, given the advantage of hindsight, it appeared that we could identify a behavioral profile associated with good treatment outcome with PRT. But in order to be certain, we needed to test our profile prospectively. We chose three new children who matched our nonresponder profile and three new children who matched the responder profile. We predicted that the children with the *responder* profile would show greater gains with PRT than the children matching the *nonresponder* profile. All of the new children were then given an intensive course of PRT treatment. As we predicted, those children who matched the responder profile showed substantial gains, while the children matching the nonresponder profile showed essentially no improvement. (It is important to emphasize here that the children were pairwise matched across conditions for level of cognitive impairment and language ability, to ensure that the different outcome was not due to the nonresponder children being generally lower-functioning than the responder children.)

At this point we had a predictive profile of specific child characteristics that allowed for a treatment decision—PRT versus no PRT. Further research has suggested that this behavioral profile is particular to PRT and is not predictive of outcome with another form of treatment, the highly structured discrete trial training (DTT). Since behavioral treatment is continually being evaluated, current research is trying to determine more precisely which behaviors are necessary for the predictive profile.[16] For instance, will the profile still work if a child's toy play is not the same as specified by the profile? Will it work if a child meets all the characteristics of the responder profile except for engaging in nonverbal self-stimulatory behavior? The idea is to look very carefully at a large array of behavioral characteristics in order to eventually develop a refined and comprehensive understanding of behavioral variables that will allow us to make treatment decisions. To appreciate the complexity and breadth of such a task, consider that we not only have to know the child characteristics that predict treatment response, but we need to know this for *each* form of treatment. Moreover, we need to continue the assessment of behavioral characteristics over time because as the child changes, it is likely that the most effective form of treatment will also change.

In addition to investigating how to individualize treatments for specific children, we also need to individualize treatment for specific behaviors. For example, Michelle Sullivan studied one behavior, immediate echolalia, the problematic form of speech anomaly where the child parrots what other people have just said.[17] We know that echolalia interferes with normal language acquisition and also serves to stigmatize the individual. While researchers and clinicians had agreed that echolalic speech served as a form of communication for these children (though an abnormal form), there was less agreement as to what kind of communication it might represent. For example, Kanner had originally speculated that echolalia was the child's way of saying "yes" ("affirmation by repetition"). However, we now know that echolalia may have different communicative functions for different children, and even for the same child in different situations.[18] Sullivan sought to identify via functional analysis the specific communicative function of echolalia in five children with autism and then to design a specific, individualized treatment strategy based upon the function. Thus for one child echolalia functioned to allow the child to avoid difficult task demands, for another it served to maintain attention, for another it served to gain access to desired items, and so on. Sullivan found that by implementing treatments that specifically targeted these functions for each child, she could readily reduce or eliminate the echolalic responding. For the child who echoed to avoid demands, she taught him another, more appropriate response that served the same communicative function. Thus this child was taught to say "Can you help me?" when faced with a difficult task. Subsequently the child used the more appropriate "Can you help me?" rather than the inappropriate echolalia to communicate to the teacher that the task was too hard. Another child was found to use echolalia to gain attention from an adult. This child was taught to say "Will you play with me?" which gained the same reward (adult attention) as did the echolalia. Again, the appropriate phrase replaced the echolalia. It should be apparent that this individualized treatment approach is ultimately far more efficient and effective than implementing the same treatment procedure (for instance, teaching the child to say "Can you help me?") with all children, since some of the children may not be using echolalia to escape from difficult demands. A one-size-fits-all treatment approach is likely to be effective for only a percentage of the children to whom it is applied.

In addition to figuring out which treatment to apply, it is apparent that treatment decisions will need to be made on a continuing basis, with attention given to the changing needs of the child. At the same time, we must consider the family variables, cultural variables, and treatment variables discussed earlier. This development and implementation of individualized, prescriptive treatments will take many years to complete, but eventually we would like to have formulas that would enable us to plug in values for the variables and then make an informed and confident decision about the application of treatment procedures. Thus if we have a child who we predict will not respond substantially to PRT, we will be able to predict a form of treatment to which the child *will* respond well.

Other Controversial Treatment Issues

Augmentative Communication Systems

Another issue that has led to debate in the field of autism treatment involves the use, and form, of augmentative communication systems. Augmentative systems are programs designed to allow for communication by individuals who cannot, or do not, communicate via speech. The most common forms of augmentative systems are *sign language* and *picture communication* systems, and both are typically trained via behavioral methodology. Sign language involves using specific hand gestures visible to a communicative partner, while picture communication involves using pictures or other iconic stimuli visible to a communicative partner. (Other augmentative systems, such as typing messages into computers that generate speech, have been applied but are not as widely used or studied as sign and picture communication.)

Sign language is familiar as a common means of communication for the deaf community. American Sign Language (ASL) is the system most often employed. In autism treatment, the child (or adult) is taught to produce signs to indicate desires, needs, or other information. Sign language was the first form of augmentative communication used for nonvocal people with developmental disabilities, and Sundberg has identified four main reasons to use sign training with developmentally disabled populations.[19] First, teaching signs may be less frustrating than teaching vocal speech, since many people with developmental disabilities have difficulty controlling their vocal cords but can often imitate actions. Because sign language is taught through imitation, it is easier for these individuals to learn. Second, sign language is a better choice for training, even if the individual has difficulty with imitation, because it is easier to prompt an action than it is to prompt a vocalization. Third, sign language involves more iconic representation than does vocal language. (For example, the sign for "eat" involves bringing the hand to the mouth as if putting food in the mouth.) Vocal language is rarely iconic. Finally, since training in sign language is easier for many of these individuals, we can avoid the negative history that often characterizes the speech efforts of the developmentally disabled. That is, if these individuals are rarely successful in their attempts to communicate in the natural environment because of poor articulation, they may find the use of vocal speech frustrating and aversive.

Sign language has been successfully used with autistic individuals for more than thirty years, and thus there is a rather extensive literature describing its training, its effects, and its general relation to language theory.[20] A comprehensive picture has emerged of both the advantages and disadvantages of using sign training with the autistic population. The advantages include the following: (1) Sign language is gestural in nature, and gestural communication has been positively associated with vocal communication in typical and autistic children and is considered a precursor to speech development. (2) It allows individuals to communicate at a conversational pace, whereas other augmentative systems do not. (3) Sign language may appear to be less unusual to others than picture communication systems, and thus less stigmatizing. People are used to seeing members of the deaf community using sign language but are probably not used to seeing people using pictures to communicate. (4) Sign language does not require extraneous stimuli (such as pictures). Signs cannot be lost or left behind as pictures can, so individuals who sign are never without the ability to communicate.

Several disadvantages of using sign language have also been identified: (1) Children with autism may have difficulty in learning signs because of their attentional and imitation deficits, and during this time they effectively have no means to communicate. (2) Another rather obvious disadvantage to signing is that the individual can only communicate with others who know sign language. (This, of course, is the same argument used by anti-sign advocates to suggest that deaf children are better served by being trained in vocal communication.) A child who uses signs in the natural environment in an attempt to communicate with others who do not recognize signs is unlikely to be rewarded for the communicative behavior. This is an argument used to promote the use of picture systems for autistic children since anyone in the environment will recognize the picture and know what the child wishes to "say." For example, if an autistic child goes into a McDonald's restaurant and signs that she wants a hamburger, the likelihood of getting the hamburger is fairly low because the person behind the counter will probably not understand the sign. However, if the child hands the person a picture of a hamburger or points to a picture of a hamburger, the likelihood of getting the hamburger increases substantially.

Picture communication systems typically involve iconic representations of words (often nouns) which the individual points to or otherwise indicates to a communicative partner. One method is for the individual to carry or have access to a communication "board" on which are displayed pictures (or iconic representations) of words; the individual points to, or otherwise indicates, what he wishes to "say." For autistic children, the most commonly used picture system is the Picture Exchange Communication System (PECS).[21] PECS uses iconic symbols (on small cards) representative of objects, verbs, prepositions, and the like which the individual physically gives to a communicative partner. The individual chooses what he wishes to communicate from a book of these PECS symbols. After selecting one picture card or multiple PECS cards (a "sentence strip"), the individual hands the cards to a communicative partner in order to communicate wishes or information.

Several advantages of PECS have been reported: (1) It does not require prerequisite skills such as imitation or attention (for example, eye contact) which may be problematic in autism and time-consuming to train. Since PECS involves only giving iconic symbol cards to another person, it is not necessary for the autistic individual to have attending, imitation, pointing, or matching skills. (2) PECS avoids problems in motivation for social reinforcement. Most other augmentative systems involve the teaching of labels and the like as the first linguistic function, and these typically involve social attention. Since autistic children are not often motivated for such attention, PECS has an advantage in that its first linguistic function is the teaching of requesting behaviors that involve concrete reinforcement. Thus the child learns to give an adult a picture of a cookie to obtain a cookie before he is asked to label "cookie." (3) PECS immediately teaches the child initiation, so that spontaneity is encouraged from the start. In contrast, other augmentative systems, such as sign language, usually begin with teaching responses to questions (for example, "What is this?") or commands ("Point to the dog"). (4) PECS encourages social initiation in that it requires the child to act in a social context. This is particularly helpful for the autistic population. (5) Rates of acquisition of PECS are faster than with sign language, perhaps because it is visually based and people with autism are often described as good "visual learners." (6) Because the pictures are highly iconic, parents and educators can easily be trained to use PECS. (7) Children with motor difficulties may find PECS easier to learn and use than signs.

However, several disadvantages of PECS have also been described. (1) Some have argued that, unlike sign language, PECS is not a true "language" in that the behavioral response (giving a picture) is identical across all communications. (2) PECS cannot usually be used at a conversational pace. (3) If the child loses or leaves behind his PECS book (with all his PECS cards), he cannot communicate. (4) As noted earlier, using PECS may be more stigmatizing than using sign language.

While it has long been apparent that these augmentative systems do achieve their goal of allowing nonverbal people to communicate, their use with autistic individuals has sparked a good deal of debate. One major issue is whether or not individuals with autism should be taught to communicate through these systems; a second issue involves the relative efficacy and benefit of the two different systems.

In regard to the first issue, the debate centers on the question of whether learning an augmentative system interferes with the acquisition of spoken language. Some people fear that if a nonverbal autistic child is taught to communicate with an augmentative system,

the child will be content to use that system and will not be motivated to learn vocal speech. This issue takes on particular importance when the child is very young. Will the child never learn to
speak if she is trained to use an augmentative system involving signs
or PECS? What about the "neuroplasticity" issue? That is, treatment conducted when the child is very young may in fact lead to
changes in the brain, and how can we best use this window of opportunity to effect permanent positive change in brain structure?
When the child is older and consistent efforts to teach vocal speech
have failed, it is sometimes more likely that an augmentative system
will be implemented. However, one could argue that by this time
the child is older, he may well have more difficulty in learning a
communication system, and he may have developed some serious
behavioral problems as a result of frustration at being unable to
communicate. Thus many parents and clinicians find themselves in
a dilemma, and the literature has not always been helpful in making
a clear recommendation.

The research results have been variable in terms of whether the
use of an augmentative system hurts or helps the development of
vocal language. This is true in the case of both sign language and
PECS. Advocates of both systems can point to some research supporting the view that the augmentative system does not hinder, and
in fact may facilitate, vocal speech development.[22] The lack of uni-
formity in research results probably reflects more the heterogeneity
of the population than the use of the systems per se.

The second issue in the use of these systems for the autistic population involves the relative merits of signs versus PECS (or other
picture-based systems). As described earlier, both systems have advantages and disadvantages, and often the decision about which
one to use is based on which system the teacher knows or which
one the parent prefers. The problem here is that the factors entering
into the treatment decision may have less to do with the best match

of treatment to the individual child and more to do with what is available or popular in a particular location at a particular time. Of course, this is a common situation with any form of treatment.

It is interesting that despite many years of studying the two systems, it is only very recently that sign language and PECS have been directly compared. The first study to provide a head-to-head comparison of the two systems when used to treat autism was conducted by Aimee Anderson, who taught six autistic children, ages 2 to 4, to use both sign language and PECS to request desired items such as food and toys.[23] The study had two main purposes: to investigate differences in child performance between sign language and PECS in terms of rate of acquisition, spontaneous use of the communication system, maintenance, generalization, eye contact, and vocalization; and to identify child characteristics that may be related to performance with each of the two augmentative systems. Regarding the first purpose of the study, there were several findings: (1) the PECS icons were more readily learned than were signs; (2) despite the fact that the pictures were learned more easily by all the children, half of the children preferred to use PECS and half preferred to use signs when given a choice of using one or the other system; and (3) PECS succeeded with a broader range of children and showed greater generalization to the requesting of untrained desired items. However, the training of signs led to higher levels of social initiation, eye contact, and vocalization. Regarding the child characteristics, the study found that children who showed higher levels of protoimperative joint attention (using joint attention to request things) learned PECS faster than children with lower levels, while children who showed higher pre-treatment levels of protodeclarative joint attention (using joint attention to direct someone's attention to something of interest but not for the purpose of requesting) learned signs faster than children with lower levels. Further, those children who had higher levels of functional play preferred sign language, and post-treatment vocalization was associated with the children's level of imitation and language level prior to treatment. Although this study found that sign language training was more likely to be associated with subsequent vocalization, we cannot conclude that sign training is superior in the promotion of vocal speech because the level of PECS training used in this study was lower than that associated with vocalization.

What does a study like this tell us? Essentially, it is a first step in the lengthy process of allowing for the prescriptive use of either sign language or PECS as an augmentative strategy in treating autism. While the study needs to be replicated with additional children, children of different ages, and so on, it serves both as a jumping-off point and as an example of the kind of research that will lead to a more effective and efficient treatment. Significantly, this study suggests that augmentative language strategies do not hinder the development of vocalization (although more research will be required here), and that different patterns of language acquisition and use may be predictable on the basis of child characteristics. Thus decisions about communication training may ultimately be made on the basis of research findings and not on the basis of whose "camp" (sign language or PECS) one may be in. Again, there is no one-size-fits-all treatment recommendation; one must look at child characteristics on an individual basis before making the training decision.

Where Do We Stand?

We can conclude that any attempt to identify the "best" treatment for autism is ultimately futile; treatments must be individualized and tailored for each child. Treatment decisions should not be based solely on what the teacher or therapist knows how to do, what the clinician likes, what the parents want, or on the latest fad. Flexibility is the key here. A good school and/or treatment program must be one that can offer an array of treatment options and can use them in a flexible manner as dictated by the needs of the individual child and family. We have a crucial window of opportunity for very young children with autism, and it is our duty to use this time wisely. It is important to be able to determine the best interventions for a child from the start so that time is not wasted on ineffective treatment.

It is also clear that anything as important as the treatment of autism will continue to be accompanied by debate, contrasting findings, conflicting claims, and calls for more research. In many ways these are good things because they are what keeps the field moving forward. Until we truly understand the etiologies and course of autism and can identify ultimate treatments (cures), we will undoubtedly remain on this roller coaster ride.

CHAPTER 10

Educate Autistic Children!

The practice of inclusion is based on the philosophy that all children have the right to learn and to belong in the mainstream of school and community life.

> —Jacob A. Burack, Rhoda Root, and Edward Zigler, in *Handbook of Autism and Pervasive Developmental Disorders* (1997)

Mainstreaming and full inclusion are positive words. They sound much better than saying that the school district can save money by partly or fully depriving a child of the special help he or she needs to best overcome a learning disability.

> —Bryna Siegel, *The World of the Autistic Child* (1996)

Because of the primarily philosophical nature of this debate and the paucity of empirical evidence clearly supporting either side of this debate, it appears that full inclusion will continue to be intensely debated well into the future.

> —Joshua K. Harrower, in *Journal of Positive Behavior Interventions* (1999)

The development of effective teaching strategies for children with autism is only part of the educational battle. While many convincingly argue that the home should be a primary educational setting for the autistic child (especially if the child is very young and the parents have been trained), the fact remains that much of the child's educational activity takes place in the classroom. Sadly, the history of educating these youngsters in classrooms is not something we can be especially proud of. When I first began to work with autistic children in the late 1960s in California, there were few school programs that would accept them. In fact, although the law mandated that children with mental retardation, physical disabilities, and other handicapping conditions had the right to be educated in public schools, children with autism were not considered to have a handicapping condition characterized primarily by mental retardation or physical disability. Thus they slipped right through the educational loophole. This meant that parents had to pay for private schools for their autistic children. Yet few of these private programs were very effective, and certainly not all families could afford them. At that time education by the parents was not yet used as an intervention, so the parents were understandably ill-equipped to teach or even manage their difficult children.

As a result of the lack of programs and parent training, many parents eventually had to make the difficult decision to place their child in some kind of residential situation, which all too frequently involved large institutional facilities. Although this was more likely to happen as the child became older and perhaps more difficult to handle, it was also the case for some young children who were more severely affected. I vividly remember the many young children I used to see in a ward for "psychotic" children at a nearby state hospital. It was truly heartbreaking to see youngsters there as young as 4 or 5, with little hope for a future outside the institution. One can only imagine how difficult it was for the parents to place them there.

As noted earlier in this book, in large part it was the parents who brought about changes in this situation. They led the charge to mandate educational programs for children with autism. They spoke out in their school districts, demanding educational rights for their children and the provision of appropriate classrooms. They organized and filed lawsuits all over the country. *Educate Autistic Children!* became their mantra; this phrase was seen everywhere on banners, bumper stickers, windows, and T-shirts. Finally many states and later the federal government (in 1975) passed legislation mandating free and appropriate education for autistic and other disabled children.

Mandating special classrooms for children with autism was of course an important victory, but unfortunately this victory was not matched by successful classrooms until several years later. When autism classrooms were finally available, our ability to provide effective educational programs for children with autism was still in the very early stages. The educational technology was running far behind the administrative improvements.

Despite the best intentions of teachers in these classrooms, the problem remained that the curricula and the specific teaching technologies being developed in clinics and laboratories were not making their way into the classroom. Over the years, a number of teaching strategies especially designed for the needs of autistic youngsters were developed and gradually were adopted in classroom settings. I have discussed some of these strategies in earlier chapters, including discrete trial training, naturalistic strategies such as Pivotal Response Training, augmentative systems such as sign language and PECS, TEACCH programs, and others.

Over the past fifteen years, the situation has changed significantly. In 1987, Lovaas published the results of his study and reported that with early intensive DTT (discrete trial training), almost half of the study's very young participants achieved "normal functioning." As described in the previous chapter, the treatment was very time- and labor-intensive; Lovaas specified that to be effective, the training had to be implemented approximately 40 hours per week. Understandably, the parents of autistic children were very enthusiastic about this treatment and began demanding that the schools either provide the treatment in the classroom or provide the funding for the treatment to be implemented at home. (Interestingly, despite the fact that the Lovaas study focused only on very young autistic children, parents of older children requested the treatment as well.)

Many schools resisted having to provide for this treatment. Not only was it very expensive (often upwards of $50,000 per year per child), but such treatment was not based on the needs of the individual student and might indeed be inappropriate for some children. Again the parents used the legal system: families began suing the schools, saying that their child's right to an appropriate education was being denied. They argued that the Lovaas study provided objective data supporting the effectiveness of the intensive treatment. In contrast, most schools did not have the data to demonstrate that their educational programming was effective; therefore they were losing the lawsuits. Many school districts were hemorrhaging money to provide the intensive services. All of this ultimately forced many school districts to develop greatly improved programs for children with autism so they could successfully defend themselves in these lawsuits. They upgraded their programs by implementing research-based curricula and intervention strategies and by developing objective evaluation techniques to demonstrate the effects of their teaching. Thus, one very positive effect of the Lovaas study and the early intervention arguments was to promote the development of effective classroom programs. In fact, today more schools are winning lawsuits. All in all, this has led to a win-win situation. The parents and children have better school programs, and the schools are not being forced to pay for costly intensive treatment in the home.

A potentially much larger battle now looms over the delivery of instruction to these children in the classroom. Of course there is no shortage of opinions about how these children should fit into the educational system, but the controversy boils down to one main issue: whether it is best to include autistic children in regular classrooms populated by typically developing students, or to provide separate special education classrooms populated by other children with autism and/or other disabilities. This is not an easy decision: the optimal choice of classroom must balance both the child's basic civil right to be fully included in the community and the child's individual needs for instruction. There are strong advocates and arguments on both sides of this debate.

The lexicon of this educational debate includes several terms in widespread use. *Mainstreaming* is a term used when a special needs child (such as a child with autism) is placed in a non–special education classroom. This often involves having the special needs student spend at least part of the day in this regular classroom while also receiving special education instruction outside this classroom with a speech pathologist, occupational therapist, or other professional, for a specified amount of time ("pull-outs" in resource rooms). *Reverse mainstreaming* involves having typical children spend part of the day in a special education classroom with special needs children. *Full inclusion* means that there is complete mainstreaming—that is, the disabled student spends the entire day in the regular classroom and may be the only such student in the class. This often involves augmented services such as speech therapy, occupational therapy, use of an aide who helps the student participate in the classroom curriculum and activities, adjusted curriculum for individual work sessions, and use of assistive equipment (such as hand calculators).

Full Inclusion Arguments—Pro and Con

There are three main arguments for fully including children with disabilities, including autism, in regular classrooms with typically developing children. Each of these arguments is compelling. One is based on the civil-rights philosophy that no individual should be denied access to the mainstream community on the basis of disability. Another argument is based on the position that being integrated with typical peers will enhance the social development of children with autism. The third argument holds that the academic achievement of autistic children will be enhanced in inclusion environments.

The Argument Based on Civil Rights

The civil rights argument says that all children have the right to be educated in settings with their peers. They have the right to learn and participate in the mainstream of school and community life. This philosophical view is rooted in the civil rights movement of the 1950s through 1970s, which asserted the fundamental rights of individuals in a variety of areas including race, gender, and disability. In the area of disabilities, this ultimately resulted in the passage of the landmark legislation PL 94-142 (Education of the Handicapped Act, 1975), the law mandating that all individuals have the right to be educated in the "least restrictive environment" possible. This legislation emphasized the normalization principle, which holds that everyone deserves to lead a life that is as normal as possible. In 1990 this law was revised and supplanted by PL 101-476, known as "IDEA" (Individuals with Disabilities Education Act). These laws dictate that every child is entitled to a free appropriate public education; every child is entitled to an individualized education plan (IEP) based on his or her specific needs; every child has a right to be educated in the least restrictive environment possible; every child's rights may be protected through due process; and parents can participate in educational decisions for their children. Thus, inclusion is based on an ethical view in that it protects the civil rights of individuals with disabilities and treats them like everyone else.

Of course, there is no rational "con" argument against the civil rights of these children. Rather, the opponents of full inclusion point out that while the philosophy is sound and appropriate, the practicality and reality of full inclusion are often less so. As will be discussed below in regard to other proposed advantages of full inclusion, the anticipated benefits to the autistic children are often not achieved, and the effects on teachers and classroom staff may be problematic.[1] These opponents also point to the large range of diversity in this population in terms of specific handicaps and range of functioning level; they believe that many children need special education programs that cannot be provided in full inclusion settings. In addition, opponents may argue that a child has a right to the program best suited to his or her needs, and perhaps for some youngsters, their needs are best met in special education settings. According to this view, a fair and appropriate education may mean a segregated setting, and it may be an infringement of the child's rights to deny provision of such a program.

Inclusion as an Aid to Social Development

A second argument for full inclusion is that putting autistic children in classrooms with typical children will enhance the social development of the autistic children. Advocates of this position hold that with appropriate support, students with special needs in integrated (as opposed to segregated) classrooms are more likely to learn to communicate, interact, and develop friendships. They also are more likely to observe and learn appropriate behaviors from their nonhandicapped peers. A related advantage is that children with disabilities are less likely to experience the stigma of being in "special ed" and thus less likely to suffer from low expectations, lack of self-confidence, and demoralization.[2] There is in fact some research that supports the positive effects of full inclusion on children with disabilities. One study found that preschoolers with disabilities showed higher rates of social interactions with peers when in an inclusive classroom than when in segregated classrooms.[3] Another study found that autistic behaviors of preschoolers with autism decreased when they were in the presence of typical peers.[4] The argument that autistic children can learn from observing peers is further supported by an experiment that my colleagues and I conducted many years ago, in which we found that low-functioning autistic children learned new tasks more rapidly when observing other autistic children performing the tasks than when we taught them via discrete trial training.

However, the opponents of full inclusion point to the fact that many of the studies on the effects of integration on social development have been conducted in laboratories or other highly controlled environments, and thus the results are not representative of what happens in real-world classrooms. Indeed, we know that just placing autistic children in proximity to typical peers does not automatically lead to increases in social interaction. Autistic children usually need to be taught how to interact, which includes teaching how to initiate social interactions and how to maintain them. This is not as easy as it sounds. As an example, a colleague and I conducted a study in which we had a very high-functioning boy, Nathan, whom we taught to interact socially with same-age typical peers. We taught the peers how to initiate social interactions with Nathan and how to respond; we also taught Nathan how to initiate social interactions and how to respond.[5] Both Nathan and his peers received reinforcement in the form of toys or snacks for their participation. Everything went well except that when we stopped rewarding the typical peers for interacting with Nathan, they ceased to do so. They went right back to their original pattern of playing by themselves and ignoring Nathan. Nathan's mother, who was observing through a one-way mirror, remarked sadly, "Look, we have to pay kids to play with Nathan."

Another important point to note is that most of the studies reporting positive social benefits with inclusive settings not only use laboratory-based environments, but most often the disabled participants are not autistic. It seems that children with autism are less likely to really benefit from these settings unless there is a good deal of extra training and support. Of course, this is not surprising; we know that difficulty with social relationships is a hallmark feature of the disorder. In addition, autistic children are less likely to imitate their peers in natural environments because they are not usually motivated to do what others do. Since imitation is so important in learning from others and constitutes a good deal of what goes on in classrooms, especially for young children, autistic children are at a particular disadvantage. Although special training and classroom support will likely help the children in this area, this is very expensive and can be difficult to achieve in a nondisruptive way without highly trained staff.

Inclusion as an Aid to Academic Development

Here the arguments for inclusion are more cautious. The advocates of inclusion maintain that children with disabilities can benefit when placed in integrated settings when their level of cognitive ability is such that the academic demands of the classroom are within their ability. However, this is more likely to be the case for children with physical disabilities or emotional problems. (These children are often placed in segregated classrooms rather than in regular classrooms.) Most agree that children with severe disabilities, such as the majority of children with autism, require supplemental assistance at some level in order to survive in an inclusive setting. It does appear that inclusion works better academically for children with more minor disabilities and for higher-functioning autistic children.

Other Issues Related to Inclusion

Several additional issues and findings about inclusion deserve mention. It appears that full inclusion is to some extent an ideal, but an ideal that has much merit. We know from years of research that inclusive settings can benefit many disabled children, and these benefits may extend to their typical peers as well. In fact, one of the virtues of full and partial inclusion (as well as reverse mainstreaming) is that nonhandicapped peers are more likely to learn tolerance and acceptance of individual differences if they have this experience.

While inclusion has been shown to be effective, especially with less severely handicapped students, an important variable relating to effectiveness is of course the classroom teacher. There is no doubt that operating an inclusive classroom is quite different from presiding over a regular classroom or even a segregated special education classroom. Each of these latter settings normally involves a basic "type" of student, and the curriculum is likely to be basically the same for all students, even with appropriate individualization. Operating an inclusive classroom involves learning and maintaining a range of programs that are geared to the range of students in attendance. What we know to be important here is strong support from school principals and other administrators, a good support staff of people who can train the teachers and also serve as resources, and the support of the parents. Of course, another concern is that the disabled student will take the teacher's time and attention away from the other children in the class, resulting in less instruction for these students. Interestingly, however, research on inclusive settings has not found this to be the case.

If full inclusion works, it is a wonderful thing. If it does not, this means we need to investigate ways to improve its effectiveness. Fortunately, there are several innovative programs, all based on behavioral research and principles, that are studying the integration of young children with autism into programs with typically developing peers. Two of the earliest such research programs are the LEAP project (Learning Experiences Alternative Program), conducted by Dr. Philip Strain at the University of Colorado, and the Walden Early Childhood Programs, conducted by Dr. Gail McGee at Emory

University. The LEAP program, begun in 1982, was one of the first programs in the country to include autistic children with typical peers, and it is widely known for its work in the area of peer-implemented social skill intervention.[6] This innovative social skill intervention is complemented by individualized curricula in a variety of areas. The Walden Program, begun in 1985, was initially developed to investigate the effects of incidental teaching (a naturalistic behavioral approach described earlier) but has evolved into integrated toddler and preschool classrooms using this teaching approach. Both the LEAP and Walden programs have demonstrated success in terms of academic and social gains made by children with autism in these inclusive settings. More recently, Dr. Aubyn Stahmer at the San Diego Children's Hospital and Health Center started an integrated Children's Toddler School to investigate effective strategies for integrating toddlers with autism and typical toddlers in a community program. She has reported positive results from this research-based behavioral program.[7] All of these innovative programs aim to take advantage of the importance of early intervention for this population by providing inclusive settings for children as young as 2 years of age.

One unresolved issue is whether autistic children need to be "ready" for entry into regular education classes. Some argue that while inclusion may be fine for older or higher-functioning autistic students, younger children, especially preschoolers, may not be behaviorally ready for inclusion. Advocates of this position fear that autistic preschoolers might not receive appropriate early intervention services in these settings and also that they may face rejection from their peers. This would certainly not be a good start for a successful educational experience. These advocates often recommend a period of individual and small-group instruction prior to placement in inclusion settings. Although this concept of readiness influences quite a few of the early education programs for autistic children, there are no data to support this position.[8] On the contrary, programs like the LEAP project, the Walden programs, and the San Diego Children's Toddler School have demonstrated outstanding progress with autistic preschoolers in inclusion settings, who leave these programs with functional communication and improved social skills, and are more likely to be mainstreamed into typical school environments.

Where do things stand in terms of full inclusion? Right now it seems that the idea of full inclusion is an outstanding one that is full of promise. We already know that many children with disabilities, including autism, can be fully included in educational settings if the situation is right. The "right" situation involves several things: the teachers must be trained in a variety of teaching methodologies appropriate to a wide range of students; these teachers must be well supported and advised; adequate support must be provided for the disabled students in terms of both academic and social assistance; and the curriculum for the disabled student should be integrated into the regular classroom activities. It is unfortunate that all too often, inclusive environments are inadvertently sabotaged because school districts do not understand that support and training are needed for inclusion to work. If the autistic youngster is thrown into a "normal" classroom without the necessary support, the situation will be a failure for the student, the teacher, and the classmates.

We know what can be accomplished in research-based settings where control over a variety of variables can be attained. Each of the three innovative programs described above is a research-based program with the resources and ability to control a number of important variables in the classroom setting. In addition, these programs are composed of a number of elements including individualized instruction, small-group instruction, parent training, and different teaching methodologies (for example, Walden uses only incidental teaching whereas the Children's Toddler Program uses discrete trial training, Pivotal Response Training, Floor Time, incidental teaching, and PECS). These differences make it difficult to make comparisons across programs and to determine the impact of any of the specific components of the programs. Moreover, follow-up research is needed in order to better determine the long-term effectiveness of these programs.

The positive results of these inclusion programs provide a tantalizing hope for what can be achieved. However, the reality is that at this time it may not be feasible for all children with autism to be educated in inclusive classrooms. There are those who argue (as Bryna Siegel does in the quotation at the beginning of this chapter) that placing children with autism in inclusive settings denies them the special attention they need to be successful in their educational program. As we have already learned, individualization of treatment may be particularly important for children with autism, and an area of concern is the extent to which individualized educational protocols can be incorporated in inclusive settings. Moreover, it will be extremely important to determine which children are most likely to benefit from an inclusive program and which will be best served within a segregated setting. The ideal and the reality are still in conflict, and the acrimonious debate continues. We can hope this is a temporary state of affairs.

Another Meaningless Debate

The decision about including a child with autism in a typical classroom versus providing the child's educational programming intensively in a home setting cannot be made according to a one-size-fits-all strategy. Decisions of this sort need to be made on the basis of the needs of the particular youngster. It is always best (and most observant of the law) for the child's educational setting to be inclusive to the fullest extent possible, depending upon her needs and abilities. We are now better able to include autistic students, and we continue to improve in our inclusion strategies. Nonetheless, failure is not a good experience for any child, and it is imperative that the decisions for each child be made on the basis of sound considerations of needs and abilities.

Similarly, the issue of whether to provide intensive one-on-one home treatment to a child must be decided on the basis of the needs and abilities of the individual child. Unfortunately, parents are often told that their child *must* have this intensive treatment, whereas we know that in many instances this is not the best strategy. I have been extremely discouraged by situations where I have seen a child spend literally all of his waking hours in one-on-one interactions with an adult. In one case I watched videotapes of a young high-functioning autistic boy who was receiving intensive DTT training provided by adults, with almost all of the training conducted in the parents' bedroom. This was a case of a very able child being denied the social interactions with peers that are so important for these children. Not only was the child not receiving exposure and training in social interactions, but it was often noted that the youngster's behavioral improvements failed to generalize outside the home or with peers. This was not surprising; the child's training was situationally restricted to the home, and all of the trained interactions were with his adult therapists. This was clearly a case where the child would be better served in a classroom setting, where he could learn in an appropriate social environment. Moreover, it is important that these children learn how to behave in a classroom and a general school setting. Imagine a case where a child has spent her early years working one-on-one with adults at home and then is placed in a first grade classroom (special or typical). My prediction would be that the child would have a very difficult time.

Of course, it is true that some autistic children may require and benefit greatly from an intensive home treatment program, especially at first and especially if the child is more severely affected. The hope would be that the child could transition to a classroom situation as early as possible. Once again, however, this decision must be made on the basis of the child's abilities and needs, not on what is fashionable, what is touted on the Internet, or what is advocated by those who may have a financial stake in the decision.

Epilogue

When looking at the historical, as well as current, debates and controversies over autism, one is struck by the sheer energy of the field. Almost every day brings some new theory, purported treatment, miracle cure, neurological finding, educational debate, or political stand. This of course makes it difficult to write a book on controversies, since it seems that before the ink is dry there is yet another new debate to talk about.

So where are we now? What do we know for sure about autism? Is there anything that is *not* controversial at this point? I believe so. I believe we can say the following with certainty: Autism is not caused by parental behavior but rather is organically based. Our ability to characterize and diagnose autism spectrum disorders is greatly improved. We are beginning to unlock the biological factors that underlie autism. While there is as yet no cure for autism, behavioral research has yielded effective treatments. There is no "one size fits all" treatment, but we are learning how to individualize treatment and education options to meet the specific needs of the child and family. Unfortunately, the lack of a known cause or cure often invites unproven claims and even acceptance of bogus treatments. However, we also can say that controversies over autism and its treatment will continue to energize this field and move it forward.

On one hand, I find the energy exciting and hopeful. All this activity, though sometimes it sends us careening in the wrong direction, is what will ultimately lead to important answers. As long as people are fascinated, intrigued, outraged, and opinionated about autism, the field will move ahead toward new discoveries. All we really need is the interest and enthusiasm to ask the important questions, and to set about finding the answers. Because autism is such a complex problem that affects the individual in so many ways, we can expect the search for answers to take some time. However, I am confident that we will continue to make significant progress.

On the other hand, I am discouraged by those who tenaciously hold on to contentious positions, even in the face of empirical evidence to the contrary. This serves only to prolong our search and delay the discovery of the answers we all seek. Going down the wrong road takes time, and this is time much better spent on finding the *right* road. Consider how many years were wasted focusing on psychodynamic theory as a basis for the etiology of autism and its treatment. Significant damage can be caused by pursuing erroneous concepts even after appropriate scientific inquiry has refuted them. We cannot afford to let hopes and desires blind us to the truth.

The energy in the field of autism has the power to drive us down many possible roads. My goal in writing this book has been to invite the reader to share my own fascination with autism and also to encourage the critical approach necessary to make sure we stay on the road to discovery. Looking at the progress we have made in recent years, I am confident that we can remain on this road and continue improving the future for those affected by autism.

Notes

1. Critical Evaluation of Issues in Autism

1. *Prime Time Live,* ABC News, January 23, 1992.
2. *60 Minutes,* CBS News, February 20, 1994.
3. D. Biklen, *Communication Unbound: How Facilitated Communication Is Challenging Traditional Views of Autism and Ability/Disability* (New York: Teachers College Press, 1993).
4. S. Epstein, *Impure Science: AIDS Activism and the Politics of Knowledge* (Berkeley: University of California Press, 1996).

2. Characteristics of Autism

1. Leo Kanner, "Autistic Disturbances of Affective Contact," *Nervous Child,* 2 (1943): 217–250. Reprinted in Leo Kanner, *Childhood Psychosis: Initial Studies and New Insights* (Washington, D.C.: V. H. Winston and Sons, 1973).
2. E. Bleuler, *Das Autistische—Undisziplinierte Denken in der Medizin und seine Überwindung* (Berlin: Spring, 1919).
3. Leo Kanner, "Autistic Disturbances of Affective Contact," reprinted in Kanner, *Childhood Psychosis,* p. 2. Quotations from Leo Kanner are reprinted by permission of the Philosophical Library, New York. Page numbers for all subsequent quotations from Kanner are given in the text and refer to the 1973 reprint of his article in *Childhood Psychosis.*
4. L. Schreibman, *Autism* (Newbury Park: Sage Publications, 1988).
5. It is important to make the distinction between "echolalia," which is

the abnormal repetition of speech, and the normal "echoic" speech of very young children during normal language development. Echolalia is pathological speech and is the term for the use of echoic responding after approximately 4 years of age.

6. See, for example, E. G. Carr, L. Schreibman, and O. I. Lovaas, "Control of Echolalic Speech in Psychotic Children," *Journal of Abnormal Child Psychology,* 3 (1975): 331–351; L. Schreibman and E. G. Carr, "Elimination of Echolalic Responding to Questions Through the Training of a Generalized Verbal Response," *Journal of Applied Behavior Analysis,* 11 (1978): 453–463; B. M. Prizant and J. F. Duchan, "The Functions of Immediate Echolalia in Autistic Children," *Journal of Speech and Hearing Disorders,* 46 (1981): 241–249.

7. See, for example, O. I. Lovaas, J. W. Varni, R. L. Koegel, and N. Lorsh, "Some Observations on the Nonextinguishability of Children's Speech," *Child Development,* 48 (1977): 1121–1127.

8. See, for example, O. I. Lovaas, A. Litrownik, and R. Mann, "Response Latencies to Auditory Stimuli in Autistic Children Engaged in Self-Stimulatory Behavior," *Behaviour Research and Therapy,* 9 (1971): 39–49.

9. B. Rimland, *Infantile Autism* (New York: Appleton-Century-Crofts, 1964).

10. National Research Council, *Educating Children With Autism,* ed. Catherine Lord and James P. McGee, Committee on Educational Interventions for Children with Autism, Division of Behavioral and Social Sciences and Education (Washington, D.C.: National Academy Press, 2001).

11. D. A. Treffert, "The Idiot Savant: A Review of the Syndrome," *American Journal of Psychiatry,* 145 (1988): 563–572.

3. Diagnosis and Assessment

1. E. Bleuler, *Dementia Praecox or the Group of Schizophrenias,* trans. J. Zinkin (New York: International Universities Press, 1950).

2. L. Bender, "Childhood Schizophrenia: Clinical Study of One Hundred Schizophrenic Children," *American Journal of Orthopsychiatry,* 17 (1947): 40–56.

3. B. Rank, "Intensive Study and Treatment of Preschool Children Who Show Marked Personality Deviations, or 'Atypical Development,' and

Their Parents," in G. Caplan, ed., *Emotional Problems of Early Childhood* (New York: Basic Books, 1955).

4. M. Mahler, "On Child Psychosis and Schizophrenia, Autistic and Symbiotic Infantile Psychoses," *Psychoanalytic Study of the Child,* 7 (1952): 286–305.

5. American Psychiatric Association, *Diagnostic and Statistical Manual of Mental Disorders, 4th ed.* (Washington, D.C.: APA, 1994).

6. World Health Organization, *Mental Disorders: Glossary and Guide to Their Classification in Accordance with the Tenth Revision of the International Classification of Diseases* (Geneva, Switzerland: WHO, 1993).

7. F. R. Volkmar, A. Klin, W. Marans, and D. J. Cohen, "Childhood Disintegrative Disorder," in D. J. Cohen and F. R. Volkmar, eds., *Handbook of Autism and Pervasive Developmental Disorders,* 2nd ed. (New York: John Wiley and Sons, 1997), pp. 47–59.

8. H. Asperger, "Die 'Autistischen Psychopathen' im Kindesalter," *Archiv für Psychiatrie und Nervenkrankheiten,* 117 (1944): 76–136.

9. A. Klin, F. R. Volkmar, and S. S. Sparrow, eds., *Asperger Syndrome* (New York: Guilford Press, 2000), p. 9.

10. T. Attwood, "Making Friends and Managing Feelings: Asperger's Syndrome and High Functioning Autism," presentation at the San Diego Children's Hospital and Health Center, San Diego, Calif., October 15, 2003.

11. F. R. Volkmar, A. Klin, and D. J. Cohen, "Diagnosis and Classification of Autism and Related Conditions: Consensus and Issues," in Cohen and Volkmar, eds., *Handbook of Autism and Pervasive Developmental Disorders,* 2nd ed., pp. 5–40.

12. L. Wing and J. Gould, "Severe Impairments of Social Interaction and Associated Abnormalities in Children: Epidemiology and Classification," *Journal of Autism and Developmental Disorders,* 9 (1979): 11–29.

13. B. Rimland, *Infantile Autism* (New York: Appleton-Century Crofts, 1964).

14. E. Schopler, R. J. Reichler, and B. R. Renner, *The Childhood Autism Rating Scale (CARS) for Diagnostic Screening and Classification of Autism* (New York: Irvington Press, 1986).

15. S. Baron-Cohen, J. Allen, and C. Gillberg, "Can Autism Be Detected at 18 Months? The Needle, the Haystack, and the CHAT," *British Journal of Psychiatry,* 161 (1992): 839–843.

16. C. Lord, M. Rutter, and A. Le Couteur, "Autism Diagnostic Interview–Revised: A Revised Version of a Diagnostic Interview for Caregivers of Individuals with Possible Pervasive Developmental Disorders," *Journal of Autism and Developmental Disorders,* 24 (1994): 659–685.

17. C. Lord, S. Risi, L. Lambrecht, et al., "The Autism Diagnostic Observation Schedule–Generic: A Standard Measure of Social and Communication Deficits Associated with the Spectrum of Autism," *Journal of Autism and Developmental Disorders,* 30 (2002): 205–223.

18. P. A. Filipek, P. J. Accardo, G. T. Baranek, et al., "The Screening and Diagnosis of Autistic Spectrum Disorders," *Journal of Autism and Developmental Disorders,* 29 (1999): 439–484.

19. Congressman John F. Tierney (*www.house.gov/tierney/press/autism 050704.shtml*), 2004; *www.autism-society.org* (2003).

20. L. A. Croen, J. K. Grether, J. Hoogstrate, and S. Selvin, "The Changing Prevalence of Autism in California," *Journal of Autism and Developmental Disorders,* 32 (2002): 207–215.

21. E. Fombonne, "Epidemiological Surveys of Autism and Other Pervasive Developmental Disorders: An Update," *Journal of Autism and Developmental Disorders,* 33 (2003): 365–382.

4. What Causes Autism?

1. The film *Refrigerator Mothers* was shown on PBS in 2001 as one of several documentaries in the PBS *Point of View* series.

2. See, for example, L. Kanner, "Autistic Disturbances of Affective Contact," *Nervous Child,* 2 (1943): 217–250.

3. B. Bettelheim, *The Empty Fortress* (New York: The Free Press, 1967).

4. M. Mahler, "On Child Psychosis and Schizophrenia, Autistic and Symbiotic Infantile Psychoses," *Psychoanalytic Study of the Child,* 7 (1952): 286–305; B. Rank, "Intensive Study and Treatment of Preschool Children Who Show Marked Personality Deviations, or 'Atypical Development,' and Their Parents," in G. Caplan, ed., *Emotional Problems of Early Childhood* (New York: Basic Books, 1955), pp. 491–501; H. Weiland and R. Rudnick, "Considerations of the Development and Treatment of Autistic Childhood Psychosis," *Psychoanalytic Study of the Child,* 16 (1961): 549–563.

5. M. Rutter and A. Cox, "A Comparative Study of Infantile Autism and Specific Developmental Receptive Language Disorder: I. The Children," *British Journal of Psychiatry,* 126 (1975): 127–145.

6. R. L. Koegel, L. Schreibman, R. E. O'Neill, and J. C. Burke, "The Personality and Family-Interaction Characteristics of Parents of Autistic Children," *Journal of Consulting and Clinical Psychology,* 51 (1983): 683–692.

7. M. Rutter and T. G. O'Connor, "Are There Biological Programming Effects for Psychological Development? Findings from a Study of Romanian Adoptees," *Developmental Psychology,* 40 (2004): 81–94.

8. C. B. Ferster, "Positive Reinforcement and Behavioral Deficits of Autistic Children," *Child Development,* 32 (1961): 437–456.

9. C. B. Ferster and M. K. DeMyer, "The Development of Performance in Autistic Children in an Automatically Controlled Environment," *Journal of Chronic Diseases,* 13 (1961): 312–345.

10. M. Rutter, A. Bailey, E. Simonoff, and A. Pickles, "Genetic Influences and Autism," in D. J. Cohen and F. R. Volkmar, eds., *Handbook of Autism and Pervasive Developmental Disorders, Second Edition* (New York: John Wiley and Sons, 1997), pp. 370–387.

11. M. Rutter, "Genetic Studies of Autism: From the 1970s into the Millennium," *Journal of Abnormal Child Psychology,* 28 (2000): 3–14.

12. R. J. Schain and D. X. Freedman, "Studies on 5-Hydroxyindole Metabolism in Autistic and Other Mentally Retarded Children," *Journal of Pediatrics,* 58 (1961): 315–320.

13. E. Geller, E. R. Ritvo, B. J. Freeman, and A. Yuwiler, "Preliminary Observations on the Effect of Fenfluramine on Blood Serotonin and Symptoms in Three Autistic Boys," *New England Journal of Medicine,* 307 (1982): 165.

14. E. Courchesne, R. Yeung-Courchesne, and K. Pierce, "Biological and Behavioral Heterogeneity in Autism: Roles of Pleiotropy and Epigenesis," in Broman and Fletcher, eds., *The Changing Nervous System: Neurobehavioral Consequences of Early Brain Disorders* (New York: Oxford University Press, 1999), pp. 292–338.

15. E. Courchesne, R. Carper, and N. Akshoomoff, "Evidence of Brain Overgrowth in the First Year of Life in Autism," *Journal of the American Medical Association,* 290 (2003): 337–344.

16. E. Courchesne, C. M. Karns, H. R. Davis, et al., "Unusual Brain Growth Patterns in Early Life in Patients with Autistic Disorder: An MRI Study," *Neurology,* 57 (2001): 245–254.

17. See E. Courchesne and K. Pierce, "Brain Overgrowth in Autism during a Critical Time in Development: Implications for Frontal Pyramidal Neuron and Interneuron Development and Connectivity," *Interna-*

tional Journal of Developmental Neuroscience (in press); M. R. Herbert, D. A. Ziegler, C. K. Deutsch, et al., "Brain Asymmetries in Autism and Developmental Language Disorder: A Nested Whole-Brain Analysis," *Brain,* 128 (2005): 213–226; D. L. Vargas, C. Nascimbene, C. Krishnan, et al., "Neuroglial Activation and Neuroinflammation in the Brain of Patients with Autism," *Annals of Neurology,* 57 (2005): 67–81.

18. S. Baron-Cohen, *The Essential Difference: The Truth About the Male and Female Brain* (London: Alan Lane, 2003).

19. J. T. Manning, S. Baron-Cohen, S. Wheelwright, and G. Sanders, "The 2nd to 4th Digit Ratio and Autism," *Developmental Medicine and Child Neurology,* 43 (2001): 160–164; S. Lutchmaya, S. Baron-Cohen, and P. Raggatt, "Foetal Testosterone and Vocabulary Size in 18- and 24-Month-Old Infants," *Infant Behavior and Development,* 24 (2002): 418–424; S. Lutchmaya, S. Baron-Cohen, and P. Raggatt, "Foetal Testosterone and Eye Contact in 12-Month-Old Human Infants," *Infant Behavior and Development,* 25 (2002): 327–335.

20. A. J. Wakefield, S. H. Murch, A. Anthony, et al., "Ileal-Lymphoid-Hyperplasia, Non-Specific Colitis, and Pervasive Developmental Disorder in Children," *The Lancet,* 351 (1998): 637–641.

21. Medical Research Council (UK), *MRC Review of Autism Research: Epidemiology and Causes* (London: MRC, 2001).

22. B. Taylor, E. Miller, C. P. Farrington, et al., "Autism and Measles, Mumps, and Rubella Vaccine: No Epidemiological Evidence for a Causal Association," *The Lancet,* 353 (1999): 2026–2029.

23. L. Dales, S. J. Hammer, and N. J. Smith, "Time Trends in Autism and in MMR Immunization Coverage in California," *Journal of the American Medical Association,* 285 (2001): 1183–1185.

24. See E. Fombonne and E. H. Cook, Jr., "MMR and Autistic Enterocolitis: Consistent Epidemiological Failure to Find an Association," *Molecular Psychiatry,* 8 (2003): 133–134.

25. T. Verstraeten, R. L. Davis, F. DeStafano, et al., "Safety of Thimerosal-Containing Vaccines: A Two-Phased Study of Computerized Health Maintenance Organization Databases," *Pediatrics,* 112 (2003): 1039–1048.

26. S. H. Murch, A. Anthony, D. H. Casson, et al., "Retraction of an Interpretation," *The Lancet,* 363 (2004): 750; Horton, R., "The Lessons of MMR," *The Lancet,* 363 (2004): 747; Horton, R. "A Statement by the Editors of *The Lancet,*" *The Lancet,* 363 (2004): 820–821.

27. Report of the National Institute of Medicine, May 18, 2004.
28. K. B. Nelson and M. L. Bauman, "Thimerosal and Autism?" *Pediatrics,* 111 (2003): 674–679; P. Stehr-Green, P. Tull, M. Stellfeld, et al., "Autism and Thimerosal-Containing Vaccines: Lack of Consistent Evidence for an Association," *American Journal of Preventative Medicine,* 25 (2003): 101–106.

5. Are There Core Deficits in Autism?

1. S. Rogers, "An Examination of the Imitation Deficit in Autism," in J. Nadel and G. Butterworth, eds., *Imitation in Infancy* (Cambridge: Cambridge University Press, 1999), pp. 254–279.
2. H. Wimmer and J. Perner, "Beliefs about Beliefs: Representation and Constraining Function of Wrong Beliefs in Young Children's Understanding of Deception," *Cognition,* 13 (1983): 103–128.
3. F. R. Volkmar, A. Carter, J. Grossman, and A. Klin, "Social Development in Autism," in D. J. Cohen and F. R. Volkmar, eds., *Handbook of Autism and Pervasive Developmental Disorders, Second Edition* (New York: John Wiley and Sons, 1997), pp. 173–194.
4. A. M. Leslie, "Pretense and Representation: The Origins of 'Theory of Mind,'" *Psychological Review,* 94 (1987): 412–426.
5. J. Osterling and G. Dawson, "Early Recognition of Children with Autism: A Study of First Birthday Home Videotape," *Journal of Autism and Developmental Disorders,* 24 (1994): 247–431. See also J. A. Osterling, G. Dawson, and J. A. Munson, "Early Recognition of 1-Year-Old Infants with Autism Spectrum Disorder versus Mental Retardation," *Development and Psychopathology,* 14 (2002): 239–251.
6. G. Baranek, "Autism during Infancy: A Retrospective Video Analysis of Sensory-Motor and Social Behaviors at 9–12 Months of Age," *Journal of Autism and Developmental Disorders,* 29 (1999): 213–224; L. Zwaigenbaum, S. E. Bryson, J. Brian, et al., "Early Behavioral Markers Predict Social-Communication Impairments in Young Siblings of Children with Autism," paper presented at the annual convention of the Society for Research in Child Development, Tampa, Florida, April 2003.
7. A. M. Leslie and D. Roth, "What Can Autism Teach Us about Meta-representation?" in S. Baron-Cohen, H. Tager-Flusberg, and D. Cohen, eds., *Understanding Other Minds: Perspectives from Autism* (Oxford: Oxford Medical Publications, 1993), pp. 83–111.

8. See H. Tager-Flusberg, "A Reexamination of the Theory of Mind Hypothesis of Autism," in J. A. Burack, T. Charmon, T. N. Yirmiya, and P. R. Zelazo, eds., *The Development of Autism: Perspectives from Theory and Research* (Mahwah, N.J.: Erlbaum, 2001), pp. 173–193.

9. Ibid.

10. U. Frith and F. Happé, "Autism: Beyond 'Theory of Mind,'" in J. Mehler and S. Franck, eds., *Cognition on Cognition*, Cognition Special Series (Cambridge, Mass.: MIT Press, 1995), pp. 13–30.

11. A. Shah and U. Frith, "An Islet of Ability in Autism: A Research Note," *Journal of Child Psychology and Psychiatry,* 24 (1983): 613–620; F. Happé, *Autism: An Introduction to Psychological Theory* (Cambridge, Mass.: Harvard University Press, 1994).

12. S. Ozonoff, "Learning and Cognition in Autism," in E. Schopler and G. B. Mesibov, eds., *Current Issues in Autism* (New York: Plenum Press, 1995), pp. 199–219; S. Ozonoff, B. F. Pennington, and S. J. Rogers, "Executive Function Deficits in High-Functioning Autistic Individuals: Relationship to Theory of Mind," *Journal of Child Psychology and Psychiatry and Allied Disciplines,* 32 (1991): 1081–1105; S. Ozonoff, D. L. Strayer, W. M. McMahon, and F. Filloux, "Executive Function Abilities in Autism and Tourette Syndrome: An Information Processing Approach," *Journal of Child Psychology and Psychiatry and Allied Disciplines,* 35 (1994): 1015–1032.

13. S. Weeks and R. P. Hobson, "The Salience of Facial Expression for Autistic Children," *Journal of Child Psychology and Psychiatry and Allied Disciplines,* 28 (1987): 137–151.

14. R. P. Hobson, "The Autistic Child's Appraisal of Expressions of Emotion," *Journal of Child Psychology and Psychiatry and Allied Disciplines,* 27 (1986): 321–342.

15. A. L. Bacon, D. Fein, R. Morris, et al., "The Responses of Autistic Children to the Distress of Others," *Journal of Autism and Developmental Disorders,* 2 (1998): 129–142.

16. P. Hobson, "Understanding Persons: The Role of Affect," in S. Baron-Cohen, H. Tager-Flusberg, and D. J. Cohen, eds., *Understanding Other Minds: Perspectives from Autism* (Oxford: Oxford University Press, 1993), pp. 204–224.

17. For a review of this literature see L. Schreibman, *Autism* (Newbury Park, Calif.: Sage, 1988).

18. L. Schreibman and O. I. Lovaas, "Overselective Response to Social

Stimuli by Autistic Children," *Journal of Abnormal Child Psychology,* 1 (1973): 152–168.

19. N. Akshoomoff, E. Courchesne, and J. Townsend, "Attention Coordination and Anticipatory Control," *International Review of Neurobiology,* 41 (1997): 575–598.

20. S. J. Hutt, C. Hutt, D. Lee, and C. Ounsted, "Arousal and Childhood Autism," *Nature,* 204 (1964): 908–909; A. M. DesLauriers and C. F. Carlson, *Your Child Is Asleep: Early Infantile Autism* (Homewood, Ill.: Dorsey Press, 1969).

21. See, for example, G. Dawson and A. Lewy, "Arousal, Attention, and the Socioemotional Impairments of Individuals with Autism," in G. Dawson, ed., *Autism: Nature, Diagnosis, and Treatment* (New York: Guilford Press, 1989), pp. 49–74; M. Kinsbourne, "Cerebral-Brainstem Relations in Infantile Autism," in E. Schopler and G. B. Mesibov, eds., *Neurobiological Issues in Autism: Current Issues in Autism* (New York: Plenum Press, 1987), pp. 107–125; M. K. Belmonte and D. A. Yurgelun-Todd, "Functional Anatomy of Impaired Selective Attention and Compensatory Processing in Autism," *Cognitive Brain Research,* 17 (2003): 651–664.

22. See, for example, E. M. Ornitz and E. Ritvo, "Perceptual Inconstancy in Early Infantile Autism," *Archives of General Psychiatry,* 18 (1968): 76–98; R. Raymaekers, J. van der Meere, and H. Roeyers, "Event-Rate Manipulation and Its Effect on Arousal Modulation and Response Inhibition in Adults with High Functioning Autism," *Journal of Clinical and Experimental Neuropsychology,* 26 (2004): 74–82.

23. E. P. Abrahamsen and J. R. Mitchell, "Communication and Sensorimotor Functioning in Children with Autism," *Journal of Autism and Developmental Disorders,* 20 (1990): 75–85.

24. G. Dawson and A. Adams, "Imitation and Social Responsiveness in Autistic Children," *Journal of Abnormal Child Psychology,* 12 (1984): 209–225.

25. M. Sigman and J. Ungerer, "Cognitive and Language Skills in Autistic, Mentally Retarded, and Normal Children," *Developmental Psychology,* 20 (1994): 293–302.

26. S. J. Rogers and B. F. Pennington, "A Theoretical Approach to the Deficits in Infantile Autism," *Development and Psychopathology,* 3 (1991): 137–162.

27. See A. Meltzoff and A. Gopnik, "The Role of Imitation in Understand-

ing Persons and Developing a Theory of Mind," in S. Baron-Cohen, H. Tager-Flusberg, and D. J. Cohen, eds., *Understanding Other Minds* (Oxford: Oxford University Press, 1993), pp. 335–366.

28. M. E. Hertzig, M. E. Snow, and M. Sherman, "Affect and Cognition in Autism," *Journal of the American Academy of Child and Adolescent Psychiatry,* 28 (1989): 195–199.

29. S. J. Rogers, S. L. Hepburn, T. Stackhouse, and E. Wehner, "Imitation Performance in Toddlers with Autism and Those with Other Developmental Disorders," *Journal of Child Psychology and Psychiatry,* 44 (2003): 763–781.

30. See, for example, D. G. Garfin, D. McCallon, and R. Cox, "Validity and Reliability of the Childhood Autism Rating Scale with Autistic Adolescents," *Journal of Autism and Developmental Disorders,* 18 (1988): 367–378.

6. Developing Treatments That Work

1. National Research Council, *Educating Children with Autism,* Committee on Educational Interventions for Children with Autism, Catherine Lord and James P. McGee, eds. Division of Behavioral and Social Sciences and Education (Washington, D.C.: National Academy Press, 2001).

2. See L. Schreibman, *Autism* (Newbury Park, Calif.: Sage, 1988).

3. P. R. Fuller, "Operant Conditioning of a Vegetative Human Organism," in L. P. Ullman and L. Krasner, eds., *Case Studies in Behavior Modification* (New York: Holt, Rinehart, and Winston, 1965), pp. 337–339.

4. O. I. Lovaas and J. Q. Simmons, "Manipulation of Self-Destruction in Three Retarded Children," *Journal of Applied Behavior Analysis,* 3 (1969): 143–157.

5. O. I. Lovaas, G. Freitag, V. J. Gold, and I. C. Kassorla, "Experimental Studies in Childhood Schizophrenia: Analysis of Self-Destructive Behavior," *Journal of Experimental Child Psychology,* 2 (1965): 67–84.

6. C. B. Ferster, "Positive Reinforcement and Behavioral Deficits of Autistic Children," *Child Development,* 32 (1961): 437–456.

7. See Schreibman, *Autism,* pp. 95–130, for a comprehensive review.

8. C. Maurice, G. Green, and S. C. Luce, eds., *Behavioral Intervention for Young Children with Autism: A Manual for Parents and Professionals*

(Austin, Texas: Pro-Ed, 1996); O. I. Lovaas, *Teaching Individuals with Developmental Delays: Basic Intervention Techniques* (Austin, Texas: Pro-Ed, 2003).

9. Some people refer to this type of training as ABA or "Applied Behavior Analysis." This is a misnomer since the term "applied behavior analysis" refers to a specific research methodology and the use of specific experimental designs; it does not refer to a form of treatment. Thus the *Journal of Applied Behavior Analysis* includes many reports that do not cover children with autism or their treatment.

10. O. I. Lovaas, R. L. Koegel, J. Q. Simmons, and J. S. Long, "Some Generalization and Follow-Up Measures on Autistic Children in Behavior Therapy," *Journal of Applied Behavior Analysis*, 6 (1972): 131–166.

11. *Reinforcement Therapy* (film) (New York: Appleton-Century-Crofts, 1966).

12. P. E. Touchette, R. F. MacDonald, and S. N. Langer, "A Scatter Plot for Identifying Stimulus Control of Problem Behavior," *Journal of Applied Behavior Analysis*, 18 (1985): 343–351.

13. E. G. Carr and V. M. Durand, "Reducing Behavior Problems Through Functional Communication Training," *Journal of Applied Behavior Analysis*, 18 (1985): 111–126.

14. See T. F. Stokes and D. M. Baer, "An Implicit Technology of Generalization," *Journal of Behavior Analysis*, 10 (1977): 349–367.

15. See, for example, R. L. Koegel, M. C. O'Dell, and L. K. Koegel, "A Natural Language Teaching Paradigm for Nonverbal Autistic Children," *Journal of Autism and Developmental Disorders*, 17 (1987): 187–200; R. L. Koegel, L. Schreibman, A. Good, et al., *How to Teach Pivotal Behaviors to Children with Autism: A Training Manual* (University of California, Santa Barbara, 1989).

16. B. Hart and T. R. Risley, "In Vivo Language Intervention: Unanticipated General Effects," *Journal of Applied Behavior Analysis*, 13 (1980): 407–423; G. G. McGee, P. J. Krantz, and L. E. McClannahan, "The Facilitative Effects of Incidental Teaching on Preposition Use by Autistic Children," *Journal of Applied Behavior Analysis*, 18 (1985): 17–31.

17. A. P. Kaiser, P. J. Yoder, and A. Keetz, "Evaluating Milieu Training," in S. F. Warren and J. Reichle, eds., *Causes and Effects in Communication and Language Intervention* (Baltimore: P. H. Brookes, 1992), pp. 9–47.

18. C. Peterson, S. F. Maier, and M. E. P. Seligman, *Learned Helplessness:*

A Theory for the Age of Personal Control (London: Oxford University Press, 1993).

19. L. Schreibman, W. M. Kaneko, and R. L. Koegel, "Positive Affect of Parents of Autistic Children: A Comparison Across Two Teaching Techniques," *Behavior Therapy,* 22 (1991): 479–490.

20. R. L. Koegel, A. Bimbela, and L. Schreibman, "Collateral Effects of Parent Training on Family Interactions," *Journal of Autism and Developmental Disorders,* 26 (1996): 347–359.

21. See, for example, J. M. Lucyshyn, G. Dunlap, and R. W. Albin, eds., *Families and Positive Behavior Support: Addressing Problem Behavior in Family Contexts* (Baltimore: P. H. Brookes, 2002).

22. R. L. Koegel, L. K. Koegel, and A. Surratt, "Language Intervention and Disruptive Behavior in Preschool Children with Autism," *Journal of Autism and Developmental Disorders,* 22 (1992): 141–153; R. L. Koegel, M. O'Dell, and G. Dunlap, "Producing Speech Use in Nonverbal Autistic Children by Reinforcing Attempts," *Journal of Autism and Developmental Disorders,* 18 (1988): 525–538.

7. Are Other Treatments Effective?

1. S. I. Greenspan and S. Wieder, *The Child with Special Needs* (Reading, Mass.: Perseus Books, 1998), p. 2.

2. National Research Council, *Educating Children with Autism,* Committee on Educational Interventions for Children with Autism, C. Lord and J. P. McGee, eds. Division of Behavioral and Social Sciences and Education (Washington, D.C.: National Academy Press, 2001), p. 168.

3. Greenspan and Wieder, *The Child with Special Needs.*

4. Ibid.

5. Ibid.

6. Letter from a parent, quoted in G. B. Mesibov, "Formal and Informal Measures on the Effectiveness of the TEACCH Programme," *Autism,* 1 (1997): 32.

7. National Research Council, *Educating Children with Autism,* pp. 169–170.

8. G. B. Mesibov and V. Shea, "The Culture of Autism: From Theoretical Understanding to Education Practice" (1998), *http://www.rmple.co.uk/eduweb/sites/autism/culture.html.*

9. E. Schopler, G. B. Mesibov, and A. Baker, "Evaluation of Treatment for

Autistic Children and Their Parents," *Journal of the American Academy of Child Psychiatry,* 21 (1982): 262–267.

10. S. Ozonoff and K. Cathcart, "Effectiveness of a Home Program Intervention for Young Children with Autism," *Journal of Autism and Developmental Disorders,* 28 (1998): 25–32.

11. S. M. Edelson and B. Rimland, eds., *Treating Autism: Parent Stories of Hope and Success* (San Diego: Autism Research Institute, 2003), p. 60.

12. S. M. Edelson and B. Rimland, *The Efficacy of Auditory Integration Training: Summaries and Critiques of 28 Reports* (San Diego: Autism Research Institute, 2001), p. 15.

13. National Research Council, *Educating Children with Autism,* p. 100.

14. *The ASHA Leader,* August 2003, p. 3.

15. A. Stehli, *The Sound of a Miracle: A Child's Triumph over Autism* (New York: Doubleday, 1991).

16. S. Bettison, "The Long-Term Effects of Auditory Training on Children with Autism," *Journal of Autism and Developmental Disorders,* 26 (1996): 361–374.

17. S. M. Edelson, "What I Would Do If I Were a Parent of An Autistic Child: Recommendations Based on 25 Years of Research Experience," in Edelson and Rimland, eds., *Treating Autism,* p. 76.

18. B. Siegel, *The World of the Autistic Child* (New York: Oxford University Press, 1996), p. 331.

19. J. Ayres, "Improving Academic Scores Through Sensory Integration," *Journal of Learning Disabilities,* 5 (1972): 338–343.

20. D. Doggett, "A Very Tough Kid," in Edelson and Rimland, eds., *Treating Autism,* pp. 137–151.

21. G. T. Baranek, "Efficacy of Sensory and Motor Interventions for Children with Autism," *Journal of Autism and Developmental Disorders,* 5 (2002): 397–422.

22. Edelson and Rimland, *Treating Autism,* p. 148.

23. National Research Council, *Educating Children with Autism,* p. 130.

24. J. Coplan, M. C. Souders, A. E. Mulberg, et al., "Children with Autistic Spectrum Disorders. II: Parents Are Unable to Distinguish Secretin from Placebo under Double-Blind Conditions," *Archives of Disease in Childhood,* 88 (2003): 739.

25. K. Horvath, G. Stefanatos, K. N. Sokolski, et al., "Improved Social and Language Skills after Secretin Administration in Patients with Autistic

Spectrum Disorders," *Journal of the Association for Academic Minority Physicians,* 9 (1998): 9–15.

26. D. McLellan, "Andrew Awakes," *Ladies' Home Journal,* vol. 116 (October 1999), pp. 162–166.

27. Coplan, Souders, Mulberg, et al., "Children with Autistic Spectrum Disorders: II.

28. B. Rimland, "Vitamin B6 (and Magnesium) in the Treatment of Autism," reprinted in Edelson and Rimland, eds., *Treating Autism,* p. 25.

29. C. Nye and A. Brice, "Combined Vitamin B6-Magnesium Treatment in Autism Spectrum Disorder," abstract, *Cochrane Review,* vol. 4, Cochrane Library (Oxford: Update Software, 2003).

30. S. Cohen, *Targeting Autism: What We Know, Don't Know, and Can Do to Help Young Children with Autism and Related Disorders* (Berkeley: University of California Press, 1998).

31. Ibid.

32. B. Rimland, "The History of the Autism Research Institute and the Defeat Autism Now! (DAN!) Project," in Edelson and Rimland, eds., *Treating Autism,* p. 22.

33. T. L. Whitman, *The Development of Autism: A Self-regulatory Perspective* (London: Jessica Kingsley, 2004), p. 221; New York State Department of Health Early Intervention Program, *Clinical Practice Guideline: The Guideline Technical Report—Autism/Pervasive Developmental Disorders Assessment and Intervention for Young Children (0–3 Years)* (Albany: New York State Department of Health Early Intervention Program, 1999).

34. R. Shattock, "Can Dietary Intervention Be Used Successfully as a Therapy in Autism?" in *Conference Proceedings: Psychological Perspectives in Autism* (Sunderland: University of Sunderland, Autism Research Unit, 1995), pp. 203–206.

35. C. Black, J. A. Kaye, and H. Jick, "Relation of Childhood Gastrointestinal Disorders to Autism: Nested Case-Control Study Using Data from the UK General Practice Research Database," *British Medical Journal,* 325 (2002): 419–421.

36. S. Lucarelli, T. Frediani, A. M. Zingoni, et al., "Food Allergy and Infantile Autism," *Panminerva Medicine,* 37 (1995): 137–141; A. Knivsberg, K. L. Reichelt, N. Nodland, and T. Hoien, "Autistic Syndromes and Diet: A Follow-up Study," *Scandinavian Journal of Educational Research,* 39 (1995): 223–236.

37. National Research Council, *Educating Children with Autism,* p. 128.

38. F. R. Volkmar, "Pharmacological Interventions in Autism: Theoretical and Practical Issues," *Journal of Clinical Child Psychology,* 30 (2001): 80–87; H. W. M. Kwok, "Psychopharmacology in Autism Spectrum Disorders," *Current Opinion in Psychiatry,* 16 (2003): 529–534.

8. Miracle Cures or Bogus Treatments?

1. B. Siegel, *The World of the Autistic Child: Understanding and Treating Autistic Spectrum Disorders* (New York: Oxford University Press, 1996).
2. A. M. Donnellan, Introduction, in P. Haskew and A. M. Donnellan, *Emotional Maturity and Well-Being: Psychological Lessons of Facilitated Communication* (Madison, Wisc.: DRI Press, 1993), p. v.
3. J. Randi, "Secrets of the Psychics." *Nova,* Public Broadcasting System, WGBH-TV, Boston, 1993.
4. D. Biklen, *Communication Unbound: How Facilitated Communication Is Challenging Traditional Views of Autism and Ability/Disability* (New York: Teachers College Press, 1993), p. 17.
5. G. Green and H. Shane, "Science, Reason, and Facilitated Communication," *Journal of the Association for Persons with Severe Handicaps,* 19 (1994): 164.
6. D. Biklen, "Facts about Facilitated Communication," Syracuse University Web site, 2004.
7. *60 Minutes,* CBS News, February 20, 1994.
8. *Prime Time Live,* ABC News, January 23, 1992.
9. For some early examples of these studies, see S. Bligh and P. Kupperman, "Evaluation Procedure for Determining the Source of the Communication in Facilitated Communication Accepted in a Court Case," *Journal of Autism and Developmental Disorders,* 23 (1993): 553–557; A. Hudson, B. Melita, and N. Arnold, "Assessing the Validity of Facilitated Communication: A Case Study," *Journal of Autism and Developmental Disorders,* 23 (1993): 165–173; H. C. Shane and K. Kearns, "An Examination of the Role of the Facilitator in Facilitated Communication," *American Journal of Speech and Language Pathology,* 50 (1994): 750–765.
10. See, for example, M. P. Mostert, "Facilitated Communication Since 1995: A Review," *Journal of Autism and Developmental Disorders,* 31 (2001): 287–313.
11. Haskew and Donnellan, *Emotional Maturity and Well-Being,* p. 13.

12. Ibid., p. 14.
13. H. C. Shane, "Letters to the Editor: The Dark Side of Facilitated Communication," *Topics in Language Disorders*, 13 (1993): ix–xv.
14. R. Pollak, *The Creation of Dr. B.: A Biography of Bruno Bettelheim* (New York: Simon and Schuster, 1997), p. 180.
15. National Institute of Mental Health, Research Task Force, *Research in the Service of Mental Health* (Rockville, Md., 1975), p. 207.
16. T. Smith, "Are Other Treatments Effective?" in C. Maurice, G. Green, and S. Luce, eds., *Behavioral Intervention for Young Children with Autism: A Manual for Parents and Professionals* (Austin: Pro-Ed, 1996), p. 52.
17. B. Bettelheim, *The Empty Fortress* (New York: Free Press, 1967).
18. National Institute of Mental Health, *Research in the Service of Mental Health* (1975).
19. M. G. Welch, *Holding Time* (New York: Simon and Schuster, 1988).
20. B. N. Kaufman, *Son-Rise* (New York: Harper and Row, 1976).
21. "Options" Web site, *www.son-rise.org*.
22. Ibid.
23. Siegel, *The World of the Autistic Child*.
24. Ibid.

9. Early Intervention, "Recovery," and "Best" Treatment

1. O. I. Lovaas, "Behavioral Treatment and Normal Educational and Intellectual Functioning in Young Autistic Children," *Journal of Consulting and Clinical Psychology*, 55 (1987): 3–9.
2. J. J. McEachin, T. Smith, and O. I. Lovaas, "Long-Term Outcome for Children with Autism Who Received Early Intensive Behavioral Treatment," *American Journal on Mental Retardation*, 97 (1993): 359–372.
3. For critiques, see F. M. Grisham and D. L. MacMillan, "Early Intervention Project: Can Its Claims Be Substantiated and Its Effects Replicated?" *Journal of Autism and Developmental Disorders*, 28 (1998): 5–13, and E. Schopler, A. Short, and G. Mesibov, "Relation of Behavioral Treatment to 'Normal Functioning': Comment on Lovaas," *Journal of Consulting and Clinical Psychology*, 57 (1989): 162–164.
4. Schopler, Short, and Mesibov, "Relation of Behavioral Treatment to 'Normal Functioning.'"

5. F. M. Gresham and D. L. MacMillan, "Denial and Defensiveness in the Place of Fact and Reason: Rejoinder to Smith and Lovaas," *Behavioral Disorders,* 22 (1997): 219–230.

6. S. J. Rogers, "Empirically Supported Comprehensive Treatments for Young Children with Autism," *Journal of Clinical Child Psychology. Special Issue: Empirically Supported Psychosocial Interventions for Children,* 27 (1998): 168–179.

7. O. I. Lovaas, "The Development of a Treatment-Research Project for Developmentally Disabled and Autistic Children," *Journal of Applied Behavior Analysis,* 26 (1993): 617–630; T. Smith and O. I. Lovaas, "The UCLA Young Autism Project: A Reply to Gresham and MacMillan," *Behavioral Disorders,* 22 (1997): 202–218; McEachin, Smith, and Lovaas, "Long-Term Outcome for Children with Autism."

8. C. Maurice, *Let Me Hear Your Voice: A Family's Triumph over Autism* (New York: Ballentine, 1993).

9. Autism Society of America, Web site: *http://www.autism-society.org* (2003).

10. S. J. Sheinkopf and B. Siegel, "Home Based Behavioral Treatment of Young Children with Autism," *Journal of Autism and Developmental Disorders,* 28 (1998): 15–23.

11. G. G. McGee, M. J. Morrier, and T. Daly, "An Incidental Teaching Approach to Early Intervention for Toddlers with Autism," *Journal of the Association for Persons with Severe Handicaps,* 24 (1999): 133–146.

12. See, for example, McGee, Morrier, and Daly, "An Incidental Teaching Approach."

13. D. J. Delprato, "Comparisons of Discrete-Trial and Normalized Behavioral Intervention for Young Children with Autism," *Journal of Autism and Developmental Disorders,* 31 (2001): 315–325.

14. A. W. Grossman, J. D. Churchill, B. C. McKinney, et al., "Experience Effects on Brain Development: Possible Contributions to Psychopathology," *Journal of Child Psychology and Psychiatry and Allied Disciplines,* 44 (2003): 33–63.

15. M. R. Sherer and L. Schreibman, "Individual Behavioral Profiles and Predictors of Treatment Effectiveness for Children with Autism," *Journal of Consulting and Clinical Psychology,* 75 (2005) .

16. L. Schreibman, A. C. Stahmer, and V. Cestone, "Turning Treatment Nonresponders into Treatment Responders: Development of Individualized Treatment Protocols for Children with Autism," paper delivered

at the International Meeting for Autism Research, San Diego, November 2001.

17. M. T. Sullivan, "Communicative Functions of Echolalia in Children with Autism: Assessment and Treatment," *Dissertation Abstracts International. Section B: The Sciences and Engineering,* 63 (2003): 4948.

18. B. M. Prizant and P. J. Rydell, "Analysis of Functions of Delayed Echolalia in Autistic Children," *Journal of Speech and Hearing Research,* 27 (1984): 183–192.

19. C. T. Sundberg and M. L. Sundberg, "Comparing Topography-Based Verbal Behavior with Stimulus Selection-Based Verbal Behavior," *Analysis of Verbal Behavior,* 8 (1990): 31–41.

20. A. E. Anderson, "Augmentative Communication and Autism: A Comparison of Sign Language and the Picture Exchange Communication System," *Dissertation Abstracts International. Section B: The Sciences and Engineering,* 62 (2002): 4269.

21. A. Bondy and L. Frost, "The Picture Exchange Communication System," *Behavior Modification. Special Issue: Autism, Part 1,* 25 (2001): 725–744.

22. See, for example, C. Kiernan, "The Use of Nonvocal Communication Techniques with Autistic Individuals," *Journal of Child Psychology and Psychiatry and Allied Disciplines,* 24 (1983): 339–375; A. S. Bondy and L. A. Frost, "The Picture Exchange Communication System," *Focus on Autistic Behavior,* 9 (1994): 1–19.

23. Anderson, "Augmentative Communication and Autism."

10. Educate Autistic Children!

1. For reviews and discussion of this point, see J. A. Burack, R. Root, and E. Zigler, "Inclusive Education for Students with Autism: Reviewing Ideological, Empirical, and Community Considerations," in D. J. Cohen and F. R. Volkmar, eds., *Handbook of Autism and Pervasive Developmental Disorders, Second Edition* (New York: John Wiley and Sons, 1997), pp. 796–807; and B. Siegel, *The World of the Autistic Child* (New York: Oxford University Press, 1996).

2. See, for example, S. Stainback and W. Stainback, "Schools as Inclusive Communities," in S. Stainback and W. Stainback, eds., *Controversial Issues Confronting Special Education* (Boston: Allyn and Bacon, 1992), pp. 29–43.

3. M. J. Guralnick and J. M. Groom, "Effects of Social Setting on the Friendship Formation of Young Children Differing in Developmental Status," *Journal of Applied Developmental Psychology,* 17 (1988): 625–651.

4. G. G. McGee, T. Paradis, and R. S. Feldman, "Free Effects of Integration on Levels of Autistic Behavior," *Topics in Early Childhood Special Education,* 13 (1993): 57–67.

5. N. J. Oke and L. Schreibman, "Training Social Initiations to a High-Functioning Autistic Child: Assessment of Collateral Change and Generalization in a Case Study," *Journal of Autism and Developmental Disorders,* 20 (1990): 479–497.

6. See P. S. Strain and M. Hoyson, "On the Need for Longitudinal, Intensive Social Skill Intervention: LEAP Follow-Up Outcomes for Children with Autism as a Case-in-Point," *Topics in Early Childhood Special Education,* 20 (2000): 116–122; P. S. Strain, G. G. McGee, and F. W. Kohler, "Inclusion of Children with Autism in Early Intervention Settings: An Examination of Rationale, Myths, and Procedures," in M. J. Guralnick, ed., *Early Childhood Inclusion: Focus on Change* (Baltimore: Brookes, 2001), pp. 337–364.

7. A. C. Stahmer and B. Ingersoll, "Inclusive Programming for Toddlers with Autism Spectrum Disorders: Outcomes from the Children's Toddler School," *Journal of Positive Behavior Interventions,* 6 (2004): 67–82.

8. Strain, McGee, and Kohler, "Inclusion of Children with Autism in Early Intervention Settings."

Index